T0319820

Transgenerational Entrepreneurship

IN ASSOCIATION WITH THE GLOBAL STEP PROJECT

The success of passing a family business from one generation to another depends not only on instilling business ideas and leadership in future generations, but, and perhaps more importantly, it depends on engendering the entrepreneurial spirit in those business leaders to come; this is the practice of transgenerational leadership. Successful Transgenerational Entrepreneurship Practices, more commonly know as the STEP Project, was put in place to help facilitate family enterprising. An innovative research initiative that spans the globe, it offers insight, partnership and solutions for current and future family leaders. In the STEP Project, academics of entrepreneurship and business collaborate with prosperous multigenerational family businesses to explore and identify those practices that will help family business grow and prosper through three key tenets: venturing – launching new businesses; renewal – revitalizing existing businesses; and innovation – introducing new products and processes. By creating a stream of powerful practices and cases that empower families to build their entrepreneurial legacies, the members of the STEP Project are rapidly moving their discoveries from research into practice.

Current STEP Partners

Europe
- Alba Graduate School of Business, Greece
- ESADE, Barcelona, Spain
- HEC, Paris, France
- Jönköping International Business School, Sweden
- Lancaster University, Lancaster, England
- UCD, Dublin, Ireland
- Universita Bocconi, Milan, Italy
- University of Edinburgh, Edinburgh, Scotland
- University of Jyväskylä, Jyväskylä, Finland
- Universitaet St. Gallen, St. Gallen, Switzerland
- Universitaet Witten/Herdecke, Germany
- Universiteit Antwerpen, Antwerp, Belgium
- University of the Western Cape, South Africa (Joint Venture with Jönköping)

Latin America
- Fundação Dom Cabral, Brazil
- Universidad Adolfo Ibáñez, Chile
- Universidad de Los Andes, Colombia
- PUCMM, Dominican Republic
- Universidad San Francisco de Quito, Ecuador
- Tecnológico de Monterrey, Mexico
- INCAE Business School, Costa Rica/Nicaragua
- IESA, Venezuela
- Inter American University of Puerto Rico
- CENTRUM, Pontificia Universidad Católica del Perú

Asia Pacific
- Chinese University of Hong Kong, Hong Kong
- Nankai University, Tianjin, P.R. China
- Sun Yat-Sen University, Taiwan
- Sun Yat-Sen University, Guangzhou, P.R. China
- Kyungpook, National University, Korea
- Waseda University, Japan
- Queensland University of Technology, Australia
- Bond University, Australia
- Indian School of Business, Hyderabad, India
- UNIRAZAK, Malaysia
- Bangkok University, Thailand

Transgenerational Entrepreneurship

Exploring Growth and Performance in
Family Firms Across Generations

Edited by

Mattias Nordqvist

Associate Professor of Business Administration, Jönköping International Business School, Sweden and Co-Director, Center for Family Enterprise and Ownership (CeFEO), Sweden

and

Thomas M. Zellweger

Assistant Professor of Entrepreneurship and Family Business, University of St Gallen, Switzerland and Managing Director, Center for Family Business, University of St Gallen, Switzerland

IN ASSOCIATION WITH THE GLOBAL STEP PROJECT

Edward Elgar
Cheltenham, UK • Northampton, MA, USA

Published by
Edward Elgar Publishing Limited
The Lypiatts
15 Lansdown Road
Cheltenham
Glos GL50 2JA
UK

Edward Elgar Publishing, Inc.
William Pratt House
9 Dewey Court
Northampton
Massachusetts 01060
USA

A catalogue record for this book
is available from the British Library

Library of Congress Control Number: 2009940735

Mixed Sources
Product group from well-managed
forests and other controlled sources
www.fsc.org Cert no. SA-COC-1565
© 1996 Forest Stewardship Council
FSC

ISBN 978 1 84720 797 5

Printed and bound by MPG Books Group, UK

Contents

Figures

Tables

Contributors

Eugenia Bieto is Associate Professor of the Business Policy Department at ESADE, Spain. She is the corporate deputy director general. She obtained a PhD in management sciences from ESADE-Universitat Ramon Llull. She founded the ESADE Entrepreneurship Institute. Her research is focused on corporate entrepreneurship.

Alain Bloch is Adjunct Professor of Entrepreneurship and Family Business at HEC Paris, France. He is co-founder of HEC Paris Family Business Centre and Director of the HEC Entrepreneur graduate program. He has a PhD in information systems and management from the University Paris-Dauphine. A Fellow of Price-Babson College Fellows Program (SEE 15), Alain Bloch is also Professor at the French Conservatoire National des Arts et Metiers, where he is head of marketing, retailing and negotiation. His own experience as an entrepreneur and a family business manager has led him to focus his research on innovation, entrepreneurship, family business and leadership.

Ethel Brundin, PhD, is Associate Professor at the Jönköping International Business School in entrepreneurship, marketing and management (EMM) and the Center for Family Enterprise and Ownership (CeFEO). Her research projects focus on entrepreneurship and family firms, the family ownership logic and projects with a focus on emotional ownership in family businesses. She has published articles on how to study micro processes, is a member of three editorial boards, publishes regularly in international journals and serves as a committee member of the world conference on emotions in organizations. She is a visiting professor at the University of the Western Cape, Cape Town, South Africa.

Alberto Gimeno is Associate Professor at the Business Policy Department at ESADE, Spain and co-director of the Advanced Management Program (AM) at ESADE Executive Education. Dr Gimeno is Visiting Professor at Witten-Herdecke Universität, Germany. He holds a PhD in management sciences from ESADE-Universitat Ramon Llull. He is a member of the Expert Group on Family Business that advises the European Commission and a member of the Body of Knowledge Committee of the Family Firm Institute (FFI). He is one of the founding partners of Family Business

Knowledge (FBK), an applied research company in the field of the family business. He acts as a consultant to family business. His research is focused on the application of the theory of complexity to family business management, with the aim of creating useful analytical models. He is the co-author of a theoretical model (the Structural Risk Model).

Timothy G. Habbershon is a Managing Director at Fidelity Investments, the largest mutual fund company in the USA and a private family controlled company. Within this company Dr Habbershon is involved in matters of organizational design and development, and succession planning for the company. He is also a coach to senior executives and teams. Prior to joining Fidelity in 2006 Dr Habbershon was the founding director of the Institute for Family Enterprising at Babson College in Wellesley, Massachusetts, and Assistant Professor of Entrepreneurship, holding the President's Term Chair in Family Enterprising. While at Babson he developed an emphasis on family based entrepreneurship called transgenerational entrepreneurship. Additionally, Dr Habbershon was a founding partner in the TELOS Group, a consulting firm that specializes in transition and strategy consultations to large family firms worldwide.

Alexandra Joseph is a PhD candidate and researcher at HEC, Paris, France. After graduating from EM Lyon she started her career in a consulting firm and joined her family business. After obtaining her DEA in industrial strategy (Sorbonne), she focused her research on strategy and entrepreneurship in the field of family business.

Ugo Lassini is Assistant Professor of General Management at Università degli Studi di Verona, Italy. He is a Member of the Centre for Research on Entrepreneurship and Entrepreneurs at Bocconi University and of the Strategic and Entrepreneurial Management Department at Sda Bocconi in Milan, Italy. He obtained a PhD in business administration and management from Bocconi University. His current research focus is on the growth patterns of small and medium enterprises (SMEs) and the evolution of entrepreneurial capabilities in closely held firms. He has published research on the dynamics of internal and external growth in SMEs and determinants of entrepreneurial behavior in family firms.

Leif Melin is Professor of Strategy and Organization and the Hamrin Professor in Family Business Strategy at Jönköping International Business School (JIBS), where he is the founding director of the Center for Family Enterprise and Ownership (CeFEO). Before joining JIBS in 1994 he was Professor of Strategic Management at Linköping University. His research interests include several topics related to strategizing and strategic change in the context of family business, applying the strategy as practice perspective. For example, strategic dialogues as an important practice. He has published in journals, such as *Strategic Management Journal, Strategic Organization, Journal of Management Studies* and *Family Business Review*, and has published several books, including recently *Strategy as Practice. Research Directions and Resources* (Cambridge University Press, 2007). He serves on the editorial boards of several journals, such as *Strategic Organization, Long Range Planning, European Management Review* and *Journal of Family Business Strategy*.

Corinne Muehlebach, PhD, is a research fellow at the University of St Gallen's Center for Family Business, Switzerland. She is a fifth generation family business manager and a family business lecturer and researcher at the University of Applied Sciences, Northwestern Switzerland.

Mattias Nordqvist, PhD, is Associate Professor of Strategy and Entrepreneurship at Jönköping International Business School where is also the co-director of the Center for Family Enterprise and Ownership (CeFEO). He has served as the co-director for the Global STEP Project between 2006 and 2009 and he is currently a visiting scholar at Babson College, Massachusetts, USA. His research on entrepreneurship and family businesses have appeared in many international journals, and he has recently guest edited an issue of *Entrepreneurship and Regional Development* on this topic. He is also an Associate Editor of the *Journal of Family Business Strategy*.

María José Parada is a researcher at the ESADE Entrepreneurship Institute. A PhD candidate in management sciences at ESADE, Spain, she is also pursuing a joint PhD degree at the Jönköping International Business School, Sweden. She holds a Master of Research in management sciences and an MBA with a major in finance from ESADE. She is a member of the Family Firm Institute (FFI) where she received the Family Business Advisor Certificate. Her current research is mainly focused on the process of developing governance structures in family businesses; values transmission and values transformation; and private equity and family business synergies.

Markus Plate has a diploma in psychology and is a research assistant at the Witten Institute for Family Business, Witten-Herdecke University, Germany. He studied psychology in Marburg and Osnabrueck. While his background is in communication, systems theory and epistemology, he now focuses on transgenerational entrepreneurship and organization science.

Carlo Salvato is Associate Professor of Strategic Management and Entrepreneurship at Università Bocconi in Milan, Italy, Vice-Director of the Centre for Research on Entrepreneurship and Entrepreneurs and Director of the Master of Science in Management. He obtained a PhD in business administration and management from Bocconi University and a PhD in entrepreneurship and management from Jönköping International Business School, Sweden. His current research focus is on the micro foundations and evolution of entrepreneurial capabilities in closely held firms. He has published research on social capital as an antecedent of entrepreneurial capabilities, determinants of entrepreneurial behavior in family firms and exit as a component of entrepreneurial processes. He has authored papers in journals such as *Organization Science, Journal of Management Studies, Entrepreneurship Theory and Practice, Entrepreneurship and Regional Development* and *Family Business Review.* He is also Associate Editor of the *Family Business Review.*

Michel Santi has been Emeritus Professor of Strategy and Business Policy at HEC School of Management, Paris since 1979. His major topics of research and teaching are innovation and entrepreneurship. Recently he developed a model for extracting, capturing and protecting value from innovations with the financial support of INPI (French IP Agency). As well as his teaching activities, he acts as an entrepreneur, a consultant and a business angel for high-tech start-ups. He is registered as expert in the innovation field within the European Community.

Christian Schiede, Dipl. Kfm., is a research assistant at the chair for Accounting and Management Control in Family Business. He studied business administration at the University of Augsburg and worked as a consultant and coach for family firms. His interests include corporate and family venturing, governance, strategy and human resource and change management.

Philipp Sieger is a PhD student at the University of St Gallen, Switzerland. He spent one semester at the BI Norwegian School of Management in Oslo, Norway and earned his Master's degree from the University of St Gallen in 2007. His research interests are entrepreneurship, psychological ownership and succession in family firms.

Frédéric Vallaud is the founder and managing director of the HEC Family Business Centre. He joined HEC Paris as program director of the HEC Executive MBA in 1994. He has created several small companies in such diverse fields as human resources, art, tourism, the building industry and consulting. His main topic of interest is family governance. He is currently in the process of completing a PhD in management science on family councils and family constitutions.

Arist von Schlippe is a psychological psychotherapist, family therapist and family psychologist. After five years working in child psychiatric hospitals he worked at the University of Osnabrueck until 2005. He received his PhD in 1986 and his licensed lecturer qualification (habilitation) in psychotherapy and clinical psychology in 2001. Between 2003 and 2004 he was representative of the chair in clinical psychology at the University of Jena. Since 2005 he has been Professor for Leadership and Dynamics of Family Business at the Witten Institute for Family Business at Witten-Herdecke University, Germany.

Thomas M. Zellweger, PhD, is Assistant Professor of Entrepreneurship at the University of St Gallen, Switzerland. He is co-founder and Managing Director of his school's Center for Family Business. His research on entrepreneurship and value management in family firms has been granted several international awards. He has served as a co-director of the STEP Project and is a research fellow at Babson College, Massachusetts, USA. He is Associate Editor of the *Journal of Family Business Strategy* and a member of the editorial board of *Family Business Review*. In 2010 he is Visiting Professor at the Sauder School of Business, University of British Columbia, Canada.

Acknowledgements

This book is the result of a true process of collaboration. As we describe in Chapter 2, we strongly believe in the importance of establishing a positive, interactive learning environment for a large, global research project in order to be successful. In the Global Successful Transgenerational Entrepreneurship Practices (STEP) Project we are fortunate to have been able to create such an environment. The content of all chapters in this book has been formed by the researchers involved in STEP both as individuals and as a group. In particular, the STEP research framework as presented in Chapter 1 is the result of many conversations between the people who form the STEP Project.

In addition to STEP as a group, we would like to extend a specific thank-you to our program manager, Robert S. Nason for his excellent work in relation to all possible (and impossible) dimensions of our global research project. Rob is truly an extraordinarily talented and likeable young professional. We are also grateful for all the support we have received from our colleagues at the Entrepreneurship Division and the Arthur M. Blank Center for Entrepreneurship at Babson College. We are especially indebted to Candy Brush, Steve Spinelli and Janet Strimaitis. We would also like to thank Per Davidsson, Michael Hitt and Tom Lumpkin who helped us with the development of the STEP Project at a critical stage. The meeting with this great group of scholars made us confident that STEP will make important contributions to the entrepreneurship and family business literature.

All in all, we believe that this book has become more than the sum of its parts. It is not a mere collection of articles like many other research anthologies, but represents a novel way of thinking about value creation and entrepreneurship in the context of family firms. As a consequence, writing this book has been a long journey for all of us, but it was more than worth it. We hope you will enjoy reading it.

Mattias Nordqvist and Thomas M. Zellweger, Boston, June 2009

Foreword

While family businesses contribute significantly to the global economy, and have done so for centuries, scholarly research is disproportionately low. More sparse are studies that explore the intersections and relationships among family, firm and entrepreneurial growth. The STEP Project is a landmark effort to better understand the nature of entrepreneurial family firms and to develop theories and hypotheses for future testing.

This project emerged from the work of Tim Habbershon, more than six years ago. Tim was committed to creating a global research project that 'addresses one of the greatest challenges faced by business families worldwide – growth and continuity that spans many generations'. To this end, he created a grand vision for this global research project that included three main aspects:

- Conduct leading edge research on the entrepreneurial capabilities and contribution of business families worldwide.
- Generate an applied stream of entrepreneurship powerful practices that lead to family business continuity and growth.
- Provide a shared learning environment where researchers and professors interact with family business leaders to generate solutions that have immediate impact.

The logic for the formation of the Successful Transgenerational Entrepreneurship Practices (STEP) Project was to bring together researchers and mid to large size family business leaders so that the research would have practical relevance to the families, as well as address important empirical and theoretical questions. The research objectives of this project are to examine how business families generate new streams of economic and social wealth.

With Babson College, the STEP Project was officially launched in 2005 by the formation of the European team at the Academic Summit at Bocconi University. By 2006 the Latin American STEP Project was underway and in 2007 STEP Asia Pacific was added to the team.

This unique research project, housed at Babson College, is already accomplishing some of the original goals stated by Tim Habbershon. The number of researchers participating in the STEP Project has reached 110, while the number of families engaging in one or more summits has reached 120. In June 2009 the STEP event brought 35 academics to campus where discussions about the multi-country survey, methodology, case writing and other topics were covered.

Global research projects are notoriously difficult to organize and manage – but through the efforts of Mattias Nordqvist and Thomas Zellweger these efforts have yielded a unique and path breaking book. Unique to this project is the frequent interface with families during the data collection process. This results in vivid and thick description of family business cases and novel insights for future research. This collection will greatly benefit family business researchers in any country. Not only is it fascinating reading in the stories of venturing and innovative family businesses brought to life, but it also highlights possibilities for theory building and theory testing.

Besides contributions to family business, this collection of chapters will add to entrepreneurship research. Many of the concepts and topics emerging from qualitative studies and explored in family business situations are of interest to entrepreneurial firms, new ventures and the entrepreneurial process.

For the past four years I observed Thomas and Mattias in their efforts to lead the STEP Project and make this book a reality. They have done a superb job and are to be congratulated for a truly terrific collection.

Candida G. Brush, Paul T. Babson Chair in Entrepreneurship, Division Chair for Entrepreneurship, Babson College, MA, USA

1. Transgenerational entrepreneurship

Timothy G. Habbershon, Mattias Nordqvist and Thomas M. Zellweger

1.1 INTRODUCTION

This book is about transgenerational entrepreneurship. This concept is introduced to the literature as a way to examine, understand and explain entrepreneurship – and especially corporate entrepreneurship – within the context of families and family businesses. We see entrepreneurship as the creation of new enterprising activities (Davidsson and Wiklund, 2001; Schumpeter, 1934), that is, innovation, new venture and strategic renewal (Sharma and Chrisman, 1999) leading to social and economic performance within firms. Following Schumpeter (1934) we consider that the creation of new streams of economic and social value through enterprising activities is crucial, not only for new firms but also for established firms, since entrepreneurship is not only important for creating but also for sustaining the firm's internal 'generative capability', defined as the capacity to renew a firm's operations through innovation in order to create new capabilities (Zahra, 2005).

In particular, we focus on established firms that are controlled by families and that have a vision of family influence beyond the founding generation (Chua et al., 1999). We argue that entrepreneurship is a key to performance and success over several generations in family firms. Our interest in multigenerational business families and family businesses is the main reason why we use the concept of transgenerational entrepreneurship. Following Gartner's (2001) view to adopt a dynamic view of entrepreneurship as a process that occurs over time, we formally define transgenerational entrepreneurship as the 'processes through which a family uses and develops entrepreneurial mindsets and family influenced capabilities to create new streams of entrepreneurial, financial and social value across generations'. As elaborated on further below, we see the entrepreneurial mindset as the attitudes, values and beliefs that orient a person or a group towards the pursuit of entrepreneurial activities (Lumpkin and Dess, 1996; Miller, 1983). By entrepreneurial capabilities we mean the resources and capabilities that a given family possesses or has access to and that may either facilitate or constrain entrepreneurial activities (Habbershon et al., 2003; Sirmon and Hitt, 2003). New streams of entrepreneurial, financial and social values refer to a broader understanding of performance and value that reaches beyond the boundaries of only economic performance outcomes in the context of families and family firms. Finally, we adopt a longitudinal perspective by looking at how value is created not only for the current stakeholders, especially the family, but for the future and, in particular, future family generations.

The aim of this chapter is threefold. First, we present the concept of transgenerational entrepreneurship and discuss its theoretical foundations. Second, we develop and present a research framework for examining and understanding transgenerational entrepreneurship in the context of family and family businesses. Third, we introduce and summarize the different chapters of this book and explicate what part(s) of the framework each chapter addresses. In the next section we provide a more detailed justification of our research in light of some tensions and limitations in extant relevant research literature.

1.2   BACKGROUND AND MOTIVATION FOR THE RESEARCH PROJECT

This book presents some early research findings from the Global STEP Project founded in 2005 by Babson College and a group of European universities and business schools. From its inception, the founding institutions envisaged STEP to be a leading international collaborative research project that would bring together a large group of scholars interested in entrepreneurship within family business contexts. From the very beginning a leading idea behind STEP was to use research methods that allowed scholars to engage deeply in the phenomenon they were studying. Thus a priority within STEP is to interact with leaders and owners of family businesses. In addition to a yearly summit where families and scholars meet to exchange experiences, this means that researchers within STEP use a qualitative in-depth case research approach, as one important method to address our overall research questions. In the subsequent chapters of this book researchers from STEP present some findings from their qualitative case research. In Chapter 2 we present and explain the key facets of our qualitative approach.

Furthermore, the Global STEP Project is motivated by at least four distinct reasons. First, families represent not just the dominant form of business organization but provide and use resources for new enterprises and entrepreneurial activities worldwide (Aldrich and Cliff, 2003). In these firms the family is a central stakeholder and its influence in the businesses they own and/or manage is thus of crucial relevance for both the firm's identity and its success. The family institution is commonly associated with specific values, interests and expectations that are different from other types of owners and managers (Lansberg, 1983; Zellweger and Nason, 2008). This assumption is, for instance, visible in the research adopting either an agency (Chrisman et al., 2004; Jensen and Meckling, 1976; Schulze et al., 2003) or a stewardship perspective (Corbetta and Salvato, 2004; Eddleston et al., 2008a) to family businesses. Both views share, however, the observation that the family is a key constituent of this type of firm. Thus it is motivated to introduce the family as the level of analysis for entrepreneurial activities. By including the family as an additional level of analysis and by investigating the family's role in entrepreneurial activities, the STEP Project develops a more comprehensive approach to study the long-term success of family firms.

In line with Davidsson and Wiklund (2001), we acknowledge that entrepreneurship occurs at and effects different societal levels simultaneously. As a result, Davidsson and Wiklund (2001) encourage research studies to consider micro and macro perspectives which incorporate multiple levels of analysis. Prior shifts in levels of analysis have given rise to new insights in the field of entrepreneurship. For example, the rise of portfolio entrepreneurship literature and the insights researchers and practitioners have derived from this research has been largely related to the shift of the level of analysis away from the firm level and towards the individual level (Scott and Rosa, 1996; Westhead and Wright, 1998). We take Birley and Westhead's (1994) considerations a step further by suggesting that there is a threat to underestimate value creation of (family) businesses if the family as a level of analysis is not taken into consideration. As elaborated on further below, introducing the family as the level of analysis enables us to look beyond a focal business and give more attention to the fact that many business families own and control several firms within a group or portfolio. Having said this, we hasten to add that the study of entrepreneurship in the context of families and family firms is distinct and different from the more traditional study of family businesses. Examining entrepreneurship within the context of families and their businesses, we are less interested in continuity, succession of ownership and leadership and stability, which has been dominant in the field of family business studies to date, as we are in change, growth and the creation of the new. In short, we are interested in families as engines for entrepreneurship.

Second, a corporate entrepreneurship study within the context of families and family businesses is motivated also because there is no agreement in the literature as to whether family businesses represent a context where entrepreneurship flourishes or is hampered (for example, Naldi et al., 2007). Certain scholars have argued that the particular culture and power structure found in many family firms may have considerable influence on the extent to which entrepreneurial activities are encouraged or held back (Hall et al., 2001; Salvato, 2004; Schein, 1983; Zahra et al., 2004). Some scholars propose that family firms present a unique setting for entrepreneurship to flourish, for example, through stewardship behavior (Eddleston and Kellermanns, 2006) family to firm-unity (Eddleston et al., 2008a) or a long-term horizon (Zellweger, 2007). Other scholars note that family firms should invoke lower levels of entrepreneurship (Levinson, 1987; Miller, 1983; Morris, 1998; Schulze et al., 2003). Considering long-term orientation, an aspect often assigned to family firms, Barringer and Bluedorn (1999) proposed that a reliance on a long-term planning horizon runs counter to the proactive nature of the entrepreneurial process and that a long-term tenure is optimal for conservative and less entrepreneurial firms (Covin, 1991; Covin and Slevin, 1991). These studies suggest that family firms are endangered, for example, by strategic simplicity and inertia, conditions that cause some managers to overuse ready-made solutions without probing the assumptions underlying the decisions they make (Cabrera-Suarez et al., 2001; Miller, 1983; Morris, 1998). In this vein, research acknowledges the serious tensions that develop within the family firm between the need for change and stability in which entrepreneurship is seen as an antidote to stability and strategic simplicity (Schulze et al., 2003). Whereas the above research provides some preliminary findings and indications on entrepreneurship in the family firm context, we see the need to further substantiate our understanding of the family firm specific contextual factors and of the what, how and why of entrepreneurship in this specific context.

Third, family business research has undertaken considerable efforts to better understand continuity and succession as well as how existing business is perpetuated in businesses (for example, Le Breton-Miller et al., 2004). In contrast, the entrepreneurship literature has focused on the creation of new enterprises, especially through new ventures, innovation and renewal within organizations (Sharma and Chrisman, 1999; Zahra, 1995). However family firms do not face just one of these challenges. Rather, they need to find ways to create new streams of value within an existing long-term oriented organizational setting, through exploration of new ways of doing things and at the same time through exploitation of existing products, service or organizational processes. Therefore we argue in line with Zahra and Sharma (2004) that there is a need for a new theoretical foundation that is able to capture and explain how families bring new streams of value to their business activities to survive and prosper across many generations. In other words, rather than examining the transfer of ownership and leadership in an existing organization from one generation to the next, we shift the focus to the use and development of entrepreneurial mindsets and capabilities across time and generations which can be deployed in existing but also new activities. What we call transgenerational entrepreneurship is about how families create new streams of value across generations – not simply how to grow and pass on a business. Since this approach is new to the literature, as researchers we face significant challenges to investigate the actual mindsets and capabilities of families involved in launching and fostering new entrepreneurial initiatives, just as the creation of financial and social value across generations.

Fourth, whereas most research in the entrepreneurship and family business context has traditionally used a descriptive approach, or single respondent and cross-sectional data analysis, we see a need for a longitudinal and multiple respondent research approach that draws upon both qualitative and quantitative methods. Given that we are striving to analyse entrepreneurial behavior and capabilities of business families in depth and across time, we need by definition to apply a multi-respondent and longitudinal research design that can benefit from the strengths of more than one research tradition. We develop this argument in greater detail in Chapter 2.

Introducing the concept of transgenerational entrepreneurship and building the research framework that we introduce below is our way of addressing these tensions and limitations in the extant literature on entrepreneurship and family businesses. There are other scholars who have approached this challenge in the literature on entrepreneurship within the context of families and family businesses. In the next section we briefly review a selection of these studies.

1.3   ENTREPRENEURSHIP IN THE CONTEXT OF THE FAMILY FIRM – A BRIEF LITERATURE REVIEW

Early academic literature viewed family business and entrepreneurship as separate but overlapping domains of interest, and noted that there was no integrated theory that explained the relationship between family and entrepreneurship (Dyer and Handler, 1994; Hoy and Verser, 1994). In what could be labeled an 'integrative approach', Poza (1988) proposed practices that support interpreneurship in the family firm context. Coining the concept of interpreneurship, Poza (1988) wanted to draw attention to how family members from different generations could contribute to growth and renewal of a family business. Brockhaus (1994) proposed a parallel development of entrepreneurship and family business research, thereby suggesting that the two need to be coordinated, but kept separate. In many ways, the entrepreneurship and family business perspectives are based upon differing and in certain ways conflicting assumptions. Whereas entrepreneurship has its roots in the context of younger and smaller or mid-sized firms, family business scholars have looked at older and often larger firms. Whereas entrepreneurship has stressed resource accumulation, family business researchers have particularly investigated resource shedding and reconfiguration (for example, Sharma and Manikutty, 2005; Sirmon et al., 2007).

In their attempts to combine the entrepreneurship and family business perspective, most authors took a common denominator approach. The common denominator attributed to both family business and entrepreneurship covers topics and issues that the two would share. This approach was aimed at finding common subjects such as small business management, entrepreneurial couples, lifestyle start-ups, founders and founder's culture, transition and succession, and some corporate entrepreneurship themes (Dyer and Handler, 1994; Hoy and Verser, 1994). However the common denominator approach is limited in terms of its explicative power. If the goal is to study family businesses through the lens of entrepreneurship, the common denominator entrepreneurship will define what actually can and will be studied in the family firm context. However the specific family related aspects, which are not covered by the individual and organizational aspects represented within entrepreneurship (entrepreneurship being the common denominator), cannot be studied with this approach.

Calls by other researchers to build an integrated approach towards studying family firms are abundant. Chrisman et al. (2003) state that if theories of entrepreneurship ignore family involvement, they might miss critical family related factors in new venture creation. Similarly, they consider it to be difficult to lay claim to developing a theory of entrepreneurship if we do not look at organizations in all of their diversity, including family firms. Habbershon and Pistrui (2002) propose the notion of enterprising families to create a true nexus between business and family. They argue for shifting the focus of corporate entrepreneurship studies from the conventional firm level of analysis to the level of the family or ownership group. Enterprising families are seen as business families that strive for transgenerational entrepreneurship and long-term wealth creation through the creation of new ventures, innovation and strategic renewal (Habbershon and Pistrui, 2002). Airing a similar trust in the capacity of families to drive both the processes and outcomes of entrepreneurship, Rogoff and Heck

(2003, p. 559) suggest recognizing the 'family as the oxygen that feeds the fire of entrepreneurship'.

Ucbasaran et al. (2001) propose that the focus of entrepreneurial research needs to include the family firm as an organizational form while Zahra and Sharma (2004) propose that family business research needs to be an integral part of the entrepreneurship literature. Aldrich and Cliff (2003) argue that families have a pervasive effect on entrepreneurship and propose a 'family embeddedness' perspective on entrepreneurial activities.

Recent literature examining the impact of family related variables on entrepreneurship delivered the first insights into our topic. For instance, Hall et al. (2001) and Zahra et al. (2004) observe the crucial role of the family influenced organizational culture in either promoting or inhibiting corporate entrepreneurship in family businesses. Kellermanns and Eddleston (2006) find that the willingness of family members to change is positively related to corporate entrepreneurship. Similarly in the same study it is demonstrated that strategic planning plays an important role on generational effects in family firms: when strategic planning is taken into account, family firms with greater generational involvement appear to experience greater corporate entrepreneurship. Naldi et al. (2007) examine risk taking as a dimension of entrepreneurship in established family businesses, and Salvato (2004) relates governance and organizational characteristics to the amount of corporate entrepreneurship in different types of family businesses. Furthermore, it has been proposed that family firms present a unique setting for entrepreneurship to flourish due to stewardship behavior, represented by harmonious (family) relations (Eddleston et al., 2008) or due to a long-term horizon (Zellweger, 2007).

The diversity of issues studied at the intersection between entrepreneurship and family business raises the question of whether an attempt towards an integrated theory of family business and entrepreneurship actually makes sense. Following Gartner (2001) we question whether a single theory can encompass such diverse issues as, for example, creation of a new firm, raising capital, succession planning and family conflicts. We think that these topics need to have different theoretical underpinnings. Therefore we revisited the calls by researchers to develop an integrative perspective of entrepreneurship and family business by asking ourselves what factors (variables, constructs, concepts) logically should be considered as part of the explanation of the phenomenon of interest, that is, entrepreneurship in the context of families and family firms. These factors need to allow a comprehensive understanding of the phenomenon, but at the same time should be parsimonious enough to capture the main points of the issue without overloading the arguments.

Building on the aforementioned literature review and considering

Whetten's (1989) arguments on the parsimony and completeness of a theoretical contribution we would like to think of the transgenerational entrepreneurship approach as an attempt to address the true nexus between entrepreneurship theory and family business studies as an appropriate way to examine and understand the role and influence of the family in reaching entrepreneurial, financial and social performance, which assures generation-spanning business activity.

To address this nexus of entrepreneurship theory and family business research we propose that transgenerational entrepreneurship comprises five key components: (1) the particular focus on the family as the unit of analysis, thereby extending the scope of analysis beyond the individual and the organizational level, (2) the entrepreneurial mindset of the family, (3) the family's influence on resource stocks and usage, (4) contextual factors like industry, community culture, family life stage and family involvement and (5) performance and value creation measured in terms of entrepreneurial, financial and social performance as antecedents to transgenerational potential, understood as the likelihood for transgenerational success of the enterprising family. To sum up and integrate, we propose the following research framework to study our phenomenon of interest, which is entrepreneurship in the context of families and family firms (Figure 1.1).

1.4   FAMILY AS THE LEVEL OF ANALYSIS

Gartner (2001) notes that 'important insights about entrepreneurship can be gained when researchers are able to conduct studies that are multi-level in nature' (p. 32). Despite the fact that researchers have proposed different modes of exploitation (Shane and Venkataraman, 2000) the challenge persists. Whereas Low and MacMillan (1988) propose five levels of analysis (individual, group, organization, industry and society), the family has not yet been considered as a distinct level of analysis despite the fact that it is the discriminatory feature of family firms. We propose that research about entrepreneurship within the context of families and their businesses should particularly investigate the family as a unit of analysis, alongside to the organization and the individual. Thereby the family needs to be seen as a key constituent in this type of firm, beyond a governance and a social institution (Davidsson and Wiklund, 2001; Zellweger and Nason, 2008). We follow Habbershon and Pistrui (2002) who proposed that researchers should envisage the family group as a key level of analysis when examining entrepreneurship, and Carter and Ram (2003) who argued that the family household is a relevant unit of analysis for entrepreneurship studies.

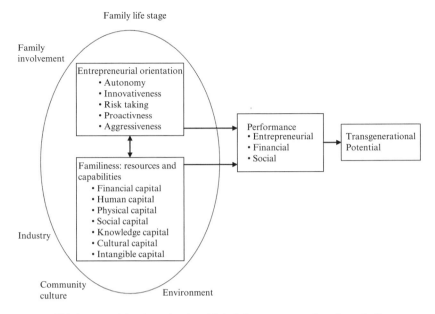

Note: This framework has been developed jointly between researchers from the European STEP partner schools during the period 2005–08.

Figure 1.1   Research framework for transgenerational entrepreneurship

One of the major problems related to solely using the firm as a level of analysis in the context of family firms is the implicit assumption that a family firm consists only of a single business entity. This oversimplification of the family business leads to a discourse about whether that specific firm either succeeds or fails in terms of remaining within family control. This perspective, however, neglects to account for family firms who control multiple firms or sell a firm, and maintain the assets to redeploy them into another business unit(s) or a newly founded or acquired firm.

In fact, according to Kellermanns (2005) and Sharma and Manikutty (2005), acquisitions and in particular (timely) divestments of resources are essential for sustaining the competitive advantage and longevity of family firms. Sharma and Manikutty (2005, p. 295) contend 'for firms desirous of longevity as family firms of interest to us, changes in the environment require strategic responses on the part of a firm (such as readjustment of the business portfolio and divestment of unproductive resources), so as to enable regeneration and renewal'. This means that divestment or closure of a business may actually be the opposite of failure, but necessary to sustain a competitive advantage and ensure longevity for a family business or a business family. In other words, whereas the 'firm' may not survive, other family related entrepreneurial activities may prosper and assure the longevity of the business family.

As a consequence from introducing the family as a level of analysis, it is further required to revisit the definition of success of a succession. If a family firm is sold or closed down, succession defined in more traditional terms will fail. However the proceedings from the sale may be redeployed in new and more value generating activities, giving family members new space for development. Similarly, a family member may choose not to take over the baton in the main company but start some new business activity by borrowing human, financial and social capital from the family, inside or outside the umbrella of a family (holding) company (Arregle et al., 2007). Consequently, applying the family level of analysis may shift how we define success or failure of family business succession.

Also, shifting to the family level of analysis may result in new insights about firm level phenomena that are not sufficiently explained by current theories, such as portfolio entrepreneurship. For example, Carter and Ram (2003, p. 372) find that 'an analysis of the wider literature suggests that for many small firms, family circumstances may influence both the decision to engage in portfolio strategies and also the processes which are used in the portfolio approach'. A growing literature around family controlled portfolio entrepreneurship challenges the sole business view (Carter and Ram, 2003; Scott and Rosa, 1996; Westhead and Wright, 1998). Accordingly, switching to the family level of analysis will provide new insights into portfolio strategies of firms.

Consequently, such a research approach that shifts to the family level of analysis touches upon the very definition of a family business. It is essential to consider the many changes in ownership, board and management structure occurring in all firms over time, which can impact on whether a firm is deemed 'family' or 'non-family'. For example, the transition from a sole family owner-manager to a non-family CEO with continued family ownership may mean that this firm loses its 'family business' title under the strictest definitions (Chua et al., 1999). Similarly, taking a firm public could mean 'failure' in terms of maintaining the family business under many definitions, but the family may retain control of that firm through voting rights or other control mechanisms (Faccio and Lang, 2002). However such a strategic move may greatly increase family wealth, business value and opportunity for further value creation with the capital influx.

Finally, shifting the level of analysis implicates reassessing the macro-economic relevance of business families and family businesses. Nowadays there is wide support beyond the family business literature that family firms make up the utmost part of all firms in developed countries (Shanker and Astrachan, 1996). However, beyond the impressive absolute and relative numbers of family firms throughout the world, there is increasing evidence that the families who are in control of these firms need to be considered as drivers and enablers of new entrepreneurial activity in their regional and national context. For example, preliminary research using the data from the Global Entrepreneurship Monitor (Volery et al., 2007) presents evidence for the plural forms of support business families provide in starting up new businesses, for instance, in terms of seed financing granted to family and non-family members. Accordingly, the true economic relevance of business families may be underestimated by simply measuring the number of family firms existing or surviving across time. With a shift of the level of analysis to the business family one may even find stronger evidence for the pivotal role of family related business activity.

1.5 ENTREPRENEURIAL ORIENTATION

To address the entrepreneurial mindset part of our model we draw upon the entrepreneurial orientation construct from the literature on corporate entrepreneurship (Lumpkin and Dess, 1996). As noted above, we view transgenerational entrepreneurship as essentially about corporate entrepreneurship within the context of families and their businesses. Entrepreneurial mindsets are the attitudes, values and beliefs that orient a person or a group towards pursuing entrepreneurial activities. This basically refers to an inclination, or spirit, of enterprising that favors growth and leads organizations to investigate opportunity when expansion is neither pressing nor particularly obvious (Penrose, 1959). As such we clearly differentiate our understanding of entrepreneurial orientation (EO) as a measure for entrepreneurial mindsets and attitudes from actual entrepreneurial performance, which is measured in terms of the sum of an organization's innovation, renewal and venturing efforts (Dess and Lumpkin, 2005; Zahra, 1995).

Corporate entrepreneurship is clearly a multidimensional concept and is best seen as an umbrella term for different aspects, levels or stages of activities and processes through which established organizations act entrepreneurially, as well as the outcomes of such activities and processes. Entrepreneurial organizations tend to engage in strategy making characterized by an active stance in pursuing opportunities, taking risks and innovation (Dess et al., 1997). This has been the focus of attention for scholars drawing on the construct of EO. Viewing entrepreneurship as a firm-level phenomenon, Miller (1983, p. 771) views an entrepreneurial firm as 'one that engages in product market innovation, undertakes somewhat risky ventures, and is first to come up with proactive innovations, beating competitors to the punch'. This definition singles out three dimensions, risk taking, innovativeness and proactiveness as the core dimensions of EO. These three dimensions have been widely adopted in subsequent, empirical and conceptual research on EO (for example, Covin and Slevin, 1989, 1991; Wiklund, 1998).

As a concept, EO is similar to Stevenson and Jarillo's (1990) notion of entrepreneurial management. Building on Miller (1983) and Stevenson and Jarillo (1990), Lumpkin and Dess (1996) provide a useful overview and integration of the EO literature. They define EO as 'the processes, practices, and decision-making activities that lead to new entry' where new entry is 'the act of launching a new venture' (Lumpkin and Dess, 1996, p. 136). They also present five dimensions of EO compared to the three dimensions originated in Miller (1983) and taken further by Covin and Slevin (1989, 1991). The five dimensions determining if a firm has an EO is the extent to which it is characterized by: proactiveness, risk taking, innovativeness, autonomy and competitive aggressiveness. We now briefly discuss these dimensions.

Proactiveness

Proactiveness refers to how a firm takes strategic initiatives by anticipating and pursuing new opportunities. It is defined as 'acting in anticipation of future problems, needs of changes'. This means a forward-looking perspective and search for new opportunities that are 'accompanied by innovative or new venture activity'. There is an important difference between proactiveness and competitive aggressiveness. The former refers to how a firm relates to market opportunities in the process of new entry whereas the latter refers to how firms 'relate to competitors, that is, how firms respond to trends and demands that already exist in the marketplace' (Lumpkin and Dess, 1996, p. 147).

Risk Taking

Firms with an EO are often said to take risks, where heavy debt and large resource commitments in relation to a new entry are examples of risky behavior. Stated formally, risk taking refers to 'the degree to which managers are willing to make large and risky resource commitments – i.e., those which have a reasonable change of costly failures' (Miller and

Friesen, 1978, p. 932). Risk-taking firms show a tendency to 'take bold actions such as venturing into unknown new markets' (Lumpkin and Dess, 2001, p. 431) without certain knowledge of probable outcomes (Covin and Slevin, 1991). Previous research on the relationship between risk taking and outcome variables such as growth and performance gives inconclusive results (Rauch et al., 2009).

Innovativeness

Innovativeness refers to 'a firm's tendency to engage in and support new ideas, novelty, experimentation, and creative processes that may result in new products, services, or technological processes' (Lumpkin and Dess, 1996, p. 142). Innovativeness is crucial to maintain a given firm's viability because it is a key source of the new ideas that lead to product introductions, service improvements and managerial practices that advance and sustain a company (Lumpkin et al., 2009). There is typically a continuum of innovativeness, both regarding the scope and pace of innovation in products, markets and technologies. Being innovative in terms of new products, process and attitudes has been found to increase growth of firms (Moreno and Casillas, 2008; Rauch et al., 2009). Innovativeness is characterized by processes where existing market structures are disrupted by the entry of new goods and services that may render previous goods and services obsolete (Schumpeter, 1934).

Autonomy

Autonomy is about the freedom granting individuals inside an organization to be creative, to push for ideas and to change current ways of doing things. Lumpkin and Dess (1996, p. 140) define autonomy as 'the independent action of an individual or a team in bringing forth an idea or a vision and carrying it through to completion'. For autonomy to be established in a firm flexible organizational structures, open communication and low power distance is important. Individuals and teams must have the ability to make decisions and take actions without being hindered by the organizational constraints or strategic norms that often impede progress (Lumpkin et al., 2009). Burgelman (1983) has shown that a certain amount of autonomous behavior by individuals and teams is needed for new venture creation within established firms. Autonomy can also refer to an external autonomy in the sense that individuals and teams are independent in relation to external constituents such as banks, financial markets, suppliers and customers. External autonomy refers to a greater sense of controlling one's destiny (Nordqvist et al., 2008).

Competitive Aggressiveness

Competitive aggressiveness refers to 'a firm's propensity to directly and intensively challenge its competitors to achieve entry or improve position, that is, to outperform industry rivals in the market place' (Lumpkin and Dess, 1996, p.148). While proactiveness is a response to opportunities competitive aggressiveness is a response to threats (Lumpkin and Dess, 2001). Competitive aggressiveness can thus be reactive. This means, for instance, a new entry that is an imitation of an existing product or service would be considered entrepreneurial if the move implies an aggressive 'head-to-head' confrontation on the market. Competitive aggressiveness also embraces non-traditional ways of competing in an industry, such as new ways of distributing or marketing products.

The literature tends to be consistent in suggesting that the five dimensions of EO are likely to be separate but related (for example, Lumpkin and Dess, 1996; Wiklund and Shepherd, 2003). This means that firms can vary in terms of how proactive, risk taking, innovative, autonomous and competitively aggressive they are. For example, a particular firm may be very competitively aggressive, but not take many risks, but still be viewed as having an EO. That is, firms can vary in the degree of each dimension so that they are not equally entrepreneurial across all five dimensions. In addition, some firms can be cautious and risk averse under some circumstances and take risks in others (Brockhaus, 1980). The five dimensions are, however, suggested to be positively correlated (Lumpkin and Dess, 1996), which also has been validated empirically (Rauch et al., 2009).

Entrepreneurial Orientation in the Family Firm Context

As outlined above, we face equivocal findings in whether family firms exhibit a context prolific or unproductive for corporate entrepreneurship to occur. Reaching beyond the diversity of findings at the level of entrepreneurship or entrepreneurial orientation in family firms, we expect that EO has specific features in family firms.

First, EO uses the business as the level of analysis. The family as the critical constituent of any family firm remains largely neglected. We argue that the importance of family and family involvement for this type of business calls for an investigation of the entrepreneurial mindset of the business family. Martin and Lumpkin (2003) contrast EO with what they call family orientation (FO) and suggest that an increasing FO will overtake the EO as the family firm is passed on through generations. Their FO dimensions are interdependency, loyalty, security, stability and tradition (Lumpkin et al., 2008). Martin and Lumpkin (2003) find decreasing levels of EO in terms of autonomy, risk taking and competitive aggressiveness as later generations are involved in the family firm in their US sample. They conclude that while founding generations are more motivated by entrepreneurial concerns, these become replaced with family concerns and an increasing FO over time and generations that appears to be in conflict with EO. Martin and Lumpkin (2003) thus argue for a tradeoff view between EO and FO where both postures cannot exist simultaneously.

This approach can be challenged. By shifting the level of analysis in line with the argument by Habbershon and Pistrui (2002) we can, for example, think of a combined EO and FO measure that addresses the EO of the family unit rather than the one of the business unit. Such a family entrepreneurial orientation (FEO) measure would more directly address EO in the family context and go after the essence of family influence on EO. Investigating FEO would, for instance, increase our understanding of different types of business families, in addition to different types of family businesses. Keeping the FO scale, additional dimensions that would be relevant to include are persistence, efficiency and reputation concerns since they are typical to many family firms and have potentially a positive impact on entrepreneurial performance.

Second, we may need to introduce new concepts to our framework in order to better understand our observations of EO in the family context. Nordqvist et al. (2008), for instance, draw on the five dimensions of EO and integrate the concept of duality to interpret what characterizes entrepreneurship in family firms over time, and how and why certain dimensions of entrepreneurship are more present and important than others for performance. They identify three dualities related to the dimensions of EO: the historical/new path duality, the independence/dependence duality and the formality/informality duality. Based on in-depth case research, they propose that the risk-taking and competitive aggressiveness dimensions of EO are less important to family firms. Conversely, they suggest that autonomy, innovativeness and proactiveness are more present dimensions of EO and have greater meaning for long-term entrepreneurial performance. This supports the assertion that EO may occur in different combinations depending on the context and that the effectiveness of EO is related to the contexts in which organizational activity takes place (Lumpkin et al., 2006).

Third, the definitions of several underlying constructs of EO might need to be revisited when applying them to the family business context. Risk taking is a key feature of entrepreneurship and the family's risk profile can play a central role for EO in family firms (Naldi et al., 2007; Zahra, 2005). Risk taking might need to be further specified given that families face a high financial risk in terms of committed and undiversified personal funds.

However, in terms of control risk, measured by leverage levels, family firms are rather risk averse. Recent studies on reference point dependent risk behavior (for example, Gomez-Mejia et al., 2007; Zellweger et al., 2008) provide a new picture of risk taking. Similarly, autonomy might be diverse when differentiating between internal (if decision making is bounded by predetermined processes) and external autonomy (in terms of independence from external stakeholders) (Nordqvist et al., 2008). A family firm can well display predetermined structures and processes internally and hence low internal autonomy, but high independence towards external stakeholders.

Fourth, EO literature assumes that the more entrepreneurial a firm is across all these dimensions, the more successful it will be in the long run. However we might, for instance, see that firms that are successful in the long run display lower levels of certain EO dimensions (for example, competitive aggressiveness and risk taking) since they have detected or actively created market niches in which they are unrivaled. Whereas high levels of EO across all dimensions might be appropriate when launching and growing a firm, such an EO pattern might not be needed or sustainable over several generations. This argument is forcefully advanced in Chapter 8 by Zellweger et al. in this volume. They argue that high degrees of entrepreneurial performance may only be necessary in specific times to regenerate and grow the business. To secure transgenerational potential and longevity in family firms, a continuously high EO in all of its five dimensions may not be optimal (Zellweger et al., 2008).

1.6   THE RESOURCE-BASED VIEW

We see the resource-based view (RBV) as the second underlying theory for our transgenerational entrepreneurship framework. The RBV holds that businesses with unique bundles of resources can create strategies that lead to a sustained competitive advantage, if they form the strategies based on resources that are valuable, rare, imperfectly imitable and non-substitutable (Barney, 1986, 1991; Wernerfelt, 1984). A central thesis in RBV is that the resource profile of a particular organization drives the success of performance outcomes of that organization (Greene and Brown, 1997). In the RBV resources are viewed as the fundamental units of value creation (Mathews, 2002). Being an elegant conceptual framework, RBV has been a popular base for theorizing in many areas of strategy and management research, including human resource management, entrepreneurship and international business (Barney et al., 2001) while empirical explorations and testing of the RBV are still very rare (Cool et al., 2002). There has been a general progression in the RBV from an interest in which resources might be valuable to an examination of how these resources are managed and leveraged. The underlying idea is that managing, in other words using, deploying and reconfiguring, resources is the key to sustainable competitive advantage (Mahoney, 1995).

Recent years have seen more scholars drawing on the RBV-related fields of entrepreneurship (for example, Alvarez and Barney, 2004) and family firms (for example, Habbershon and Williams, 1999; Sirmon and Hitt, 2003). In the entrepreneurship literature some have argued that the actual processes associated with the ability to seek, capture and exploit opportunities can be a resource in its own right (Alvarez and Busenitz, 2001). In family business research the interaction between the family and the business is argued to give rise to unusually complex and difficult to imitate resources (Cabrera-Suarez et al., 2001; Chrisman et al., 2005; Habbershon and Williams, 1999; Sirmon and Hitt, 2003). Habbershon and Williams (1999) use the RBV to coin the notion of 'familiness' and to argue that complex and unique resources and family involvement in a firm's strategic business activities can generate a competitive advantage. Family influence can thus become the root to heterogeneity since it leads to idiosyncrasies of the individual family firms. These family driven idiosyncrasies become part of the competitive advantage of a firm when they are valuable and inimitable by other firms. The value and inimitability of these idiosyncratic resources and capabilities is due to their socially complex, path dependent and often tacit nature.

However not all family influenced resources enhance performance. Rather 'some family firm attributes provide advantages in the resource management process, while others limit this ability' (Sirmon and Hitt, 2003, p. 340). Therefore Habbershon et al. (2003) suggest that family involvement can either drive or constrain performance depending on the nature of the resources, as well as the particular business activity in focus. In other words, a specific family influenced resource can either represent distinctive familiness ('f+') for influences that support an advantage to emerge, or restrictive familiness ('f−') for influences that constrain and lead to a disadvantage, and 'f0' for family influences that are neutral in relation to desired outcomes (Habbershon et al., 2003). The notion of familiness in relation to the RBV thus aims to capture the source of what is idiosyncratic in the resource profile of each family firm and provides a conceptual path for examining the way in which family influence may lead to a business creating heterogeneous performance outcomes.

There has been a great deal of confusion on the appropriate usage of the term familiness. The term has originally been defined as the unique firm level bundle of resources and capabilities resulting from family involvement (Habbershon et al., 2003). In recent publications authors have undertaken significant efforts to clarify the nature and the domain of the construct (Pearson et al., 2008; Sharma, 2008). However, due to the still fragmentary and incomplete knowledge about the concept, we see a need to clarify our understanding of familiness, thereby contributing to the concept's nomological net (Pearson et al., 2008).

In line with the more general RBV we understand familiness as a concept that addresses both the 'what' and the 'how' of family involvement in firms. On the side of the content, hence the 'what' dimension, familiness informs about the type and amount of resource stocks available within family influenced firms. Scholars have particularly underlined the relevance of particular resources in the family firm context, such as social capital (Pearson et al., 2008; Sharma, 2008), human capital (Puhakka, 2002), financial capital (Sirmon and Hitt, 2003) and physical capital (Miller and Le Breton-Miller, 2005; Steier, 2007). In addition, researchers have investigated the explicit and in particular the implicit knowledge resources embedded in the family business system (Carney, 2005; Sirmon and Hitt, 2003), which can be particularly strong and critical for these firms due to the path-dependent development and their dependence on governance and ownership structures.

Furthermore, our research shows that family firms often exhibit a particular corporate culture that can be influenced by the family's sustained presence in the firm, often referring back to the attitudes and beliefs of the founders of these companies (Poutziouris et al., 1997). Finally, we see intangible resources and in particular reputation as a further key resource in this type of firm (Dyer and Whetten, 2006). Several scholars have investigated the performance implications of personal, family and corporate reputation, but there are equivocal findings they report about the reputation–performance link (for example, Anderson et al., 2003; Naldi et al., 2008; Zellweger and Kellermanns, 2008). As such, we consider family firms to have unique social, human, financial, physical, knowledge, cultural and intangible resource stocks due to family involvement in the firm. Here we see the necessity to apply a trans-unit of analysis perspective since part of the resources at the firm and family level are provided by either family or firm system. As Sharma (2008) correctly points out, we need to consider capital flows between family and firm system to understand the competitive advantages or disadvantages of family firms. In such a trans-unit of analysis perspective, family and firm can both serve as lenders and borrowers of resource stocks.

Whereas recent developments in family business theory have provided some insights into the relevance of different resource stocks, the RBV has traditionally also stressed the relevance of resource management and leveraging as outlined above. Accordingly, the second dimension of our understanding of familiness, the 'how' dimension, relates to the ways in which owners and managers of family firms are actually able, or competent, to bundle and leverage their resource bases to create competitive advantages (Sirmon and Hitt, 2003). In this regard, Naldi et al. (2008) stress that family involvement in strategy-making processes may be seen as a moderator that impacts on whether intangible resources such as knowledge and reputation can be deployed at their full potential to create financial performance. Adding to this contingency perspective, Kellermanns (2005) and Sharma and Manikutty (2005) stress that family firms might be biased by the personal preferences of family members when it comes to resource adding and shedding. Eddleston et al. (2008b) show that family firms can benefit from emphasizing the positive aspects of kinship and from developing innovative capacities. As such, they demonstrate that not only do firm-specific resources contribute to family firm performance, but also that family relationships based on reciprocal altruism, which could be seen as a family firm-specific form of bonding social capital, can be a source of competitive advantage for a family firm.

In summary, combining these two perspectives in the transgenerational entrepreneurship framework, we therefore consider the relevance of studying family influence on both resource stocks and usage. As such, we stress family influence on resources, and do not see the family as a resource on its own. Also we do not see familiness as a pure firm-level phenomenon, as originally defined by Habbershon et al. (2003), but as a trans-unit of analysis phenomenon, due to the interrelation of the family and the firm in resource availability and usage.

1.7 THE INTERRELATIONSHIP BETWEEN RESOURCES AND ENTREPRENEURIAL ORIENTATION

Traditionally, entrepreneurship scholars have argued that while the RBV focuses on heterogeneity of resources, entrepreneurship theory focuses on the heterogeneity of beliefs about the value of these resources. Hence the focus on heterogeneity in firms' strategic profiles can be seen as a common denominator between the RBV and entrepreneurship. Thus combining the RBV with an entrepreneurship framework such as EO may, we argue, allow researchers to address the essence of the question why some firms stay competitive and continue to grow while other firm decline or even become obsolete.

In line with Habbershon (2006), we may argue that the interactions between the family, its firm and individuals in the family and/or firm create resources that either promote or inhibit entrepreneurial orientation. It is conceivable, for example, that a family influenced social network might foster entrepreneurial behavior. A certain leadership style as a resource may very well facilitate EO in one generation, while constraining it in another. Another family influenced resource that may affect EO is governance. Family firms are often assumed to have rather informal governance and organizational structures with quick, sometimes intuitive, decision making (Carney, 2005; Hall et al., 2006). These characteristics, Lumpkin and Dess (1996) argue, promote EO. Poza (1988), however, looks at 'interpreneurship', defined as intergenerational entrepreneurial activities in family firms and argues that formalized governance and especially the presence of non-family board members are conducive to promote continued growth over the long term. Brunninge and Nordqvist (2004) do not find empirical support for the hypothesis that non-family board members promote corporate entrepreneurship. Other examples of family influenced resources that have been argued to have an impact on the entrepreneurial capacity of family firms is organizational culture (Hall et al., 2001; Zahra et al., 2004), knowledge (Chirico, 2008) and trust (Steier, 2003). Wiklund and Shepherd (2003) stress the role of intangible resources for entrepreneurial activities and orientation. Furthermore, kinship ties within social capital can facilitate opportunity recognition and exploitation (Aldrich and Cliff, 2003). Finally, Eddleston et al. (2008a) found that family to firm unity moderates the relationships between human capital and corporate entrepreneurship, whereby a lack of human capital can be offset by higher levels of family unity. Given these considerations, some of the chapters in this book are explicitly dedicated to further explore these specific resource aspects of entrepreneurial orientation in the family and the family firm context.

Despite some noteworthy exceptions presented above, we consider that there is still a dearth of research untangling the relationship between family influenced resources and the entrepreneurial orientation of firms. In particular, we challenge the unidirectional nature of the relationship, where (prior) resource allocations should serve as an indicator of an entrepreneurial posture (Lyon et al., 2000). Also the opposite way is conceivable: for example, if a firm displays high levels of autonomy towards internal and external stakeholders, it will most likely experience lower levels of social capital. However the reliance on internal processes and ways of doing things might, in contrast, be prolific to develop tacit knowledge. Furthermore, being aggressive towards competitors might impact reputational resources, both at the family and the firm level. Moreover, an innovative posture might not only be positively impacted by the firm's human capital and knowledge-based resources. Innovativeness might also fuel the levels of human capital and knowledge-based resources through learning effects.

Accordingly, we see entrepreneurial postures and resources as inter-related, the first one representing the attitudes to take an active stance in doing things, and the latter representing the means to undertake the required actions. We therefore see both as being important drivers of a firm's performance and value creation potential and, ultimately, success across several generations. This view is driven by the insight that resources and entrepreneurial orientation taken on their own are necessary but not sufficient conditions for long-term success. Without resources entre-preneurial orientation lacks the means to be realized. Thus without an entrepreneurial posture resources are unexploited, become slack and lack rejuvenation. Our transgenerational perspective proposes that only the combination of resources and entrepreneurial orientation will carry family firms and business families into a successful future.

1.8   CONTEXTUAL FACTORS

An important aspect of theory development is setting the boundaries for its application and accounting for the contextual factors in which the theory holds or is investigated. Lumpkin and Dess (1996) argue that the strength of the five different dimensions of EO may differ depend-ing on the characteristics of the firm or types of firm. Besides industry, they suggest size, ownership and age as other possible contextual factors that may impact EO in a particular firm. But they also underline that little empirical research has so far been done to untangle these relation-ships. Also there have been arguments within the EO literature to further explore the EO–performance relationships (Dess et al., 1997; Zahra, 1993). Lumpkin and Dess (1996) suggest that organizational factors such as size, structure, strategy, strategy-making processes, firm resources and culture and top management team characteristics should moderate the relationship. Furthermore, Lumpkin and Dess (1996) argue that environ-mental factors such as dynamism, munificence, complexity and industry characteristics might interfere.

Beyond these arguments, Lyon et al. (2000) suggest that time might be a further contextual issue in the relationship between EO and performance, since entrepreneurial attitudes and initiatives often do not create immedi-ate performance effects. A recent meta-analysis explored the extent to which the different dimensions of EO are positively or negatively related to performance (Rauch et al., 2009). Broadly speaking, the literature tends to be consistent in suggesting that firms with higher EO levels are more likely to do well in traditional performance measures, such as growth and profitability.

In a similar way, within the RBV scholars have called for more attention to be paid to the boundaries of the theoretical concept (Priem and Butler, 2001) and to the contexts within which particular resources were determined to be more or less valuable (Miller and Shamsie, 1996). Again industry is seen as such a contextual factor, but also community culture (Hofstede, 1991) and the temporal orientation (Powell, 1992).

Following these calls, we introduce a series of contextual factors within the transgenerational entrepreneurship research framework that are intended to capture the variance in the context and to set the boundaries of our research (Whetten, 1989). Accordingly, in the STEP Project we include contextual factors that have been identified in previous studies of EO and the RBV, such as industry, community culture and the environment (captured through dynamism, munificence and complexity). Furthermore, we also include contextual factors that we have observed in the first phases of the qualitative case research such as family life stage and family involvement. By family life stage we mean the number of generations the family has been in control of the specific firm. Partly in line with Martin and Lumpkin (2003) we see that business families may differ in their resources and entrepreneurial posture depending on the generation they are in. In an attempt to account for generational differences, Cruz and Nordqvist (2008) study how the determinants of proactiveness, risk taking and innovativeness differ depending on the family generation in charge of the business. They argue that while the founders drive EO to a great extent in the first generation, EO is more subject to managers' interpretations of the competitive environment in the second generation. In the third generation and beyond, access to non-family resources is increasingly important to maintain an EO in family firms (Cruz and Nordqvist, 2008).

We investigate family involvement, in particular through the family's involvement in equity, management and, if available, governance board. Our cases show very heterogeneous ways in which families are involved in their firms, as is evident in the studies forming the chapters in this book.

Capturing the temporal dimension that has been stressed is an important contextual factor both in EO and RBV theory. We investigate the evolution of family involvement across time, but also the evolution of the portfolio of the businesses making part of the family business group. Furthermore, we are investigating the entrepreneurial performance of the family firms under investigation across time. As such we are able, at least partly, to overcome the limitations related to a cross-sectional design of EO and RBV studies.

1.9   PERFORMANCE

Within our framework we expect that performance is a necessary ante-cedent for successful business activity that spans generations. Due to numerous assertions that family firms strive for multiple performance dimensions (Chrisman et al., 2005; Zellweger and Nason, 2008), we dif-ferentiate between three types of performance outcomes: entrepreneurial, financial and social performance outcomes. As such we see performance in the family firm context as a multidimensional construct. Before describing the three performance dimensions we hasten to add that we see these per-formance dimensions as interrelated. As elaborated on below, we conceive that one performance dimension will impact the other ones, for instance, through substitution but also synergistic effects. Family harmony through hiring of a family member might only be achievable at the expense of financial performance. But family reputation, a performance outcome on the side of the family, may also nurture corporate financial perform-ance through access to clients and industry networks. Moreover, we also consider these performance dimensions to be interrelated in the tempo-ral dimension. For example, entrepreneurial performance in terms of renewal or venturing might take years to manifest itself in financial terms. We now explain what we mean by entrepreneurial, financial and social performance.

Entrepreneurial Performance

In line with our consideration that entrepreneurship is an important engine for generation-spanning business activities, we consider that entre-preneurial performance is one of the key performance measures for our study. Entrepreneurial performance is defined as 'the sum of an organi-zation's innovation, renewal, and venturing efforts where innovation involves creating and introducing products, production processes and organizational systems. . . renewal means revitalizing the company's oper-ations by changing the scope of its business, its competitive approaches, and acquiring new capabilities and then creatively leveraging them to add value for shareholders. . .venturing means that the (organization) will enter new businesses by expanding operations in existing or new markets' (Zahra, 1995, p. 227; for similar definitions see Davidsson and Wiklund, 2001; Dess and Lumpkin, 2005).

   The entrepreneurship view on performance considers that the relative performance advantage over competitive firms, as strategic manage-ment scholars hold (Venkataraman, 1997), is not a sufficient measure for entrepreneurial performance. This is related to the insight that a performance advantage may be insufficient to compensate for the opportunity cost of other alternatives, a liquidity premium for time and capital and a premium for uncertainty bearing (Shane and Venkataraman, 2000). Entrepreneurship researchers rather consider performance as the degree to which valuable opportunities (for example, new entry) are exploited, thereby creating entrepreneurial rents.

The above definition of entrepreneurial performance as the 'sum of an organization's innovation, renewal, and venturing efforts' might create confusion with the measure of entrepreneurial orientation. EO is defined as an indication of entrepreneurial attitudes and practices at the firm level. As such, EO determines a firm's inclination to be entrepreneurial, and is a measure of the firm's attitude to undertake entrepreneurial efforts. To avoid confusion between the two terms, we see entrepreneurial performance as the actual entrepreneurial initiatives in terms of innovation, renewal and venturing, and hence as the manifestation of the entrepreneurial stance or efforts. Even though there might be a high positive correlation between EO and entrepreneurial performance, we see them as distinct and separate constructs. For example, a firm can display a low level of entrepreneurial performance despite high levels of EO since the organization is unable to transform its entrepreneurial posture into actual entrepreneurial performance (for example, new products), or due to the temporal distance between the entrepreneurial behavior and the actual entrepreneurial performance.

Considering the differences between entrepreneurship in the context of established firms as opposed to newly founded organizations, for example, in terms of resource stocks, we expect to discover distinct patterns of entrepreneurial performance. Whereas for newly founded firms creating new products and introducing them to new markets is the key to overcoming liability of newness, in the context of long-established firms different types of innovation activities might become essential for survival and prosperity. For example, a top selling product that has a loyal customer base does not have to be reinvented or replaced by a new product, even if it is 'old'. Rather, long-term successful goods or services need to be rejuvenated and need not to be replaced to satisfy today's customers. Accordingly, we expect long-term established firms to display different types of entrepreneurial performance, with presumably lower levels of innovation in terms of new products or markets, but higher levels of renewal. As such, we see entrepreneurial performance not as a manifestation of the firm's need to overcome liability of newness, but to overcome 'liability of oldness', defined as the liability faced by established firms to keep up with changes in their environmental and organizational setting. In a similar way, we might find that established firms are challenged more with shrinking the product portfolio that has become excessively diversified over the years. In contrast to the traditional entrepreneurship perspective, we see such moves as equally entrepreneurial as adding new products.

Financial Performance

Traditionally, management scholars have evaluated performance of organizations in financial terms. Whereas financial performance is certainly a crucial outcome of any business activity, we understand it as a result of entrepreneurial performance, and thereby entrepreneurial activities being the engine or the driver of financial success.

Performance of family firms has been assessed using objective measures such as return on equity, return on assets, return on sales and gross margin, or growth measures of the aforementioned ratios and figures. In the absence of objective measures, subjective performance measures have been used since prior research suggests that there is a high level of correlation between actual performance and the self-reported subjective performance data (Dess and Robinson, 1984; Love et al., 2002; Venkatraman and Ramanujam, 1987). In addition, subjective measures allow inclusion of perks and the financial freedom for family members to develop a reliable performance measure. In the context of publicly quoted firms, stock market performance has been investigated or Tobin's Q, the market value of the firm divided by the replacement costs of the assets.

There is a wide array of studies investigating the financial performance of privately held and publicly quoted family firms. Since Anderson and Reeb (2003) found that family firms are outperforming their non-family counterparts on the stock market, a large number of performance studies on family firms have emerged (Rutherford et al., 2008; for an overview see Miller and Le Breton-Miller, 2005). These studies provide ambiguous findings. A large number of studies examining the impact of family in ownership conclude that family ownership does not impact financial performance (Cho, 1998; Demsetz and Lehn, 1985; McConaughy et al., 2001; McConnell and Servaes, 1990; Morck et al., 1988; Stulz, 1988). Other studies suggest that it is paramount to distinguish between founding ownership (that is, first-generation family influence) and descendant ownership (that is, influence of the family via second or later generations). Several authors (for example, Adams et al., 2005; Fahlenbrach, 2006; McConaughy et al., 1998; Morck et al., 1988; Villalonga and Amit, 2006) agree that family firms are outperforming their non-family counterparts when the founder remains active in the firm. However this issue has not received unequivocal support either.

Whereas studies investigating family ownership and governance provide ambiguous findings, there seems to be some support for the case that family firms are financially outperforming their non-family counterparts when family is active in the management of the firm (Sraer and Thesmar, 2007; Zellweger, 2006). This is tied to lower salary levels, the long-term tenure of employees and related innovation and efficiency effects and trust-based manager relations.

This literature review on performance studies is far from being complete. However, all in all, studies investigating the financial performance of family firms provide very diverse results. We consider that this variety is not only related to the diversity and fuzziness of the applied family firm and performance definitions. At least as important, we consider that these frontal attempts to measure family firm performance, for example, through artificially dichotomizing family versus non-family firms, overlook how families can be drivers of entrepreneurial activities and sources of distinctive familiness which ultimately fuels financial performance. Therefore within our research model we will particularly investigate how business families' mindsets, resources and capabilities will affect the performance of these firms.

Social Performance

A common theme in family business literature is that financial outcomes may have been inaccurately assumed to be the primary or even sole performance objective of a family business (Alvarez and Barney, 2004; Anderson and Reeb, 2003; Chrisman et al., 2003, 2004; Dunn, 1995; Lee and Rogoff, 1996; Sharma, 2004; Westhead and Cowling, 1997; Zellweger and Astrachan, 2008). Scholars have suggested that family firms have multiple and changing goals rather than a singular and constant goal, and that this type of firm displays a stronger preference towards non-pecuniary outcomes like independence, prestige, tradition and continuity than non-family firms (Corbetta and Salvato, 2004; Dunn, 1995; Sharma et al., 1997; Sorenson, 1999; Stafford et al., 1999; Tagiuri and Davis, 1982; Ward, 1997). We describe these non-financial performance outcomes as social performance. Thereby it is important to note that we do not define social performance according to its financial or non-financial nature. Social performance, for example, in philanthropy or giving to environmental groups, is mostly financial in nature. However, given the use of the funds for social aims we consider them as part of social performance.

Litz (1997) and Sharma (2004) have proposed that stakeholder theory might be useful in investigating family firms. Indeed, we also believe that the stakeholder framework is useful to investigate the social performance dimension, since family firms have a natural inclination to satisfy multiple stakeholders that follow social alongside financial goals. We see three distinct reasons for this (Zellweger and Nason, 2008).

First, in contrast to non-family enterprises, family firms by definition have an additional stakeholder group, the family. In addition, the family stakeholder group has unique goals, many of which can be considered social, such as harmony, jobs for family members and family control.

A second reason why family firms have a natural inclination to satisfy multiple stakeholders is related to the tight overlap between the individual owner-manager, the family and the firm. Given that entrepreneurs in family firms often make part of all three stakeholder categories, we should expect that these decision makers have a higher incentive to ensure the particular satisfaction of the related individual stakeholders and stakeholder groups who form the reputation of the organization (Dyer and Whetten, 2006; Hogg et al., 1995).

Third, family enterprises have been reported to display strong community relations and display richer social capital due to their transgenerational outlook (Sirmon and Hitt, 2003). The transgenerational outlook and patient capital allow these firms to devote the proper time to cultivate the necessary relationships with societal stakeholders, allowing these firms to establish more effective relations with support organizations (for example, banks), while maintaining legitimacy with other important constituencies and societal stakeholders (Lounsbury and Glynn, 2001).

Applying the stakeholder paradigm to assess the social performance of family firms provides insight into the question of which social performance outcomes family firms will actually produce to satisfy key constituents. However, beyond the question of which performance dimensions should be produced to satisfy the multiple stakeholders, family firms need to answer the question of how they should efficiently produce the diverse performance outcomes originating from these multiple stakeholders. This question is related to the observation that certain outcomes of business activity have the capacity to satisfy multiple stakeholder categories and impact each other (Chrisman and Carroll, 1984). Thereby we follow Dess et al. (2003) who propose that a stakeholder analysis need not implicitly involve tradeoffs among the various stakeholders, but rather that other, for example, symbiotic, relationships may exist and that stakeholder groups can be satisfied in other matters. Zellweger and Nason (2008) have extended this line of thinking by showing that beyond substitution effects, in which non-economic performance dimensions offset economic performance, this relation can be synergistic, causal (one performance dimension causing multiple other performance dimensions) or overlapping (one performance dimension satisfying multiple stakeholders).

Despite the relevance of social performance in the context of family firms, only recently have scholars investigated this performance dimension in more detail (for example, Dyer and Whetten, 2006; Zellweger and Astrachan, 2008). By investigating the social aspects of performance, alongside entrepreneurial and financial performance, we follow calls by Chrisman et al. (2005) to further investigate the issue.

1.10   BRIEF INTRODUCTION TO THE CHAPTERS OF THE BOOK

Having laid out the major building blocks of our transgenerational entrepreneurship framework, we believe that the approach chosen exhibits a good fit between the theoretical foundations and the object of investigation. The following chapters introduce the methodology of our case study approach and the preliminary findings from the European STEP team.

In Chapter 2 the STEP Project's qualitative research approach is presented and discussed. In addition to explaining the need for more in-depth, theory generating research in the area of entrepreneurship in family businesses, Mattias Nordqvist and Thomas Zellweger describe the main aspects of the case research method we have applied. We cover the sampling criteria, details about data collection as well as the process of data analysis. We also briefly explain the importance of creating an interactive learning environment within a large, global research project as well as the role of the yearly summits.

In Chapter 3 the Italian team from Bocconi University, Milan, investigates the resource perspective within the transgenerational entrepreneurship framework. Ugo Lassini and Carlo Salvato argue that, although a focus on specific resources is attractive since it offers a parsimonious explanation of what determines family firms' value creation potential, there is widespread agreement among scholars that the gradual development of firm-specific resource stocks over generations may also be a source of inertial forces blocking family firm's entrepreneurial potential. Despite this awareness, little research to date has been carried out on how controlling families can leverage the pool of unique firm-specific resources they develop, while overcoming the inertial risks they carry. Lassini and Salvato present a pioneering study that investigates how some family firms attain this difficult balance between the positive features of idiosyncratic resources cumulated over generations and their inertial potential.

The German team, from the University of Witten-Herdecke, represented by Markus Plate, Arist von Schlippe and Christian Schiede, presents in Chapter 4 a single case analysis of the processes and conditions of portfolio entrepreneurship within a large multinational family firm, and identify resources that enable portfolio entrepreneurship. In their study the authors strive to answer two research questions. First, how do the portfolio of ventures emerge in the family context? This analysis includes the processes, conditions, motives and strategy of the portfolio entrepreneurship process. Second, the authors investigate which resources (influenced by the family and the entrepreneur) enable the development of successful portfolio entrepreneurship practices. This analysis takes a resource-based view, with a special focus on the bundle of resources influenced and provided by the entrepreneur and the business family. The study is an important early attempt to better grasp the dynamics of family portfolio entrepreneurship.

In Chapter 5 the Swedish team, from Jönköping International Business School, represented by Ethel Brundin, Mattias Nordqvist and Leif Melin, aims at increasing the understanding of how entrepreneurial orientation is transferred and translated to the next generation family members in strong family business cultures. The purpose of their chapter is to illustrate and discuss the role of culture as a key element for entrepreneurial orientation to travel over generations. More specifically, the Swedish team shows how autonomy and proactiveness can both support and hamper such a process. Based on findings from two in-depth case studies and the transgenerational entrepreneurship framework, they explore the role of culture, seen as a family influenced resource, on entrepreneurial orientation. Moving beyond conventional life cycle reasoning, they show that founder-centric cultures can return in later stages of the firm's life cycle. They introduce the concept of 'owner-centric culture' as an alternative way of thinking about and conceptualizing strong family businesses cultures and their impact on the entrepreneurial orientation of a business.

In Chapter 6 the French team, from HEC School of Management, Paris, represented by Alain Bloch, Michel Santi and Alexandra Joseph, analyses two French family business case studies. In both families children were faced with the sudden and early death of their fathers which left them unprepared to be in charge. They nevertheless kept the ownership of the company within the family and developed the family business successfully. In both cases they find that entrepreneurial performance followed a very similar path. In their cases firm life stage did not follow family life stage, which unleashed additional entrepreneurial performance in both firms. Both families had to face a breakout in the succession process and both families answered the same way: maintaining the firm under the family control without necessarily occupying a management position. They succeeded in maintaining the family firm's entrepreneurial performance despite a generational breakthrough within the family life stage.

The Spanish team, from ESADE, Barcelona, represented by Eugenia Bieto, Alberto Gimeno and María José Parada, focuses in Chapter 7 on how familiness evolves over time. These authors specifically deal with entrepreneurial teams as a key resource within the family's pool of resources which tends to weaken over time mainly due to family complexities. Through an in-depth study, their chapter analyses the role of succession, governance structures and relations in entrepreneurial teams. A thorough analysis of interview material from family owners/managers and non-family executives of two family firms suggests that the three aforementioned elements play a critical role in the evolution of the leadership team as a distinct resource. These firms evolved from solo-founder to top management teams (teams of siblings) up to the entrepreneurial management team (team of family and non-family managers). Their chapter contributes to the family business and familiness/RBV literature by approaching the familiness advantage from a dynamic point of view, proposing an explanation about how some of the resources that create the familiness advantage are sustained or diluted.

Finally, in Chapter 8 the Swiss team, from the University of St Gallen, represented by Thomas Zellweger, Philipp Sieger and Corinne Muehlebach, investigates EO in the context of family firms that have been successful over long periods of time, in their case more than 80 years. These researchers question whether EO is a suitable concept to explain the success of transgenerational family firms. Thereby, the Swiss team investigates the levels and patterns of EO in these firms and questions whether EO really is a necessary condition for long-term organizational success in that context, as implicitly suggested by many corporate entrepreneurship studies (for example, Dess et al., 2003; Rauch et al., 2009). The Swiss team shows that the levels of EO alter across the life cycle of these firms, phases of low levels of EO followed by phases of higher levels of entrepreneurial activity. On average, the three family firms they investigate show rather moderate levels of EO across time. They also discuss the shortcomings of the traditional subdimensions of EO and propose refined measures that are better suited to explain the patterns of entrepreneurship in long-living family firms.

In summary, the chapters in this book explore parts of the building blocks and relationships within the transgenerational entrepreneurship framework. As such, these chapters do not strive to provide a complete overview on all aspects that can potentially be explored within the transgenerational entrepreneurship framework. We hope, however, that they stimulate further reflections and research about one of the most central questions in investigating family firms: what makes these firms successful in the long run?

REFERENCES

Adams, R.B., H. Almeida and D. Ferreira (2005), 'Powerful CEOs and their impact on corporate performance', *Review of Financial Studies*, **18**(4), 1403–32.

Aldrich, H.E. and J.E. Cliff (2003), 'The pervasive effects of family on entrepreneurship: toward a family embeddedness perspective', *Journal of Business Venturing*, **18**(5), 573–96.

Alvarez, J.L. and L. Busenitz (2001), 'The entrepreneurship of resource-based theory', *Journal of Management*, **27**(6), 755–75.

Alvarez, S.A. and J.B. Barney (2004), 'Organizing rent generation and appropriation: toward a theory of the entrepreneurial firm', *Journal of Business Venturing*, **19**(5), 621–35.

Anderson, R.C. and D.M. Reeb (2003), 'Founding-family ownership and firm performance: evidence from the s&p 500', *Journal of Finance*, **58**(3), 1301–28.

Anderson, R.C., S.A. Mansi and D.M. Reeb (2003), 'Founding family ownership and the agency cost of debt', *Journal of Financial Economics*, **68**(2), 263–85.

Arregle, J.-L., M.A. Hitt, D.G. Sirmon and P. Very (2007), 'The development of organizational social capital: attributes of family firms', *Journal of Management Studies*, **44**(1), 73–95.

Barney, J.B. (1986), 'Strategic factor markets: expectation, luck, and business strategy', *Management Science*, **32**(10), 1231–41.

Barney, J.B. (1991), 'Firm resources and sustained competitive advantage', *Journal of Management*, **17**(1), 99–120.

Barney, J.B., M. Wright and D.J.J. Ketchen (2001), 'The resource-based view of the firm: ten years after 1991', *Journal of Management*, **27**(6), 625–41.

Barringer, B.R. and A.C. Bluedorn (1999), 'The relationship between corporate entrepreneurship and strategic management', *Strategic Management Journal*, **20**(5), 421–44.

Birley, S. and P. Westhead (1994), 'A taxonomy of business start-up reasons and their impact on firm growth and size', *Journal of Business Venturing*, **9**(1), 7–31.

Brockhaus, R.H. (1980), 'Risk taking propensity of entrepreneurs', *Academy of Management Journal*, **23**(3), 509–20.

Brockhaus, R.H.S. (1994), 'Entrepreneurship and family business research: comparisons, critique, and lessons', *Entrepreneurship Theory and Practice*, **19**(1), 25–38.

Brunninge, O. and M. Nordqvist (2004), 'Ownership structure, board composition and entrepreneurship: evidence from family firms and venture-capital-backed firms', *International Journal of Entrepreneurial Behaviour and Research*, **10**(1/2), 85–105.

Burgelman, R.A. (1983), 'A process model of internal corporate venturing in the diversified major firm', *Administrative Science Quarterly*, **28**(2), 223–44.

Cabrera-Suarez, K., P. De Saa-Perez and D. Garcia-Almeida (2001), 'The succession process from a resource- and knowledge-based view of the family firm', *Family Business Review*, **14**(1), 37–48.

Carney, M. (2005), 'Corporate governance and competitive advantage in family-controlled firms', *Entrepreneurship Theory and Practice*, **29**(3), 249–65.

Carter, S. and M. Ram (2003), 'Reassessing portfolio entrepreneurship', *Small Business Economics*, **21**(4), 371–80.

Chirico, F. (2008), 'Knowledge accumulation in family firms: evidence from four case studies', *International Small Business Journal*, **26**(4), 433–62.

Cho, M. (1998), 'Ownership structure, investment, and the corporate value: an empirical analysis', *Journal of Financial Economics*, **47**(1), 103–21.

Chrisman, J.J. and A.B. Carroll (1984), 'Corporate responsibility – reconciling economic and social goals', *Sloan Management Review*, **25**(2), 59–65.

Chrisman, J.J., J.H. Chua and L.P. Steier (2003), 'An introduction to theories of family business', *Journal of Business Venturing*, **18**(4), 441–8.

Chrisman, J.J., J.H. Chua and R.A. Litz (2004), 'Comparing the agency costs of family and non-family firms: conceptual issues and exploratory evidence', *Entrepreneurship Theory and Practice*, **28**(4), 335–54.

Chrisman, J.J., J.H. Chua and P. Sharma (2005), 'Trends and directions in the development of a strategic management theory of the family firm', *Entrepreneurship Theory and Practice*, **29**(5), 555–75.

Chua, J.H., J.J. Chrisman and P. Sharma (1999), 'Defining the family business by behavior', *Entrepreneurship Theory and Practice*, **23**(4), 19–39.

Collins, J.C. and J.I. Porras (1994), *Built to Last: Successful Habits of Visionary Companies*, New York: HarperCollins.

Cool, K., L.A. Costa and I. Dierickx (2002), 'Constructing competitive advantage', in A. Pettigrew, H. Thomas and R. Whittington (eds), *Handbook of Strategy and Management*, London: Sage Publications, pp. 55–71.

Corbetta, G. and C. Salvato (2004), 'Self-serving or self-actualizing? Models of man and agency costs in different types of family firms: a commentary on "comparing the agency costs of family and non-family firms: conceptual issues and exploratory evidence"', *Entrepreneurship Theory and Practice*, **28**(4), 355–62.

Covin, J.G. (1991), 'Entrepreneurial versus conservative firms: a comparison of strategies and performance', *Journal of Management Studies*, **28**(5), 439–62.

Covin, J.G. and D.P. Slevin (1989), 'Strategic management of small firms in hostile and benign environments', *Strategic Management Journal*, **10**(1), 75–87.

Covin, J.G. and D.P. Slevin (1991), 'A conceptual model of entrepreneurship as firm behavior', *Entrepreneurship Theory and Practice*, **16**(1), 7–24.

Cruz, C. and M. Nordqvist (2008), 'Entrepreneurial orientation in family firms: a generational perspective', Paper presented at the 8th Annual Ifera Conference, Nyenrode, Breukelen, NED.

Davidsson, P. and J. Wiklund (2001), 'Levels of analysis in entrepreneurship research: current research practice and suggestions for the future', *Entrepreneurship Theory and Practice*, **25**(4), 81–100.

Demsetz, H. and K. Lehn (1985), 'The structure of corporate ownership: causes and consequences', *Journal of Political Economy*, **93**(6), 1155–77.

Dess, G.G. and G.T. Lumpkin (2005), 'The role of EO in stimulating effective corporate entrepreneurship', *Academy of Management Executive*, **19**(1), 147–56.

Dess, G.G. and R.B. Robinson (1984), 'Industry effects and strategic management research', *Journal of Management*, **16**(7), 7–27.

Dess, G.G., G.T. Lumpkin and J.G. Covin (1997), 'Entrepreneurial strategy making and firm performance: tests of contingency and configurational models', *Strategic Management Journal*, **18**(9), 677–95.

Dess, G.G., R.D. Ireland, S.A. Zahra, S.W. Floyd, J.J. Janney and P.J. Lane (2003), 'Emerging issues in corporate entrepreneurship', *Journal of Management*, **29**(3), 351–78.

Dunn, B. (1995), 'Success themes in Scottish family enterprises: philosophies and practices through the generations', *Family Business Review*, **8**(1), 17–28.

Dyer, W.G. and W. Handler (1994), 'Entrepreneurship and family business: exploring the connections', *Entrepreneurship Theory and Practice*, **19**(1), 71–84.

Dyer, W.G. and D.A. Whetten (2006), 'Family firms and social responsibility: preliminary evidence from the s&p 500', *Entrepreneurship Theory and Practice*, **30**(6), 785–802.

Eddleston, K.A. and F.W. Kellermanns (2006), 'Destructive and productive family relationships: a stewardship theory perspective', *Journal of Business Venturing*, **22**, 545–65.

Eddleston, K., F.W. Kellermanns and T. Zellweger (2008a), 'Corporate entrepreneurship in family firms: a stewardship perspective', Paper presented at the USASBE, San Antonio.

Eddleston, K.A., F.W. Kellermanns and R. Sarathy (2008b), 'Resource configuration in family firms: linking resources, strategic planning and technological opportunities to performance', *Journal of Management Studies*, **45**(1), 26–50.

Faccio, M. and L.H.P. Lang (2002), 'The ultimate ownership of Western European corporations', *Journal of Financial Economics*, **65**(3), 365–95.

Fahlenbrach, R. (2004), *Founder-CEOs and stock market performance*, unpublished working paper, Wharton School, University of Pennsylvania.

Gartner, W.B. (2001), 'Is there an elephant in entrepreneurship? Blind assumptions in theory development', *Entrepreneurship Theory and Practice*, **25**(4), 27–39.

Gomez-Mejia, L.R., K.T. Haynes, M. Nunez-Nickel, K.J.L. Jacobson and J. Moyano-Fuentes (2007), 'Socioemotional wealth and business risks in family-controlled firms: evidence from spanish olive oil mills', *Administrative Science Quarterly*, **52**(1), 106–37.

Greene, P.G. and T.E. Brown (1997), 'Resource needs and the dynamic capitalism typology', *Journal of Business Venturing*, **12**(3), 161–73.

Habbershon, T.G. (2006), 'Commentary: a framework for managing the familiness and agency advantages in family firms', *Entrepreneurship Theory and Practice*, **30**(6), 879–86.

Habbershon, T.G. and J. Pistrui (2002), 'Enterprising families domain: family-influenced ownership groups in pursuit of transgenerational wealth', *Family Business Review*, **15**(3), 223–37.

Habbershon, T.G. and M.L. Williams (1999), 'A resource-based framework for assessing the strategic advantages of family firms', *Family Business Review*, **12**(1), 1–25.

Habbershon, T.G., M. Williams and I.C. MacMillan (2003), 'A unified systems perspective of family firm performance', *Journal of Business Venturing*, **18**(4), 451–65.

Hall, A., L. Melin and M. Nordqvist (2001), 'Entrepreneurship as radical change in the family business: exploring the role of cultural patterns', *Family Business Review*, **14**(3), 193–208.

Hall, A., L. Melin and M. Nordqvist (2006), 'Understanding strategizing in the family business context', in P. Poutziouris, K.X. Smyrnios and S.B. Klein (eds), *Handbook of Research on Family Businesses*, Cheltenham, UK and Northampton, MA, USA: Edward Elgar Publishing, pp. 253–68.

Hofstede, G. (1991), *Cultures and Organizations: Software of the Mind*, London: McGraw Hill.

Hogg, M.A., D.J. Terry and K.M. White (1995), 'A tale of two theories: a critical comparison of identity theory with social identity theory', *Social Psychology Quarterly*, **58**(4), 255–69.

Hoy, F. and T.G. Verser (1994), 'Emerging business, emerging field: entrepreneurship and the family firm', *Entrepreneurship Theory and Practice*, **19**(1), 9–23.

Jensen, M.C. and W.H. Meckling (1976), 'Theory of the firm: managerial behavior, agency costs, and ownership structure', *Journal of Financial Economics*, **3**, 305–60.

Kellermanns, F.W. (2005), 'Family firm resource management: commentary and extensions', *Entrepreneurship Theory and Practice*, **29**(3), 313–19.

Kellermanns, F.W. and K.A. Eddleston (2006), 'Corporate entrepreneurship in family firms: a family perspective', *Entrepreneurship Theory and Practice*, **30**(6), 809–30.

Lansberg, I.S. (1983), 'Managing human resources in family firms: the problem of institutional overlap', *Organizational Dynamics*, **12**(1), 39–46.

Le Breton-Miller, I., D. Miller and L.P. Steier (2004), 'Toward an integrative model of effective FOB succession', *Entrepreneurship Theory and Practice*, **28**(4), 305–28.

Lee, M. and E.G. Rogoff (1996), 'Research note. Comparison of small businesses with family participation versus small businesses without family participation: an investigation of differences in goals, attitudes, and family/business conflict', *Family Business Review*, **9**(4), 423–7.

Levinson, R.E. (1987), 'Problems in managing a family-owned business', in C.E. Aronoff and J.L. Ward (eds), *Family Business Sourcebook*, Detroit: Omnigraphics, pp. 169–74.

Litz, R. (1997), 'The family firm's exclusion from business school research: explaining the void; addressing the opportunity', *Entrepreneurship Theory and Practice*, **21**(3), 55–71.

Lounsbury, M. and M.A. Glynn (2001), 'Cultural entrepreneurship: stories, legitimacy, and the acquisitions of resources', *Strategic Management Journal*, **22**(6/7), 545–64.

Love, L.G., R.L. Priem and G.T. Lumpkin (2002), 'Explicitly articulated strategy and firm performance under alternative levels of centralization', *Journal of Management*, **28**(5), 611–27.

Low, M.B. and I.C. MacMillan (1988), 'Entrepreneurship: past research and future challenges', *Journal of Management*, **14**(2), 139–61.

Lumpkin, G.T. and G.G. Dess (1996), 'Clarifying the entrepreneurial orientation construct and linking it to performance', *Academy of Management Review*, **21**(1), 135–72.

Lumpkin, G.T. and G.G. Dess (2001), 'Linking two dimensions of entrepreneurial orientation to firm performance: the moderating role of environment and industry life cycle', *Journal of Business Venturing*, **16**(5), 429–51.

Lumpkin, G.T., W.J. Wales and M.D. Ensley (2006), 'Assessing the context for corporate entrepreneurship: the role of entrepreneurial orientation', in M. Rice and T.G. Habbershon (eds), *Praeger Perspectives on Entrepreneurship*, Vol. III, Westport, CA: Praeger Publishers.

Lumpkin, G.T., W. Martin and M. Vaughn (2008), 'Family orientation: individual-level influences on family firm outcomes', *Family Business Review*, **21**(2), 127–38.

Lumpkin, G.T., K. Brigham and K. Moss (2009), 'Long-term orientation: implications for the entrepreneurial orientation and performance of family businesses', *Entrepreneurship and Regional Development*, forthcoming.

Lyon, D.W., G.T. Lumpkin and G.G. Dess (2000), 'Enhancing entrepreneurial orientation research: operationalizing and measuring a key strategic decision making process', *Journal of Management*, **26**(5), 1055–85.

Mahoney, J.T. (1995), 'The management of resources and the resource of management', *Journal of Business Research*, **33**(2), 91–101.

Martin, L. and T. Lumpkin (2003), 'From EO to "family orientation": generational differences in the management of family businesses', Paper presented at the 22nd Babson College Entrepreneurship Research Conference, Babson College, Massachusetts.

Mathews, J.A. (2002), 'A resource-based view of Schumpeterian economic dynamics', *Journal of Evolutionary Economics*, **12**(1/2), 29–54.

McConaughy, D.L., M.C. Walker, G.V. Henderson and C.S. Mishra (1998), 'Founding family controlled firms: efficiency and value', *Review of Financial Economics*, **7**(1), 1–19.

McConaughy, D.L., C.H. Matthews and A.S. Fialko (2001), 'Founding family controlled firms: performance, risk, and value', *Journal of Small Business Management*, **39**(1), 31–49.

McConnell, J.J. and H. Servaes (1990), 'Additional evidence on equity ownership and corporate value', *Journal of Financial Economics*, **27**(2), 595–612.

Miller, D. (1983), 'The correlates of entrepreneurship in three types of firms', *Management Science*, **29**(7), 770–91.

Miller, D. and P.H. Friesen (1978), 'Archetypes of strategy formulation', *Management Science*, **24**(9), 921–33.

Miller, D. and I. Le Breton-Miller (2005), *Managing for the Long Run: Lessons in Competitive Advantage from Great Family Businesses*, Boston, MA: Harvard Business School Press.

Miller, D. and J. Shamsie (1996), 'The resource-based view of the firm in two environments: the Hollywood film studios from 1936 to 1965', *Academy of Management Journal*, **39**(3), 519–43.

Morck, R., A. Shleifer and R.W. Vishny (1988), 'Management ownership and market valuation: an empirical analysis', *Journal of Financial Economics*, **20**, 293–315.

Moreno, A.M. and J.C. Casillas (2008), 'Entrepreneurial orientation and growth of SMEs: a causal model', *Entrepreneurship Theory and Practice*, **32**(3), 507–28.

Morris, M.H. (1998), *Entrepreneurial Intensity: Sustainable Advantages for Individuals, Organizations, and Societies*, Westport, CT: Quorum Books.

Naldi, L., M. Nordqvist, K. Sjöberg and J. Wiklund (2007), 'Entrepreneurial orientation, risk taking, and performance in family firms', *Family Business Review*, **20**(1), 33–47.

Naldi, L., M. Nordqvist and T.M. Zellweger (2008), 'Intangible resources and family firm performance: the moderating role family involvement in strategy making', Paper presented at the Babson Kaufmann Entrepreneurship Research Conference, Chapel Hill, North Carolina.

Nordqvist, M., T.G. Habbershon and L. Melin (2008), 'Transgenerational entrepreneurship: exploring EO in family firms', in H. Landström, H. Crijns and E. Laveren (eds), *Entrepreneurship, sustainable growth and performance: frontiers in European Entrepreneurship Research*, Cheltenham, UK and Northampton, MA, USA: Edward Elgar Publishing.

Pearson, A.W., J.C. Carr and J.C. Shaw (2008), 'Toward a theory of familiness:

a social capital perspective', *Entrepreneurship Theory and Practice*, **32**(6), 949–69.

Penrose, E.T. (1959), *The Theory of the Growth of the Firm*, Oxford: Basil Blackwell.

Poutziouris, P., K. O'Sullivan and L. Nicolescu (1997), 'The (re)-generation of family-business entrepreneurship in the Balkans', *Family Business Review*, **10**(3), 239–62.

Powell, T.C. (1992), 'Strategic planning as competitive advantage', *Strategic Management Journal*, **13**(7), 551–8.

Poza, E.J. (1988), 'Managerial practices that support interpreneurship and continued growth', *Family Business Review*, **1**(4), 339–59.

Priem, R.L. and J.E. Butler (2001), 'Is the resource-based "view" a useful perspective for strategic management research?', *Academy of Management Review*, **26**(1), 22–40.

Rauch, A., J. Wiklund, G.T. Lumpkin and M. Frese (2009), 'Entrepreneurial orientation and business performance: an assessment of past research and suggestions for the future', *Entrepreneurship Theory and Practice*, **33**(3), 761–87.

Rogoff, E.G. and R.K.Z. Heck (2003), 'Evolving research in entrepreneurship and family business: recognizing family as the oxygen that feeds the fire of entrepreneurship', *Journal of Business Venturing*, **18**(5), 559–66.

Rutherford, M.W., D.F. Kuratko and D.T. Holt (2008), 'Examining the link between familiness and performance: can the f-pec untangle the family business theory jungle?', *Entrepreneurship Theory and Practice*, **32**(6), 1089–109.

Salvato, C. (2004), 'Predictors of entrepreneurship in family firms', *Journal of Private Equity*, **7**(3), 68–76.

Schein, E.H. (1983), 'The role of the founder in creating organizational culture', *Organizational Dynamics*, **12**(1), 13–28.

Schulze, W.S., M.H. Lubatkin and R.N. Dino (2003), 'Toward a theory of agency and altruism in family firms', *Journal of Business Venturing*, **18**(4), 473–90.

Schumpeter, J.A. (1934), *The Theory of Economic Development*, Cambridge, MA: Harvard University Press.

Scott, M. and P. Rosa (1996), 'Has firm level analysis reached its limits? Time for a rethink', *International Small Business Journal*, **14**(4), 81–9.

Shane, S.A. and S. Venkataraman (2000), 'The promise of entrepreneurship as a field of research', *Academy of Management Review*, **25**(1), 217–26.

Shanker, M.C. and J.H. Astrachan (1996), 'Myths and realities: family businesses' contribution to the U.S. economy – a framework for assessing family business statistics', *Family Business Review*, **9**(2), 107–18.

Sharma, P. (2004), 'An overview of the field of family business studies: current status and directions for the future', *Family Business Review*, **17**(1), 1–36.

Sharma, P. (2008), 'Commentary. Familiness: capital stocks and flows between family and business', *Entrepreneurship Theory and Practice*, **32**(6), 971–7.

Sharma, P. and J.J. Chrisman (1999), 'Toward a reconciliation of the definitional issues in the field of corporate entrepreneurship', *Entrepreneurship Theory and Practice*, **23**(3), 11–27.

Sharma, P. and P.G. Irving (2005), 'Four bases of family business successor commitment: antecedents and consequences', *Entrepreneurship Theory and Practice*, **29**(1), 13–33.

Sharma, P. and S. Manikutty (2005), 'Strategic divestments in family firms: role of family structure and community culture', *Entrepreneurship Theory and Practice*, **29**(3), 293–311.

Sharma, P., J.J. Chrisman and J.H. Chua (1997), 'Strategic management of the family business: past research and future challenges', *Family Business Review*, **10**(1), 1–35.

Sirmon, D.G. and M.A. Hitt (2003), 'Managing resources: linking unique resources, management, and wealth creation in family firms', *Entrepreneurship Theory and Practice*, **27**(4), 339–58.

Sirmon, D.G., M.A. Hitt and R.D. Ireland (2007), 'Managing firm resources in dynamic environments to create value: looking inside the black box', *Academy of Management Review*, **32**(1), 273–92.

Sorenson, R.L. (1999), 'Conflict management strategies used by successful family businesses', *Family Business Review*, **12**(4), 325–40.

Sraer, D. and D. Thesmar (2007), 'Performance and behavior of family firms: evidence from the French stock market', *Journal of the European Economic Association*, **5**(4), 709–51.

Stafford, K., K.A. Duncan, S. Dane and M. Winter (1999), 'A research model of sustainable family businesses', *Family Business Review*, **12**(3), 197–208.

Steier, L. (2003), 'Variants of agency contracts in family-financed ventures as a continuum of familial altruistic and market rationalities', *Journal of Business Venturing*, **18**(5), 597–618.

Steier, L. (2007), 'New venture creation and organization: a familial sub-narrative', *Journal of Business Research*, **60**(10), 1099–107.

Stevenson, H.H. and C.J. Jarillo (1990), 'A paradigm of entrepreneurship: entrepreneurial management', *Strategic Management Journal*, **11**, 17–27.

Stulz, R. (1988), 'Managerial control of voting rights: financing policies and the market for corporate control', *Journal of Financial Economics*, **20**, 25–54.

Tagiuri, R. and J.A. Davis (1982), 'Bivalent attributes of the family firm', Working paper, Harvard Business School, Cambridge, Massachusetts. Reprinted 1996, *Family Business Review*, **9**(2), 199–208.

Ucbasaran, D., P. Westhead and M. Wright (2001), 'The focus of entrepreneurial research: contextual and process issues', *Entrepreneurship Theory and Practice*, **25**(4), 57–80.

Venkataraman, S. (1997), 'The distinctive domain of entrepreneurship research', in J. Katz (ed.), *Advances in Entrepreneurship, Firm Emergence and Growth*, Greenwich, CT: JAI Press, pp. 119–38.

Venkatraman, N. and V. Ramanujam (1987), 'Measurement of business performance in strategy research: a comparison of approaches', *Academy of Management Review*, **11**(4), 801–14.

Villalonga, B. and R. Amit (2006), 'How do family ownership, control and management affect firm value?', *Journal of Financial Economics*, **80**(2), 385–417.

Volery, T., H. Bergmann, M. Gruber, G. Haour and B. Leleux (2007), Global Entrepreneurship Monitor, Bericht 2007 zum unternehmertum in der schweiz und weltweit. St Gallen: KMU-HSG.

Ward, J.L. (1997), 'Growing the family business: special challenges and best practices', *Family Business Review*, **10**(4), 323–37.

Wernerfelt, B. (1984), 'The resource-based view of the firm', *Strategic Management Journal*, **5**(2), 171–80.

Westhead, P. and M. Cowling (1997), 'Performance contrasts between family and non-family unquoted companies in the UK', *International Journal of Entrepreneurial Behaviour and Research*, **3**(1), 30–52.

Westhead, P. and M. Wright (1998), 'Novice, portfolio, and serial founders: are they different?' *Journal of Business Venturing*, **13**(3), 173–204.

Whetten, D.A. (1989), 'What constitutes a theoretical contribution?', *Academy of Management Review*, **14**(4), 490–5.

Wiklund, J. (1998), *Small Firm Growth and Performance: Entrepreneurship and Beyond*, Jönköping: Jönköping International Business School.

Wiklund, J. and D. Shepherd (2003), 'Knowledge-based resources, entrepreneurial orientation, and the performance of small and medium-sized businesses', *Strategic Management Journal*, **24**(13), 1307–14.

Zahra, S.A. (1993), 'Environment, corporate entrepreneurship, and financial performance: a taxonomic approach', *Journal of Business Venturing*, **8**(4), 319–40.

Zahra, S.A. (1995), 'Corporate entrepreneurship and financial performance: the case of management leveraged buyouts', *Journal of Business Venturing*, **10**(3), 225–47.

Zahra, S.A. (2005), 'Entrepreneurial risk taking in family firms', *Family Business Review*, **18**(1), 23–40.

Zahra, S.A. and P. Sharma (2004), 'Family business research: a strategic reflection', *Family Business Review*, **17**(4), 331–46.

Zahra, S.A., J.C. Hayton and C. Salvato (2004), 'Entrepreneurship in family vs. non-family firms: a resource-based analysis of the effect of organizational culture', *Entrepreneurship Theory and Practice*, **28**(4), 363–81.

Zellweger, T.M. (2006), *Risk, Return and Value in the Family Firm*, St Gallen: University of St Gallen.

Zellweger, T.M. (2007), 'Time horizon, costs of equity capital, and generic investment strategies of firms', *Family Business Review*, **20**(1), 1–15.

Zellweger, T.M. and J.H. Astrachan (2008), 'On the emotional value of owning a firm', *Family Business Review*, **21**(4), 347–363.

Zellweger, T.M. and F.W. Kellermanns (2008), 'Family firm reputation concern: antecedents and performance outcomes', Paper presented at the Academy of Management Conference, Anaheim, California.

Zellweger, T.M. and R.S. Nason (2008), 'A stakeholder perspective on family firm performance', *Family Business Review*, **21**(3), 203–16.

Zellweger, T.M., C. Mühlebach and P. Sieger (2008), 'How much and what kind of entrepreneurial orientation is needed for family business continuity?', Paper presented at the 8th Annual Ifera Conference. Nyenrode, Breukelen, NED.

2. A qualitative research approach to the study of transgenerational entrepreneurship

Mattias Nordqvist and Thomas M. Zellweger

2.1 THE NEED FOR QUALITATIVE RESEARCH IN ENTREPRENEURSHIP AND FAMILY BUSINESS STUDIES

The main idea behind the research project on Successful Transgenerational Entrepreneurship Practices (STEP) as a collaborative and comparative research project is to use a mixed methods strategy to investigate and understand the phenomenon of transgenerational entrepreneurship. By drawing on both quantitative and qualitative research tools and techniques, we generate a rich understanding of transgenerational entrepreneurship as a process through which families develop and use entrepreneurial mindsets, and family influenced capabilities to create new streams of entrepreneurial, financial and social value across generations. Our research strategy was to start with rather open-ended, case-oriented qualitative research and then successively move into quantitative data collection and analysis. Starting with the qualitative research phase allows for emerging findings from the case research to feed into the construction of a survey instrument for the quantitative phase (Eisenhardt, 1989). All the chapters included in this book build upon the qualitative, case-oriented research. This chapter describes the qualitative research approach.

Why did we start out with a qualitative research approach? Scholars from the entrepreneurship and family business area argue that more in-depth, qualitative research is needed to better understand how entrepreneurship in the family business context relates to important social and economic value creation. Several early and pioneering studies on entrepreneurial processes in established companies (Burgelman 1983; Stopford and Baden-Fuller, 1994) revealed how in-depth research on a small number of companies leads to a detailed and rich understanding of corporate venturing, innovation and strategic renewal. There are four major reasons why we chose a qualitative methodology.

1. Entrepreneurial orientation (EO) scholars point out the need to explore in greater depth and detail the characteristics and strengths of EO and its dimensions in various types of organizations and stakeholder contexts (Lumpkin and Dess, 1996, 2001; Wiklund and Shepherd, 2005). The underlying assumption is that EO might differ in important ways between organizations depending, for instance, on their history, culture and the priorities and interests of their ownership and management. There is a growing recognition that the role of EO and the importance of its dimensions may change over time. This means that cross-sectional studies need to be complemented with more longitudinal research studies in order to better grasp and conceptualize the characteristics and dimensions of EO and how they unfold across time (Lumpkin and Dess, 1996; Lyon et al., 2000). An important intention of the STEP Project is to contribute to the research on entrepreneurial orientation with studies that draw upon a qualitative research approach, and to use the case study as its main research tool.

2. We also believe the qualitative case research approach is apt to capture the complexities related to the concept of familiness, that is, family influenced resources and capabilities. As explained in Chapter 1, the resource-based view (RBV) posits uniqueness of resources. In the STEP Project what resources are important for family business entrepreneurship is a key question, as well as how and why these resources emerged. Therefore we propose that family influence on resources and capabilities that may be used for entrepreneurial activities can represent either an advantage or a disadvantage. It is fair to say that it is difficult to capture the nature and impact of the family influence on these resources and capabilities (Habbershon et al., 2003; Sirmon et al., 2007) using any research method. A qualitative research approach allows the researcher to get close to the actors that constitute the family influence on the firm's resource base and unveil the very nature of resource interactions between business and family. By applying a case-based research approach STEP thus has the possibility to generate findings and reveal new insights that add and extend in important ways the still rather limited number of empirical studies of RBV in the family business (cf. Pearson et al., 2008).

3. To understand entrepreneurial processes, a prominent call within entrepreneurship research has been to conduct studies not only at the level of the individual entrepreneur or the firm level, but to integrate different levels of analysis (Davidsson and Wiklund, 2001; Shane and

Venkataraman, 2000). Beyond the five levels of analysis proposed by Low and MacMillan (1988) (individual, group, organization, industry and society), studying transgenerational entrepreneurship in family firms requires the inclusion of the family level of analysis. The family as a key stakeholder, the relevance of family influenced entrepreneurial activity taking place outside the boundaries of the focal firm, as well as the systemic interactions between business, the family and individuals (Habbershon et al., 2003). We see qualitative case studies as particularly suited to explore entrepreneurship across levels of analysis.

4. We opted for a qualitative research approach because of the increasing awareness of the heterogeneity of the family businesses population. Even if often treated as similar and routinely compared to 'non-family businesses', thereby artificially dichotomizing these organizations, family businesses are in fact different amongst themselves, that is, there are many different types of family firms (for example, Westhead and Howorth, 2007). More in-depth research can help to generate insights with regards to the specific challenges and characteristics of different forms of family businesses rather than default to a lumping together of them all (Nordqvist et al., 2009).

In summary, given that family firms represent a specific context for entrepreneurship, the conceptual youth of some of the key constructs of our transgenerational entrepreneurship research framework, the necessity to study how entrepreneurial processes unfold across time, the scarcity of prior work on the relationships across levels of analysis, in particular in a RBV world, and the heterogeneity of family firms, we opt for a qualitative research approach to assure methodological fit (Edmondson and McManus, 2007). In doing so we follow recent calls in the family business literature for 'alternative research methodologies; micro level collection and alternative data sources' (Heck et al., 2008, p. 325), and a broader use of the arsenal of research methodologies and techniques available for social scientists (Sharma, 2004). In essence, our qualitative research approach aims to build and extend theory on important phenomena that are still relatively unexplored in the research literature on entrepreneurship and family business.

2.2   THE CASE RESEARCH METHOD WITHIN STEP

The basis for the qualitative research approach in STEP is the use of comparative, exploratory case studies. We follow Yin (1994) who suggests that a case study is an empirical inquiry that investigates a contemporary phenomenon within its real-life context, especially when the boundaries between phenomenon and context are not clearly evident. This methodology enables researchers to study actors, processes and events both closely and holistically (Eisenhardt, 1989; Stake, 1999). It is appropriate for procedural, contextual and longitudinal studies (Hartley, 1994) and can give insight through rich detail. Orum et al. (1991) summarize the advantages of case studies in four points. First, they permit the grounding of observations and concepts about social action and structures by studying actors' day-to-day activities at close hand in their natural settings. Second, they provide information from a number of sources and over an extended period of time, thus allowing for a study of complex social processes and meanings. Third, they highlight the dimensions of time and history to the study of social life. In that way, a researcher can examine continuity and change in 'life-world patterns'. Finally, case studies encourage and facilitate theoretical and conceptual development.

Our case research method is comparative because each team of researchers in a given country or institution conducted and analysed a number of cases. It is also comparative because the shared research approach facilitated possible comparisons across cases from different countries and institutions. This offers the opportunity to learn from the uniqueness of each case and to compare and analyse similarities and differences in patterns across several cases in different national, cultural and industry contexts.

For this project all STEP researchers use a shared conceptual framework (outlined in the previous chapter) as a point of departure. Initially the researchers were encouraged to be open to capture and interpret additional, emerging aspects and dimensions of importance for transgenerational entrepreneurship. Our approach can thus be described as 'abductive', that is, a mix between a traditional inductive or deductive approach that allows for an iterative process between theory development and data collection and analysis (Alvesson and Sköldberg, 2000; Suddaby, 2006).

An open, comparative and exploratory case research strategy was also deemed crucial in order to better grasp the overall research questions of research project in a real-life, empirical context. Such a research approach helped us to 'generate an understanding of the concepts and theories held by people you are studying . . . it provides you with an understanding of the *meaning* that these phenomena and events have for the actors who are involved in them, and the perspectives that inform these actions' (Maxwell, 1998, pp. 79–80, emphasis in original). The purpose of our case research was thus to both compare our initial theoretical understanding with real-life cases, and to use the emerging empirical observations to refine, develop and improve the theoretical pre-understanding. In practice, this means that we allow for the emerging research findings to have an impact both on the overall research framework and especially on the development of the survey instrument for the quantitative research phase.

2.3   SAMPLING CRITERIA

A goal of the STEP Project is to produce high quality qualitative research based on comparative case research. In order to select cases that could form the basis for relevant comparisons, the sampling criteria was an important issue. After discussions within the European group of researchers we agreed upon a set of criteria that each family business had to fulfill in order to become a STEP research case. These criteria were consistent with the objective of better understanding the processes through which a family uses and develops entrepreneurial mindsets and family influenced capabilities to create new streams of entrepreneurial, financial and social value across generations.

We selected the criteria keeping in mind common definitions of family business in the literature, in particular those of Westhead and Cowling (1997) and Chrisman et al. (2005). In general, we wanted to sample family firms that operated in typical industries representative of the family firm population in a given country. The following are the sampling criteria for a STEP research case:

- The family must see their business as a family business.
- Family ownership in the main operating business above 50 per cent (voting share).
- The family must have at least one active operating business, not only being a passive shareholder or investor.
- At least second generation involved in ownership and/or management.
- At least 50 employees in the main operating business.
- The family has a transgenerational intention, that is, an ambition to pass on the business to the next generation of family members.

Knowing that the family business landscape is often different between countries and regions in the world, we allow for some regional adaptation regarding the size of the firm (that is, we allow smaller firms to participate in the study in Latin America). In addition to these formal criteria all research teams ensured that each research case was conducted and developed for the specific purpose of the STEP Project, and they did not utilize case research or teaching cases previously collected as input to the STEP

Project. However a research team was allowed to use the same cases and contacts, that is, the same owner-family and/or family firm that fulfill the formal selection criteria to conduct a case study.

We created a purposeful sample to attain our research goal. There is a notable variation of cases. There are very large firms (multi-billion dollar in sales volume), very old firms (more than 175 years under the control of the same family) and very entrepreneurial firms (five parallel running business entities making part of a portfolio of activities). It is the variation of these cases that makes them so powerful to examine transgenerational entrepreneurial processes.

2.4   DATA COLLECTION

Case study research often benefits from multiple sources of empirical material to build a case story and interpretations that are as rich, lush and fine-grained as possible. In the STEP Project researchers agreed on primarily collecting empirical material through personal interviews with key actors and through secondary data sources, such as websites, annual reports and media articles.

Interviews

An interview is the primary tool for gathering empirical material. Conducting interviews is an acknowledged and useful way to investigate how actors experience and interpret their everyday life (Fontana and Frey, 1994; Pettigrew, 1997), even if some argue that interviews are too politicized and rarely give 'correct' interpretations (for example, Silverman, 1993). In the STEP Project each research team was expected to conduct five or more interviews with key actors in each case. These actors should, in any combination, include the following:

- A controlling owner(s) working as CEO and/or chairman of the board in the main business.
- The CEO/President of the firm's main business whether family or non-family.
- At least one more family member owner (if existing) who is active in the firm's main business (as board member and/or employee).
- At least one family member active in the main business (as board member and/or employee) who represents a different generational perspective from the people mentioned above (the point is to get a multigenerational leadership perspective).

- At least one non-family member active at the top management level of the main business.
- A significant non-family owner that is considered strategically relevant as a representative if existing.

The research goal was to get the 'story of each case' and thus the interviews were open-ended and flexible. Respondents were encouraged to reflect, elaborate and extend, rather than provide short, direct and closed answers. This is seen as an essential feature of the interviews in order to be able to generate new insights and findings that do not already exist in the literature. The length of the interviews are between one and two hours. All interviews are tape-recorded and transcribed verbatim to facilitate subsequent analyses.

Interview Guide

To assist the researchers in conducting the interviews a STEP interview guide was used based on the overall theoretical framework For each conceptual element of our research framework we developed questions. The interview guide includes questions related to the following overall themes:

- The history of the business and business family
    - Key strategic decisions and critical incidents
    - Most influential family and non-family actors in the historical development.
- Ownership evolution and governance structures.
- Guiding values, vision and goals of the family.
- The entrepreneurial character of the family.
- The entrepreneurial character of the business.
- The extent to which entrepreneurship is maintained and developed across generations.
- The family's risk profile.
- The five dimensions of entrepreneurial orientation (innovativeness, proactiveness, risk taking, autonomy and competitive aggressiveness).
- Resource profile, important resources for competitive advantage (for example, leadership, culture, knowledge and networks).
- The nature of the family influence on these resources.
- Contingencies (for example, industry and environment).
- Performance: financial, entrepreneurial and social.

Below are two examples of questions from the STEP interview guide,[1] the first one pertaining to the risk-taking dimension and the second one to the autonomy dimension within EO. These two examples used the traditional wording of EO questions and asked for the deeper relevance of the dimensions on growth and goal achievement, how the family impacts this aspect of EO and the relationship of the EO dimension with resources and capabilities.

Do you generally take new initiatives/strategic actions and invest where the outcome is highly uncertain, or do you prefer to invest where less resource is at stake and you know fairly well the result (e.g. introduce new product, new service, new processes, renewal actions, or opening new markets and launch new ventures)?
The answer should cover, if relevant, the following issues:

(a) If this (the answer) facilitates or hinders further growth and/or the accomplishment of vision and goals.
(b) How and why the family influence and/or involvement impacts this.
(c) What resources and capabilities enable or constrain this.

To what extent are individuals and teams in your firm given freedom to be creative, to push for new ideas and to change current ways of doing things in order to come up with new initiatives/strategic actions (e.g. introduce new product, new service, new processes, renewal actions, or opening new markets and launch new ventures)?
The answer should cover, if relevant, the following issues:

(a) If this (the answer) facilitates or hinders further growth and/or the accomplishment of vision and goals.
(b) How and why the family influence and/or involvement impacts this.
(c) What resources and capabilities enable or constrain this.

Using the interview guide researchers were encouraged to ask process questions, that is, researchers follow up the first answers that informants gave by asking 'how and why questions'. Asking these questions provided an an attempt to go somewhat deeper and to investigate, for example, how and why things happens, events unfold and what 'lies behind' the first answers that informants give. In good case research it is typically in the answers to such process questions that new insights into the studied phenomena are generated. When conducting the STEP cases research teams were free to add other questions or issues for investigations outside the realm of STEP only if this did not negatively affect the focus and quality of research being done for the STEP Project.

Secondary Empirical Materials

Secondary empirical materials were used in the STEP case research to collect material to construct the overall profile of the owner-family and firm, such as:

- to map out major strategic and entrepreneurial moves;
- to describe important contingencies (for example, industry, tax regime, environment);
- to document relevant outcomes/financial statements, annual reports and so on (for example, growth, profitability);
- to understand the ownership and family governance structures and reporting relationships, besides the information gathered through interviews;
- to accomplish 'triangulation', that is, to corroborate relevant information gathered through interviews.

The more secondary materials that the researchers were able to use, the more interviews could focus on discussion about the actual entrepreneurial processes and the influences on and outcomes of this process. The secondary materials that we use in the STEP research include financial statements, books and publications on the company's and the family's history, press releases and media information. In some cases researches have also gathered board meeting minutes and internal memos with relevance for strategic development.

2.5 REPORTING THE EMPIRICAL MATERIAL – CASE REPORT FORM AND MASTER CASE

To ensure that the information collected in the interviews was accessible for our research purposes the STEP researchers saved the verbatim interview transcripts in a Word document in their original language (one for each interview). Verbatim interview transcription were not translated into English in the first phase. The next step, and likewise the first level of analysis, was to construct rich and thick *master cases* out of the raw data. These master cases were structured around the themes and categories from the interview guide and also follow the different questions. Larger amounts of data at this stage facilitated the generation of many possible routes for exploration in later stages of analysis and interpretation.

In a separate section, after the different themes from the interview guide, researchers included emergent analytical ideas, possible interpretations and other reflections that emerged whilst working with the data. This is a very important part of qualitative case research and was supported from the start. Here researchers 'diverted' from the overall theoretical framework and research model and encouraged lines of thought and reflections that added to, contradicted or provided alternative explanations of initial theoretical points.

In developing the 30–50-page master case documents, the researchers followed the structure provided in the *case report form*.

1. Executive summary.
2. Information about the firm and the interviewers and interviewees.
3. Short description of the firm, its industry and products.
4. History of the firm and the family.
5. Core values and vision.
6. Entrepreneurial orientation.
7. Familiness.
8. Performance.
9. Emerging themes from the specific case.

The master cases were primarily descriptive and not analytical, that is, researchers described their findings under each of the sections and themes and did not report their analytical thoughts and interpretations as they went along in the text. Instead there was a part at the end of each report for analytical discussions, conclusions and propositions. The purpose of the master case was thus to give a wider set of STEP researchers an opportunity to develop an initial understanding of each case. The master cases were also intended to provide STEP researchers with enough data to identify themes which could be further developed and deepened in separate research papers. The chapters in this book are a result of the investigations of such master cases.

The master cases were translated into English and made available in a shared database, which is based on a software package for qualitative research (NVivo) in order to support subsequent interpretations of the cases. This work method particularly facilitated coding and later comparisons between cases and countries, even if the first aim was to understand the uniqueness and story of each individual case. The database is also a way to create a format for the empirical material that is easy for all to work with and at the same time safeguarding the quality and trustworthiness of the whole research process.

2.6 ANALYSING THE EMPIRICAL DATA – AN EXAMPLE

The ambition of STEP's qualitative research was clearly to be analytical and go beyond case descriptions. Following Yin (1994) the overarching goal was to develop analytical or theoretical generalization by both drawing on existing and developing new theory. Here the basis of generalization is not from a sample to a population, but from the case to theory. 'The way this is accomplished is not by teasing out efficient causations between variables, but, instead by teasing out the deeper generative mechanisms that account for observed patterns in the event' (Garud and Van de Ven, 2001, p. 224).

To provide a better idea of the process used by STEP researchers to develop master cases and derive new theoretical insights, we outline the methodology that the Swiss STEP team applied in their research. The Swiss team's research goal was to develop pertinent propositions for further inquiry about levels and patterns of EO in long-living family firms. The team conducted five semi-structured interviews with both family and non-family members in top echelon positions (for example, CEO, CFO, head of marketing and so on) in three family firms, each of the firms corresponding to the STEP sampling criteria. Each interview lasted between 60 and 90 minutes. Two researches asked the respondents to touch upon both EO at the firm level and specific family involvement. All interviews were audiotaped and the team gathered secondary data from company websites, annual reports, press releases and company documents to map out major strategic entrepreneurial actions, describe important contingencies (industry, tax structure or environment), document relevant outcomes and accomplish 'triangulation' (that is, corroborate relevant information gathered through the interviews).

The interviews were then transcribed and coded by a PhD student who, although not involved in the interviews, was familiar with both EO and family business literature and with case writing. This resulted in three master case documents. The team chose a third person for this part of the study to further increase the reliability of their findings and interpretations and to ensure divergent perspectives (Eisenhardt, 1989). They did not use specific coding software because the number of interviews was limited and their lengths not excessive. As the interviews were conducted on a semi-structured basis, the PhD student could rapidly identify and access defined constructs under consideration.

The three master cases, each with a length of about 30 pages, were enriched with several tables, highlighting the family's and the firm's history and evolution, the finances of the company, and an overview of the five EO dimensions, including related statements of the interviewees. This helped the researchers to become intimately familiar with each case and enabled unique patterns to emerge before cross-case comparison (Eisenhardt, 1989). By integrating the information gained through the interviews with information gained through secondary materials, the research team measured EO using a combination of firm behavior and managerial perceptions (Lyon et al., 2000). The first version of the master case derived was organized according to the guidelines provided in the case report form. The master case and the audiotapes were then sent to the two interviewers, who independently reviewed and adapted the protocols.

Each of the three researchers independently assessed the levels of the five EO dimensions at the point of investigation for every company using a nine-point scale ranging from 1 (low) to 9 (high). To avoid overspecification, the researchers formed three categories: low (score 1–3), medium (score 4–6), and high (score 7–9). This resulted in a graphical illustration of all five EO dimensions for every company by each researcher (nine total EO profiles). The three researchers then met, discussed the case study protocols, and agreed on a final version that varied only marginally from the original version. After comparing identified EO patterns, the researchers agreed upon one profile for each firm, reflecting the researchers' shared understanding. Of the 45 judgments of EO levels (3 researchers × 3 cases × 5 dimensions), the team reached initial agreement in nearly all cases (> 40); the rare disagreements were resolved, since they referred to adjacent classifications. Consequently, the team considered that inter-rater reliability was not a main concern in their study. In addition, researchers together considered possible shortcomings and extensions of the existing EO measures, resulting in a refined conceptual grid on EO in the context of long-living family firms (cf. Denzin and Lincoln, 2000).

As a further test of the reliability of the findings, and in line with suggestions by Denzin and Lincoln (2000), the research team performed a member check by cross-checking its work with managers' perceptions. The interviewees had the opportunity to read and comment on the case study protocols and the assessment of the EO patterns of their companies. This procedure not only is in accordance with Yin's (1994) recommendation about construct validity, but also increases the study's reliability. The interviewees had only minor comments, which were incorporated in the analysis. The resulting findings are provided in the corresponding chapter within this book.

Even though the above research methodology is an example, it highlights the rigor that STEP researchers applied within their research efforts. This rigor was included in creating an interactive learning environment for the researchers, which is outlined in the next section.

2.7 INTERACTIVE LEARNING ENVIRONMENT

A critical step in the development of valuable and trustworthy research from a large global project is the interactive learning among all researchers involved. To create an interactive learning environment, as we learned, is neither achievable through sharing of conceptual models and research guidelines (that is, interview guide and case report form), nor is a single contact sufficient to create a common understanding about the goals of such a research project, and the research questions deriving thereof. The STEP Project placed a high priority on face to face meetings to facilitate collaboration in the research process. The first meeting of the European STEP researchers took place in the fall of 2005 in Milan. At that time the project was in a 'storming' rather than a 'forming' phase – it took the European team three more meetings to come up with a somewhat accepted research framework, which is still regularly and vividly debated at most STEP meetings. However, from these in-person meetings, the methodology and research framework emerged and further refined through discussion. This chapter reflects the results of a collaborative research effort as well. While gaining momentum with an increasing number of schools and researchers joining the project, we developed a plan for researchers' learning as well. The interactive learning included the following elements:

1. Theoretical concepts. We developed a common understanding about the key elements of the transgenerational entrepreneurship research model, in particular EO, the resource-based view, performance outcomes and potential interrelationships. We discussed the issue of diverging levels of analysis and the difference of our research approach to the more traditional study of succession.
2. Use of interview guide and case report form. We ensured that researchers were trained in the use of the interview guide and the case report form. We provided guidance about the selection of firms and the conduct of interviews, for example, about the questions to be posed to different people, depending on their specific roles in the family firm. Also we addressed potential ethical concerns, given the inherent tension to gain good access to firms and family members, on the one hand, but to stay critical and distant to ensure research rigor, on the other hand. Since researching a family firm also meant researching a family we had to address confidentiality issues of the data we gathered.
3. Writing the master case. We shared information about what we considered to be a rich, comprehensive master case. Within the European team we spent several rounds in reading each other's cases and

improving them by revisiting the firm we had originally visited and by further enriching our descriptions. We paid particular attention to make sure that the researchers did not adopt an uncritical, positive admiring tone.

4. Qualitative research analysis. We ensured that researchers were familiar with qualitative research methods, supporting them in conducting qualitative research analyses and interpretations based on the data gathered. We mutually reviewed each other's master cases and discussed findings across case studies. We benchmarked previously published qualitative research to our studies developed from the master cases to improve our skills and learn the craft of publishing case study research.

STEP research teams agreed to be fully committed and to follow the shared, agreed upon research guidelines to maintain quality and trustworthiness of the research conducted and presented. At the very least, the researchers contributing to STEP were exposed to two days of structured learning events in the four outlined domains. Most researchers, however, were trained beyond this level through multiple research meetings, with iterative rounds of discussion about each other's research experience, thereby fostering self-reflection, mutual learning and improvement of research output. Moreover, most researchers had the opportunity to participate in STEP summits, defined as joint learning events between families and firms. This particularity of STEP is outlined in the next section.

2.8   SUMMITS

The mixed methods strategy of the STEP Project includes both quantitative and qualitative research approaches. There was an element of applied research present in the STEP Project since its inception. A STEP summit is where researchers and representatives from the case family businesses meet and share experiences. At the summits researchers presented their emerging findings to the family members who were given the opportunity to reflect on the findings. These events were designed to be joint learning events whereby knowledge is refined and co-produced between families and researchers. Even though these events were intended to have practical implications they were not traditional executive education seminars. With these events we follow the advice of Pettigrew et al. (2002, p. 480) 'to help practitioners to think more creatively about the complex, shifting world in which they operate'. The aim of the summits was thus to achieve a process of mutual knowledge creation between researchers and practitioners.

During the two-day summit events we discussed different aspects of the research framework, the interrelationships between concepts and the findings from the case research with the practitioners. Most often, the practitioners attending a summit were also the respondents who were interviewed in the case research. By establishing an interactive dialogue, we hoped to enhance the ability of critical and reflective thinking among and between researchers and practitioners. Such a dialogue can be a powerful source of development and change. At the summit our ambition was not to be normative, but to exchange and jointly create increased knowledge and understanding. This dialogue and exchange allowed the academics to do research and to theorize in a more informed way, and the practitioners to reflect upon and perhaps alter the way they act in the managing and governing of their business. As an illustration, Box 2.1 contains the agenda of the third European STEP summit which was held in Milan in August 2008. At this summit there were equal numbers of academics and practitioners present, in total about 60 people. The agenda of this summit looked as follows overleaf.

2.9   THE EMERGENCE OF THE CHAPTERS IN THIS BOOK

Many international collaborative research projects produce an edited book to report the final results of the research project. For the STEP Project we hoped to stimulate researchers to work on different emerging research themes and topics rather early in the research process. Knowing the long lead times at most scientific journals today, we also wanted to provide a way for the researchers within the STEP Project to share some of their unique findings and results with a broader audience. During 2005–08 the STEP Project grew rapidly with an impressive number of institutions, academics and family businesses involved. We therefore offer a book that is representative of the early research work that we are doing within the project, and that we can share with other interested people, both within and outside the STEP Project.

The idea is to edit one book per region that includes a set of research papers written by the STEP researchers of that region. Since the European team was the first STEP team to form, the Europeans are also the first to publish a book of their research findings. In 2007 we asked researchers from all the European STEP founding partners to select and explore one theme of particular interest and importance that they saw emerging in one or more of their cases, tie it to the research framework and examine this aspect in more depth. For this, researchers expanded on the literature

---

BOX 2.1   AGENDA OF THE THIRD EUROPEAN
           STEP SUMMIT

Morning Day 1   **Company introductions: posters**
                   Each family will have a poster arranged
                       around the room.
                   Participants will be encouraged to browse
                       posters and socialize.
                   STEP introduction and Impact Panel
                   An overview and introduction to STEP and
                       summit purpose.
                   2 Family Members, 2 Academics, 1
                       Facilitator.
                   To address the following questions:
                   ● What have we found in our first three
                       years?
                   ● How has STEP impacted your family
                       and business?
                   ● What do we need to look at more in
                       the future?
                   ● Introduction of parallel sessions

Afternoon Day 1   **Parallel sessions: choose theme 1 or 2**
                   1. Culture: how to use organizational culture
                       as a driver for entrepreneurship.
                   2. Entrepreneurial succession: how to
                       empower next generation entrepreneurs
                       and sustain entrepreneurial capacity
                       across generations.

Morning Day 2   **Parallel sessions: choose theme 1 or 2**
                   1. Building a business portfolio: how to
                       leverage a pool of resources to grow a
                       portfolio of new ventures.
                   2. Governance structures which constrain or
                       stimulate entrepreneurship.

Afternoon Day 2   **The STEP future**
                   Summit wrap up

review regarding the selected topic, conducted a focused analysis of the empirical material from the case research that related to the topic, and provided an expansion and elaboration of the conceptual framework in order to offer a theoretical contribution to the wider literature on entrepreneurship and family business. Every chapter followed the research approach outlined in this current chapter. All chapters went through several rounds of reviews by the editors, and a review by at least one other colleague outside the editorial team. Drafts have also been presented and discussed at several meetings.

In the end, the quality of our research will be judged by the readers of this book, be they researchers or practitioners. To all of you, we wish you a lot of fun and hopefully some attention-grabbing insights while reading the subsequent chapters.

NOTE

1. The complete interview guide can be downloaded from http://www.stepproject.org.

REFERENCES

Alvesson, M. and K. Sköldberg (eds) (2000), *Reflexive Methodology: New Vistas for Qualitative Research*, New York: Sage.

Burgelman, R.A. (1983), 'A process model of internal corporate venturing in the diversified major firm', *Administrative Science Quarterly*, **28**(2), 223–44.

Chrisman, J.J., J.H. Chua and P. Sharma (2005), 'Trends and directions in the development of a strategic management theory of the family firm', *Entrepreneurship Theory and Practice*, **29**(5), 555–75.

Davidsson, P. and J. Wiklund (2001), 'Levels of analysis in entrepreneurship research: current research practice and suggestions for the future', *Entrepreneurship Theory and Practice*, **25**(4), 81–100.

Denzin, N.K. and Y.S. Lincoln (2000), *Handbook of Qualitative Research*, Thousand Oaks, CA: Sage Publications.

Edmondson, A.C. and S.E. McManus (2007), 'Methodological fit in management field research', *Academy of Management Review*, **32**(4), 1155–79.

Eisenhardt, K.M. (1989), 'Building theories from case study research', *Academy of Management Review*, **14**(4), 532–50.

Fontana, A. and J.H. Frey (1994), 'Interviewing: the art of science', in N. Denzin and Y. Lincoln (eds), *Handbook of Qualitative Research*, Thousand Oaks, CA: Sage, pp. 361–77.

Garud, R. and A.H. Van de Ven (2001), 'Strategic change processes', in A. Pettigrew, H. Thomas and R. Whittington (eds), *Handbook of Strategy and Management*, London: Sage Publications, pp. 206–31.

Habbershon, T.G., M. Williams and I.C. MacMillan (2003), 'A unified systems perspective of family firm performance', *Journal of Business Venturing*, **18**(4), 451–65.

Hartley, J. (1994), 'Case studies in organizational research', in C. Cassell and G. Symon (eds), *Qualitative Methods in Organizational Research*, London: Sage, pp. 208–26.

Heck, R., F. Hoy, P. Poutziouris and L. Steier (2008), 'Emerging paths of family entrepreneurship research', *Journal of Small Business Management*, **46**(3), 317–30.

Low, M.B. and I.C. MacMillan (1988), 'Entrepreneurship: past research and future challenges', *Journal of Management*, **14**(2), 139–61.

Lumpkin, G.T. and G.G. Dess (1996), 'Clarifying the entrepreneurial orientation construct and linking it to performance', *Academy of Management Review*, **21**(1), 135–72.

Lumpkin, G.T. and G.G. Dess (2001), 'Linking two dimensions of entrepreneurial orientation to firm performance: the moderating role of environment and industry life cycle', *Journal of Business Venturing*, **16**, 429–51.

Lyon, D.W., G.T. Lumpkin and G.G. Dess (2000), 'Enhancing entrepreneurial orientation research: operationalizing and measuring a key strategic decision making process', *Journal of Management*, **26**(5), 1055–85.

Maxwell, J.A. (1998), 'Designing a qualitative study', in L. Bickman and D.J. Rog (eds), *Handbook of Applied Social Research Methods*, Thousand Oaks, CA: Sage, pp. 69–100.

Nordquist, M., A. Hall and L. Melin (2009), 'Qualitative research on family businesses: the relevance and usefulness of the interpretative approach', *Journal of Management and Organization*, **15**(3), 294–308.

Orum, A.M., J.R. Feagin and G. Sjoberg (1991), 'Introduction: the nature of the case study', in J.R. Feagin, A.M. Orum and G. Sjoberg (eds), *A Case for the Case Study*, Chapel Hill, NC: University of North Carolina Press, pp. 1–26.

Pearson, A.W., J.C. Carr and J.C. Shaw (2008), 'Toward a theory of familiness: a social capital perspective', *Entrepreneurship Theory and Practice*, **32**(6), 949–69.

Pettigrew, A.M. (1997), 'What is a processual analysis?' *Scandinavian Journal of Management*, **13**(4), 337–48.

Pettigrew, A., H. Thomas and R. Whittington (eds) (2002), *Handbook of Strategy and Management*, London: Sage Publications.

Shane, S.A. and S. Venkataraman (2000), 'The promise of entrepreneurship as a field of research', *Academy of Management Review*, **25**(1), 217–26.

Sharma, P. (2004), 'An overview of the field of family business studies: current status and directions for the future', *Family Business Review*, **17**(1), 1–36.

Silverman, D. (ed.) (1993), *Interpreting Qualitative Data: Methods for Analysing Talk, Text, and Interaction*, London: Sage.

Sirmon, D.G., M.A. Hitt and R.D. Ireland (2007), 'Managing firm resources in dynamic environments to create value: looking inside the black box', *Academy of Management Review*, **32**(1), 273–92.

Stake, R.E. (1999), *The Art of Case Study Research*, New York: Sage.

Stopford, J.M. and C.W.F. Baden-Fuller (1994), 'Creating corporate entrepreneurship', *Strategic Management Journal*, **15**(7), 521–36.

Suddaby, R. (2006), 'What grounded theory is not', *Academy of Management Journal*, **49**(4), 633–42.

Westhead, P. and M. Cowling (1997), 'Performance contrasts between family and non-family unquoted companies in the UK', *International Journal of Entrepreneurial Behaviour and Research*, **3**(1), 30–52.

Westhead, P. and C. Howorth (2007), '"Types" of private family firms: an exploratory conceptual and empirical analysis', *Entrepreneurship and Regional Development*, **19**(5), 405–31.

Wiklund, J. and D. Shepherd (2005), 'Entrepreneurial orientation and small business performance: a configurational approach', *Journal of Business Venturing*, **20**(1), 71–91.

Yin, R.K. (1994), *Case Study Research: Design and Methods*, Thousand Oaks, CA: Sage.

3. Balancing familiness resource pools for entrepreneurial performance

Ugo Lassini[1] and Carlo Salvato[2]

3.1 INTRODUCTION

Maintaining an entrepreneurial orientation (EO) over generations is a primary concern for many family firms. Family controlled businesses (FCBs) may face several challenges to their entrepreneurial potential and, ultimately, to their survival. Factors such as nepotism, altruism, adverse selection and family conflicts harm the FCBs' potential for entrepreneurial renewal and longevity (Anderson and Reeb, 2003; Carney, 2005; Kets de Vries et al., 2007; Miller and Le Breton-Miller, 2004). It is not surprising that recent family business research is increasingly focused on the antecedents of the family firm's long-term entrepreneurial potential.

Building on the resource-based view (RBV) of the firm (for example, Barney, 1991), recent efforts describe the resources appropriate for achieving competitive advantage. Valuable, rare, inimitable and non-substitutable resources are central to these explanations. Possessing unique resources and leveraging them in line with the firm's business model, FCBs attain competitive advantage and subsequent value creation (Cabrera-Suàrez et al., 2001; Habbershon and Williams, 1999; Sirmon and Hitt, 2003).

Focusing on specific resources is attractive, however, as it offers a parsimonious explanation of what determines FCBs' value creation. There is widespread agreement among scholars that the gradual development of firm-specific resource stocks over generations may also be the source of inertial forces blocking the FCBs' entrepreneurial potential (Collins and Porras, 1994; Gersick et al., 1997). In general, the development of distinctive resources and capabilities increases the firm's likelihood to survive and flourish. However gaps between current environmental requirements and a firm's core resources and capabilities emerge. Highly specific, currently valuable knowledge that sustains competitive advantage may be less relevant in the future and hard to adapt in the short run. Resources and capabilities that served the firm well in the past, and appropriate for some current entrepreneurial initiatives, may not satisfy the new requirements of a shifting competitive landscape (Levinthal, 1997). Firms confront a paradox: core resources and capabilities facilitate the exploitation of new entrepreneurial opportunities, but can easily turn into sources of rigidity (Leonard Barton, 1992).

This problem is relevant to all organization types. However it becomes particularly salient for family firms, as family control – through owner-ship, governance or managerial mechanisms – is more likely to favor path-dependent forces than in non-family firms. Therefore the presence of the family and the strong influences derived from its culture, knowledge and leadership within the organization may generate inertia, thereby turning once valuable resources and competencies into dangerous rigidities (Miller and Le Breton-Miller, 2004; Sharma and Irving, 2005).

Despite this awareness, research to date has rarely addressed how con-trolling families can leverage the pool of unique firm-specific resources they develop and overcome inertial risks. A focus on the possession of unique resources has prevented a detailed understanding of the specifics of strategic practices and processes allowing FCBs to balance positive and negative aspects of the family specific pool of resources, also known as distinctive and constrictive familiness, respectively (Habbershon and Williams, 1999; Habbershon et al., 2003).

This study investigates how some FCBs attain this difficult balance between the positive features of idiosyncratic resources accumulated over generations and their inertial potential. An integrated model is proposed, based on the contrasting theoretical approaches offered by the RBV of the firm and population ecology theory.

We conduct an in-depth study of the Veronesi Group, a multigenera-tional Italian family firm, and its entrepreneurial initiatives over time. As our data reveal, family controlled firms can actively manage the difficult balancing act between the value-creating and inertial potential inherent in the pools of resources they develop over generations.

There are three relevant contributions. First, the family has a strong and systematic influence on the firm's EO throughout the entire company history. Second, the interaction of the family and the business has both a positive and a negative influence on EO, termed, respectively, distinctive versus constrictive familiness (Habbershon et al., 2003). Third, organiza-tional 'balancing mechanisms' allow the family business to mitigate con-strictive familiness while emphasizing the role of distinctive familiness in sustaining entrepreneurial performance over time.

The chapter is structured as follows. We first develop a conceptual argument about the need to balance both innovative and inertial potential inherent in family specific resource pools by contrasting the conflicting prescriptions derived from the RBV and population ecology theories with the relationship between an organization's age and its vitality in achieving good financial, entrepreneurial and social performance. Next, we present the empirical setting, the Veronesi Group, and our data collection and data analysis processes. We then illustrate our analysis of the relationship between the familiness resource pools and entrepreneurial performance and discuss the results. We conclude with an illustration of implications for future research and entrepreneurial practice.

3.2   GUIDING THEORY

A central proposition in organization theory is the balance between opposites such as stability and change, inertia and transformation, the present and the future. The ability of opposites to balance rather than trade off is an important, though rare, organizational capability (Rumelt, 1995). This is particularly true in the context of family firms, which are frequently depicted as navigating between uncontested tradition and untested change (Collins and Porras, 1994). Veronesi is a particularly instructive example of how some multigeneration family firms gradually develop an ability to leverage the benefits of long-lasting tradition, while at the same time overcoming inertial forces ensuing from repeating the same activities.

Long-lasting tradition – a characteristic feature of many generational family firms – has no clear-cut impact on long-term performance, according to mainstream organizational literature. Within organizations continuous replication of successful strategies produces the accumulation of resources and competencies – that, according to the RBV, are key factors in building a firm's competitive advantage (Barney, 1991; Prahalad and Hamel, 1990). In contrast, alternative frameworks, such as population ecology, assume that the creation of routines necessary for the firm to make decision processes reliable and replicable will, over time, create inertial elements, which become embedded in the organization and hard to remove (Singh et al., 1986; Hannan and Freeman, 1989).

This chapter investigates the family specific mechanisms that allow the resource accumulation process to generate family specific core competencies and transgenerational entrepreneurship, while avoiding the organizational inertia and core rigidities that hamper risk taking and innovation. Although relevant to all types of organizations, this question is particularly salient for the family firm, as the presence of the family in the business is more likely to favor path-dependent forces than in non-family counterparts.

According to the RBV, financial, entrepreneurial and social performance depends on the firm's ability to accumulate asset stocks. These are labeled internal resources (Wernerfelt, 1984), distinctive competencies (Barney, 1986), core capabilities (Grant, 1991), accumulated asset stocks (Amit and Schoemaker, 1993) and firm-specific assets (Dierickx and Cool, 1989; Prahalad and Hamel, 1990).

A firm's survival and performance levels over time established by its internal resources, not just by the external competitive context, was first explicitly emphasized by Wernerfelt (1984). Similarly, Barney (1986) suggested that a firm's ability to survive and over-perform is not a consequence of its competitive positioning within the industry, but of the set of resources and competencies acquired on factor markets and adapted for alignment with environmental needs. Prahalad and Hamel (1990) state that firms, over time, continuously trigger collective processes of learning, thus inducing organizations to modify and improve their competencies. These become distinctive and guarantee future strengthening patterns in different and unclear scenarios. The relationship between age and vitality can be positive: core competencies will deteriorate if not used (see Nelson and Winter, 1982 on the issue of 'rustiness') and strengthen each time they are utilized.

Leonard-Barton (1992) questions the positive relationship between the age and vitality of a firm by introducing the concept of core rigidities as the other side of core capabilities. The more competencies are firm specific, the more they generate rigidities. Firms face a paradox: core capabilities facilitate and, at the same time, hinder the creation of new products and new processes. In this context, the presence of the family and the strong influence of its culture, knowledge and leadership may generate inertia, thereby inverting the relationship between a firm's age and vitality. According to this view, there is no a priori 'net effect'; it is therefore important to verify the creation of intentional balancing acts and activities to limit inertia.

To sum up, although Leonard-Barton (1992) highlighted the tradeoff between specificity and rigidity embedded in resource process accumulation, the RBV posits that the engine of change lies within the organization, which can innovate and grow through managerial activities and the continuous creation of new resources that leverage old ones. The nature of the process of resource and competency accumulation allows the relationship between an organization's age and its vitality to be not only positive, but also exponential, since the isolating mechanisms can overlap over time (Figure 3.1).

There are, however, alternative explanations of the relationship between firm age and firm vitality, with results less positive about the increasingly productive role of firm resources and competencies. Population ecology, in particular, offers an interesting contrast to the RBV in explaining the

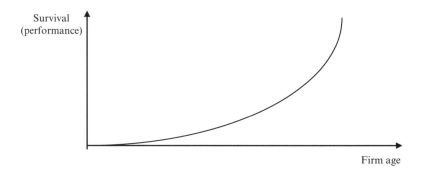

Figure 3.1   The relationship between firm age and firm vitality according to resource-based theory

role of family firm resources and competencies. This alternative explanation is premised on three concepts: liability of newness and smallness; liability of adolescence; and liability of aging.

The liability of newness hypothesis (for example, Stinchcombe, 1965) suggests that younger firms have higher mortality rates due to their having to learn new rules and create organizational routines when resources are spent in different tasks and processes. Moreover, new firms lack adequate power to influence the 'rules of the game' and the possibility of leveraging a consolidated network of relationships with other industry actors. Consequently, firms endure a sort of weakness during their start-up phase, since they experience difficulties in accessing the resources available in their environment. For these reasons, mortality rate has a reverse correlation with the age of the organization (Figure 3.2).

The liability of adolescence hypothesis (for example, Bruderl and Schussler, 1990) proposes a U-shaped relationship between firm age and vitality (Figure 3.2). At the beginning, the new organization has an initial stock of resources (goodwill, positive expectations, commitment of workers, financial resources and so on) that prevent it from bankruptcy. The higher the initial stock of resources, the longer this period of protection lasts. Consuming this stock without building the adequate routines that enable the organization to survive leads to liability of adolescence and, eventually, causes the firm to die. In contrast with liability of newness, there is a period of survival that is correlated with the stock of resources that owners allocate to the firm. The highest rate of failure, hence, occurs at some distance from the time of foundation, whereas both liability of newness and liability of smallness suggest that mortality rates decrease as the firm grows older and bigger. Both hypotheses consider that firms learn and build new routines during their early stages.

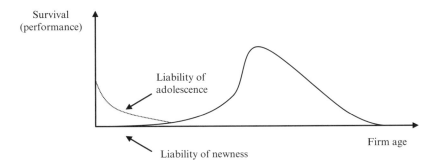

Figure 3.2   The relationship between firm age and firm vitality under the three population ecology hypotheses

The third hypothesis, liability of aging (for example, Baum, 1997), which predicts a high rate of mortality for older organizations (Figure 3.2), is based on the idea that a firm is established using resources and technologies coherent with a stated period. Over time, the organization yields its place to another, which will achieve better performance using a different, often new, bundle of resources provided by a changed environment.

Throughout its life span, a firm reflects the environment dominant at the moment of its founding. The harmony between the organization and its industrial field is eroded by different factors, among which are information asymmetries, limited rationality and inertia, making it difficult, if not impossible, for the firm to change its routines and adapt to mutated environmental elements. These changes offer newcomers the chance to enter the business and to undermine competitive advantages established by incumbent firms (Carroll, 1985). Paradoxically, attempts at realigning the organization to the environment may increase the risk of failure if managerial skills are limited. If so, change may yield lower performance since it reduces the firm's reliability while breaking down established relationships with clients, suppliers and customers.

Considering the population ecology approach, the rational search for coherence among the firm's activities generates rigidity, which derives from specific and idiosyncratic investments in routines. However it is exactly these investments and routines that, according to the RBV, give the firm its distinctive identity and the ensuing chance to out-distance competitors. It is interesting to identify the factors yielding sources of competitive advantage rather than the organizational inertia that limits family firm survival and performance over time (Figure 3.3).

According to the STEP model, which guides our analysis, the answer lies in the familiness resource pools and in the impact these resources have on

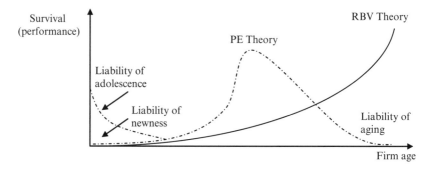

Figure 3.3   The relationship between firm age and firm vitality according to both population ecology and resource-based theory

EO and, together with EO, on entrepreneurial performance (Habbershon and Pistrui, 2002; Habbershon et al., 2003). Our research aims at exploring how familiness resource pools accumulated by the founder and subsequent generations may influence EO across generations. Entrepreneurial orientation has emerged as a major concept within the entrepreneurship literature. Several innovative firms attribute their success to EO, which is defined as an approach to decision making that draws on entrepreneurial skills and capabilities such as innovativeness, proactiveness, risk taking, autonomy and competitive aggressiveness (for example, Lumpkin and Dess, 1996, 2001; Lumpkin et al., 2009). An EO keeps firms alert by exposing them to new technologies, making them aware of marketplace trends and helping them evaluate new possibilities. Hence firms that exhibit a strong EO are often better performers (Naldi et al., 2007; Rauch et al., 2009).

In particular, we are interested in understanding how certain family controlled firms overcome the inertial qualities of some resources and competencies, while keeping a fresh stock of assets constantly in tune with the competitive needs of their shifting industry environment. Our main argument is that, over time, as an increasing number of family members and generations are involved in the business, the family should act to balance inertia and make future competitive advantage possible.

3.3   METHODS

To address our research questions, we performed an in-depth longitudinal case study, following the STEP case methodology (see Chapter 2). This allowed us to develop a holistic view of the processes under review, to obtain a deep, comprehensive understanding of them, and to generate theory about such processes. As this research is aimed at theory generation, the case was selected according to the principles of theoretical sampling, allowing focal topics to be studied in contexts enabling transparent observation.

We therefore chose to analyse a family business with three characteristics: (1) a relevant and extensive presence of the family in the business, through ownership, governance and management; (2) the co-existence of more than one generation active in the business; and (3) a demonstrated ability to obtain clear and positive financial, competitive and social results over time. The second and third requirements are motivated by the need to verify conditions under which the relationship between familiness resource pools and entrepreneurial performance is positive across generations (Habbershon and Pistrui, 2002; Habbershon et al., 2003).

The first aspect is fundamental when analysing a context in which a family has a significant impact on the resource accumulation process within different familiness resource pools. It also allowed us to address the issue of the definition of family business by requiring a significant role played by the family in controlling the business and clear evidence of an intention to transfer the business to subsequent generations (Harris et al., 1994; Klein, 2000; Litz, 1995).

3.4   EMPIRICAL SETTING

The Veronesi Group is a suitable case to address the main research questions in our study. Veronesi is both family owned and family managed (although there are also external managers). Altogether, the family comprises 34 members (the founder, five members of the second generation, 15 members of the third and 13 of the fourth); 13 of them are actively involved in the business. There is a Family Council composed of 21 family members of the first, second and third generations, and an active Board of Directors (composed of ten family members and four non-family directors).

The Veronesi Group was founded by Apollinare Veronesi in 1958. The founder not only established a new company; he started an industry new to Italy. Veronesi SPA (the Group's first company chronologically) was the first company active in the large-scale production of livestock feed. Today it boasts a national market share of around 19.5 percent, which makes it the leading firm in the food industry in Italy, the ninth most important producer in Europe, and the twenty-third in the world in this field.

The Veronesi Group was entirely devoted to the concept of 'food made in Italy' and, starting from the livestock sector, it expanded business by integrating different animal products. In 1968 AIA was established to deal in the breeding, processing and marketing of chickens, turkeys, rabbits, eggs, guinea hens and trout. In 1975 the Group entered the pork and beef sector by operating a series of farms and purchasing the leading firm and several other cold meat and salami factories in Italy (such as Montorsi, Negroni and Fini).

The Group is currently composed of more than 20 companies operating in different food businesses. It has eight factories (known as the '8 stars'), which have brought prosperity to the city that is home to the Veronesi farm, as well as a consolidated net revenue of 1 978 613 000 euros in 2007. The Group has 6513 employees (over 10 000 considering all related industries), total assets of about 1 278 045 000 euros and an EBITDA approaching 191 million.

Since the beginning, the Veronesi family has been involved in business ownership, governance and management. The founder (ninth of ten sons) is still alive and interested in his creation, although he is no longer active. The Group is totally owned by his five children – two daughters (members of the Board of Directors) and three sons (president and vice-presidents of the firm). Ten members of the third generation (15 in total) are active as managers in different roles (vice-CFO, marketing manager, export sales manager, purchasing manager, quality control manager, legal affairs director, project manager and so on).

3.5   ANALYSIS AND DISCUSSION

The main objective of this study is to understand the differential positive or negative impact of family related resource pools on the family firm's long-term entrepreneurial viability. This is a central concern in recent family business literature, but it has rarely benefited from accurate empirical treatment. We address this issue by an in-depth analysis of the entrepreneurial history of the Veronesi Group, a large FCB, currently in its third generation. The aim is to understand how this firm managed to overcome the different liabilities inherent in being a family controlled entity, while at the same time leveraging the strengths that copious literature credits to firms actively controlled by entrepreneurial families.

We focus on three bundles of familiness resource pools,[3] which proved to be central in explaining Veronesi entrepreneurial history: leadership, culture and governance. However we acknowledge the existence of other relevant familiness resource pools of capital (financial, physical, human, social and intangible) (see Chapter 2). For each of these three resource pools, we describe how they influenced the family firm's EO and the

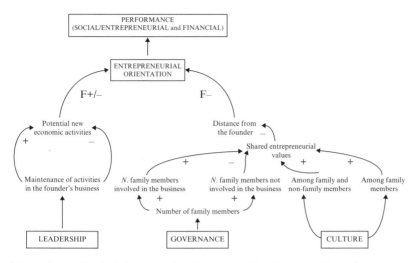

Figure 3.4   The link between familiness and the Veronesi Group's performance

specific 'balancing acts' the firm intentionally adopted in order to limit constrictive familiness.

This interpretive framework is illustrated in Figure 3.4. In this section we first define performance in the Veronesi case.

Second, we separately analyse the impact that leadership, culture and governance have on EO and how such impact is balanced – when needed – in order to obtain a positive link between the EO of the Group and its performance.

Entrepreneurial Performance

In the 55 years since its founding the Veronesi Group has achieved impressive goals in the financial field and, in particular, in the four different dimensions that describe entrepreneurial performance over time: innovation, renewal, new venture creation and social success (Table 3.1).

Innovation has been the key to success since the firm's inception when livestock feed did not exist as an industry in Italy. The Group's founder, after World War II, applied his knowledge of proteins to the increasing need of farmers to improve the health and productivity of their stock. Consequently, Veronesi did not simply enter a business – it started a new industry, being the first to operate in the production of livestock feed. Today, it boasts a national market share of around 19.5 percent, which makes it the leading firm in the food industry in Italy, the sixth most

*Table 3.1   Financial, entrepreneurial and social performance of the
            Veronesi Group (1952–2007)*

Performance		
International Brand		**Veronesi Mangimi, AIA, Montorsi, Negronl, SO.GE.MA**
Financial	Annual Sales	1 978 613 000
	Net income	75 867 000
	# of Employees	6 513
	% Sales Growth	+45% over the last 3 years
	Ebitda	190 081 000
	Total assets	1 278 045 000
Entrepreneurial	# of New Products	Many: through acquisitions and internal product innovation
	# of New Services	Many, thanks to an intensive integration strategy targeted at the final client
	# of New Markets Entered	Leader in Italy: segment leader in Europe; added a new industry, as well as a related market, to the original business
	# of Acquisitions	> 10 (2 significant ones in order to penetrate into the new industry)
	# of Renewal Programs	Implementation of a strategy of integration and internationalization which led to a strong renewal of the competitive strategy in terms of 'where'
Social	Community	Third firm in the food industry in Italy
		Eight factories known as the '8 stars', which brought richness to the city which hosted the Veronesi farm
		More than 10 000 employees on the territory thanks to the Veronesi Group's activities
	Family	Those family members involved are totally focused on the business
		Those who are not are free to follow their calling
		Respect each other's needs
		Each family member of each generation counts (directly or throughout mechanisms of representation) in business decisions and perceives Veronesi as their firm

	Performance
International Brand	**Veronesi Mangimi, AIA, Montorsi, Negronl, SO.GE.MA**
Individual	The founder received all sorts of awards (from *laurea ad honoris* to 'Work Cavalier for Italy')
	Employees are proud to be part of the Veronesi project
	All five second generation family members fulfilled themselves both in their jobs and in their personal needs and aspirations
	All 15 third generation family members are free to choose whether to contribute or not to the business and receive respect from the others, inside and outside the family

important producer in Europe and the twentieth worldwide in this sector. Product innovation by leveraging new science discoveries and improving production processes through new technology is a constant of the Group's factories. The renewal of competitive strategy was also relevant and, periodically, some key choices were decisive in achieving long-term success. An example is the decision in the early 1970s to transform scale production by building the biggest factory in Italy, aimed at the national market.

Although remaining strongly linked to the values of its place of origin (Verona), the Group expanded in order to compete internationally, particularly in Europe but also in Japan, North and South America, and the Middle East. One figure summarizes and reflects the presence of the Group in the world today: 2100 trucks, which run daily over 300000 km, seven times the Earth's circumference. The logistics division includes two platforms, 13 distribution centers and 26 nationwide transit points, totaling an overall surface of more than 67000 square meters, and employing more than 650 people. Deliveries are made by over 1000 lorries that move more than one million tons of products a year. This system boasts the largest structure in Italy for distributing fresh and extra-fresh food (expiration within 7–10 days), whose range embraces the entire nation and much of Europe. In 2007 production exceeded the 2.8 million ton threshold, with 730000 fattened pigs, 28000 tons of salami, 125 million chickens, 1.6 billion eggs and so on.

Another example is the decision to be totally devoted to the concept of 'food made in Italy' and to expand the operations of the original business. Since the foundation of Veronesi spa, the Group's first company, established in 1958, the Group has increased sales through expansion in the livestock feed business; it has entered the poultry and meat industry and the restaurant business through both organic growth and acquisitions. Many new ventures were created, and today there are more than 20 companies that, starting from the livestock sector, expanded the business by integrating different animal products. In 1968 AIA was established to deal in the breeding, processing and marketing of chickens, turkeys, rabbits, eggs, guinea hens and trout. In 1975 the Group entered the pork and beef sector by operating a series of farms and purchasing the leader and several other cold meat and salami factories in Italy (such as Montorsi, Negroni and Fini).

The combination of narrow diversification and vertical integration within the food industry boosted expansion and brought Group activities nearer to the end customer. This also led to a new mentality and the development of skills suitable not only for the business to business approach (clearly evident in livestock feed production, chicken farming and cattle breeding), but also for the business to consumer approach. Vertical integration allowed the Group to absorb and hold value from different and 'richer' levels of the food value chain.

A central belief of the founder, embedded in the whole organization, clarifies the dimension of entrepreneurial performance that is predominant for the Veronesi Group: 'The best social performance is the only way to achieve good entrepreneurial and financial performance.' In accordance with this principle, Veronesi factories in Italy were built in small villages characterized by severe unemployment rates. After Veronesi Group investments these locations typically flourished and the firm gained the gratitude and loyalty of employees and the local community, coupled with low labor costs. The Veronesi family is convinced that social goals are so central that they cannot be sacrificed to improve economic or financial performance. 'Continuity of core values' is the underlying philosophy guiding firm choices, with the aim of creating wealth in the long run not only for the owners but, more broadly, for managers, employees, the local community and the entire nation. The following quotes vividly exemplify this attitude.

Year-end managers meeting – livestock feed division
Founder: 'The best social performance yields the best entrepreneurial and financial performance. It is not Veronesi which creates job opportunities; Veronesi clients do. In a way, our clients are also our employers.' 'The firm must be considered in the

light of the long-term continuity of the activities of the people it relates with. All employees must think that their work is both useful in itself, and for its related salary, which is obviously important. Continuity of the firm and of its activity in the social context in the long run is the most relevant goal, for clients, for suppliers, for everyone.'

CEO: 'Our main concern is to create wealth in a broad sense, for employees, the population, the region, the country. I imagine this philosophy can be seen from outside as a view that generates constraints to the development of the firm. But this is the deepest belief of the founder and I also believe that it is right to be satisfied with an honest profit and to look at the firm's future as an opportunity to further improve social performance, more than the financial one.'

Senior Employees Award – livestock feed and poultry division

Founder: 'Our final goal is not year-end group earnings, but allowing the group to increase its reputation.' 'I do not care much about when and what kind of economic performance we have. I do not attribute a relevant value to them. Our main asset is represented by people. I am touched by this commitment to the firm: what you are doing is not only for the future performance of this Group; you are improving the nation's wealth and knowledge.' 'I am proud since we are accomplishing our social role. We carried out this progress in agriculture, in aviculture, in all operational activities.' 'In my life I have always worked for common, rather than individual wealth.' 'The client is our employer. We should consider mainly which kind of contribution we can make to our client's activities: they help us, and we must respect them.'

The Veronesi Group's global results highlight the success of an approach based on the deep belief that social performance has a strong positive relationship with both competitive and financial performance over time.

Leadership

Our data reveal that among familiness resource pools leadership has an enormous impact on EO. Existing research has been equivocal about the importance of CEOs in affecting firm-level outcomes. Our data suggest that a transformational leader plays an important role, particularly in promoting corporate entrepreneurship. This result is in line with the outcome of the few studies that have addressed the transformational role of leadership within organizational settings different from the family firm (for example, Ling et al., 2008; Schein, 2004; Waldman et al., 2001). From the outset the family had a strong, systematic influence on the business, both in ownership (the percentage of non-family owners is currently lower than 2 percent) and in management. Fourteen members of two generations are involved in the firm, three of them with the highest managerial responsibilities (see Appendix: Veronesi family genogram).

In order to understand how leadership may impact EO over time, the founder's characteristics and those of his sons must be considered.

Table 3.2 offers an illustration of the role leadership played in driving most of the crucial historical events of the Group, and in determining both the initial growth and later development of the firm over the first and the second generations.

As illustrated in Table 3.2, the founder, inspired by a sort of revenge against those who did not believe in his intuition and especially stimulated by the desire to demonstrate his own abilities, was able to absorb technical knowledge and to create and sell a new and innovative product that marked the beginning of the livestock feed industry in Italy.

In this way, he was not only able to create value out of what his father had left him (that is, wheat, which, in the 1930s was not as valuable as the mill or the maize his two brothers inherited), but he also undertook amazing entrepreneurial activity, which currently makes Veronesi the third largest firm in the food industry in Italy. From the beginning, the expansion of the Group was guided by a clear idea – keeping activities in the original business (those related to the activity at the base of the food industry value chain): 'Doing well [that is, our best every day in producing], we do good [that is, for people in general since we deliver food which is a primary need for everyone].'

This driving principle, stemming from the founder's leadership, was transmitted to his sons involved in the management of the business, and over the last 50 years it has acted both as an impulse and as a constraint on EO. Table 3.3 illustrates some positive and negative effects of 'continuity within the original business' on the five dimensions of EO.

The 'unwritten law' that business activities should be strictly related to the original business represents a core value of the Group. Over time, it has generated both distinctive and constrictive familiness (Habbershon et al., 2003). An example from Table 3.3 clarifies this issue. In 1967, when the firm's main client, operating in the poultry industry, said that Veronesi's livestock feeds were too expensive and declared it was going to produce them internally by integrating upstream, the distinctive familiness based on the founder's leadership emerged, positively influencing EO. As the

Table 3.2   *The role of leadership in driving the growth of the Veronesi Group: crucial historical events*

Year	Historical Event	Founder (and Successors) Leadership
1911	28 August: the founder (Apollinare Veronesi) is born, the ninth of ten children (seven female and three male).	'I was the youngest son: my first brother inherited the mill, the second the maize and I received just the wheat, but later I found a way to create value from this product!'
1923–26	The founder's father splits from his brothers and sets up his own activity together with his three sons (Angelo, Alfonso, Apollinare), creating the first 'industrial mill' in the region.	'My father was my first teacher: I learned the art of milling and to love my job. I was forbidden to go to school since my father thought I could help in some way.'
1927	The first balance sheet of the family business is developed.	'I had to study after dinner, or to attend lectures on accounting and commerce, and on agriculture. Learning from these my second and third teachers, I started thinking as an entrepreneur within the existing family business and I decided to develop what was our first balance sheet'.[4]
1937–47	The family business started a pattern of narrow diversification.	'The activities of our family were growing, we were introducing new and more productive technology. I put in the family business every competence, ability and commitment I had. We started a narrow diversification, selling oil and brewer's yeast. Using a truck dating back to World War I, I commercialized every kind of product and sales increased significantly.'
1940	The founder becomes the point of reference for his brothers and sisters, a fundamental help for his father, and the family's spokesman with both regional and national political institutions.	'Although I was the youngest son, I was responsible for the whole family. For example, when politicians decided to move the street down from our valley to the plain, I began to act as a protester.[5] The economic loss we would face

Table 3.2   (continued)

Year	Historical Event	Founder (and Successors) Leadership
		was oppressing me. The family was large, but I held the reins of it, unfortunately: it was a stressing responsibility, but I had to do it.'
1952	The founder develops his own business, investing money inherited by his wife.	'Within the existing family business, I bought a piece of land and I started up an activity in order to create and sell new and innovative livestock feed. I invested my wife's inheritance in the most disreputable piece of land in the valley: since the amount of money was not big, I could not make another choice and anyway I thought that you never know, maybe things were going to change in the future.'
1958	The founder's two elder brothers ask him to separate his business (livestock feed) from the family one (home made bread making).	'On May 1st I set up my own firm (Veronesi Apollinare snc) operating in livestock feed, since my father, my brothers and nephews did not believe in the livestock feed industry and they also considered it not prestigious.'[6]
1967	The founder started diversification in the poultry industry.	'Reacting to our main client – Polli Arena – who integrated upstream by starting a business in livestock feed, I decided to enter his industry and founded AIA, which produces and sells chickens, turkeys, eggs, rabbits, guinea-hens and trout.'
1974	A new plant is set up for livestock feed production.	'I was convinced that we should pursue strong expansion within the original industry. Our plant is still the biggest farm in Italy in this industry.'
1984	Creation of Veronesi Finanziaria S.p.a., a financial holding entirely owned by the founder's five children (three male and two female).	'I decided to take a step back and to enhance the succession process by giving shares to all my five children and in particular an increasing responsibility to the three males, who were actively involved in the business.'

Year	Historical Event	Founder (and Successors) Leadership
1976– 2007	Setting up of new plants and 17 acquisitions of firms in the poultry and the meat industry (such as Montorsi and Negroni, two of the main actors in their industry).	'We progressed along the pathway started by our father, pursuing the improvement of the competitive positioning of the Group in Europe both in the original businesses of livestock feed and poultry. We also increased diversification by performing acquisitions in the meat industry and by enlarging activities in the gastronomy business. We took the responsibility of three different divisions within the Group: livestock feed, aviculture and pork meat.'

competitor encroached on the Veronesi arena, Veronesi retaliated by expanding its activities in the competitor's territory and pursuing opportunities in the poultry industry (vertical integration). In that case, the personal characteristics of the founder (aggressiveness and risk taking, in particular) help us to understand his simple reply to this competitive threat: 'Therefore, I am going to raise battery chickens!' And so he did, helped by his three sons who were in their twenties. The firm entered the poultry industry, building over time the brand AIA, which produces and sells chickens, turkeys, eggs, rabbits, guinea hens and trout and is a leader, not only in Italy, but throughout Europe.

More recently, the ownership was asked to join a start-up that hoped to play an important role in a completely different industry (highway catering). The same personal characteristics that drove growth in the poultry business led the ownership to pose a simple question to the potential partner: 'How many sausages can we sell?' Since food was not the main value driver of this initiative, leadership limited the growth of the Group in non-correlated business. In fact, the Group preferred to seek opportunities correlated only to the original business and did not join this start-up (which became the leading brand in Italy, Autogrill), even if risk was limited and the expected financial (*ex post* realized) and economic revenues were enormous.

Since then the founder and the reputation he built among direct customers, suppliers, employees and end customers (the collectivity) anchored the activities of the firm to the original business, even in the 1980s and

Table 3.3   The impact on EO of maintaining activities in the original business

Negative Impact (F−)	EO Dimensions	Positive Impact (F+)
Vice-President: 'We do not act this way: if you want to acquire another firm, first we have to meet and discuss all together and then we will decide.'	Autonomy	President: 'Within the food industry, you can start any sort of initiatives to discover and create value for our customers.'
Founder: 'The farmer could not believe that I created for him an innovative livestock feed: in this industry before getting people used to an innovation, lots of time must pass. We have to be patient!'	Innovativeness	Founder: 'Every person is an encyclopedia. Where I could learn, there I always was. Once a month I listened to the lesson of a professor of agriculture: he was really an honest person and used to talk about a new food integrator. I understood that this was the future for my original business: livestock feed. Still now, you have to listen to your clients and don't care about what competitors are doing. In this industry our customers are our employers and they will suggest where we can be innovative. We will leverage on past experience to find out how.'
CFO: 'Things at the moment go on as I said: we won't make this diversification even if the expected revenues and the partner of the joint venture are definitely alluring. We will add another step only after the previous one is completed.'	Risk taking	Founder: 'Since I was a child my mother gave to me all the weak chickens. I was not afraid of the responsibility of saving them from death since I simply observed that by using small worms instead of only vegetables they would survive and grow. What I am saying is that we started this industry 50 years ago and now it is our duty to assume risk and to invest in every kind of project that can improve knowledge and allow us to offer better products.'

Negative Impact (F−)	EO Dimensions	Positive Impact (F+)
Founder: 'When I began to operate in this business, I went to Mass at six a.m., before the others so that I was free to stay out and sell products to my clients. I could not be absent when they got out from their Mass, since some of them made more than 40 kilometers on foot! In this way I made myself popular with everybody. Starting from those farmers, today the Group has expanded its image all over the world and built a strong reputation. In my view, if we start operating in other industries different from agriculture, breeding and at the most gastronomy, we will confuse our actual suppliers and clients.'	Proactiveness	CEO: 'Listening to some new projects that scientists back in the seventies were developing on proteins, I immediately understood that these innovations had the potential of turning the industry upside down. But I also clearly knew that science was still undeveloped. So my effort was to believe that science would improve and complete the discovery and in order to make me able to use it in my industry.' 'The European common market is near. For us who are operating exclusively in different links of the food chain this means that we must reach the same technical knowledge in production of our most advanced global competitors. It is urgent: either we keep ourselves up to date or we will perish!.'
Founder's son discussing with Benetton Group the opportunity of starting up a diversification in the national highway food delivery services: 'The expected financial revenues are impressive and the risk is not very high: this is definitely a great opportunity. But how many sausages can we sell in this way? Not so many. . .and this is our priority: to serve our industry.'	Aggressiveness	Founder: Talking to the main client of livestock feed products: 'Are you perhaps threatening us with entering the livestock feed business? That's fine, so we will start chicken farming, your business.'

early 1990s, when three members of the second generation had important responsibilities in the organization. In this sense, it may be observed that the choices concerning corporate strategy and, in particular, the portfolio decisions, were guided by the founder's vocation: to contribute to global welfare through responsible performances in agriculture and the food industry. This started an intense accumulation process of skills and resources, generating core competencies within the Group and the total commitment of all stakeholders in the business activities. At the same time, the strong leadership of the founder generated organizational inertia and core rigidities that limited the autonomy of other members of the family in exploiting various opportunities for the Group to expand outside the original business.

From 1984 onwards, the need to balance the restrictive influence of familiness related to leadership became evident. It was emphasized more recently by two shocking external factors which occurred in the industry, SARS and mad cow disease, which strongly reduced the revenues of the Group in its original businesses and undermined its future expansion potential.

In that year, although growth opportunities within the original industry were still present, a financial holding was created, entirely owned by the founder together with his five children (and their families): three sons, who had been active in the business since the 1940s and are now top managers, and two daughters, who were never active in the firm and are shareholders.

The holding structure created two effects. First, it opened up the decision-making process, distancing it a little further from the founder's background and experience, thus permitting his leadership to acquire balance (and enrichment). As a consequence, firms in both the poultry and the meat industry were established or acquired, leveraging on the competencies the three sons had developed in these businesses. In particular, after the creation of the holding, the Group acquired two firms that are segment leaders in the meat industry, with two relevant brands at the international level.

In this way, it was possible to enlarge the diversification process from narrow dimensions to less correlated businesses through a vertical integration that put Veronesi Group in contact with the end consumer. This expansion also allowed the third generation to specialize in marketing activities. It is no accident that the majority of third generation family members are involved in the marketing division. The good entrepreneurial performance achieved by the second generation, both in the original business as well as in narrow and uncorrelated businesses, is opening up new opportunities for the third generation to contribute to the future development of the Group. The last generation, in fact, is acquiring the skills and competencies in marketing that are no longer involved in essential products for a business to business logic (managed by the family members of the first and second generation). In the meat industry and in particular the restaurant line of products communication with the end customer has more relevance in facing global competition.

The second effect of the creation of the Veronesi financial holding is that even non-active family members (not involved in the operative decision process) were brought into the team. Investment opportunities not related to the business were considered in order to create value for all the shareholders.

In 2002 a new organizational structure of the entire Group was formed as a result of the new direction of investments. Four divisions were created, managed by the three sons together with the top managers, and coordinated by a CEO exploring opportunities far outside the original business.

Distance From the Founder

The joke about family business is that the first generation creates wealth, the second maintains it and the third squanders it. Researchers have developed statistics that support this anecdote (Colli, 2003; Ibrahim et al., 2001; Littunen et al., 2000; Nicholson, 2008; Stein, 2001).

Similar studies generally analyse the ability of firms to survive over time, without expressly comparing family versus non-family owned businesses. The statistics presented reflect the predictable death rate of organizations facing competitors, during strategic and financial troubles.

With regard to family firms it is useful to identify two areas: the number of generations involved in ownership, governance or management and 'distance from the founder'.

The presence of more than one generation active in the business is itself a sign of success over time and is definitely correlated with a chronological dimension. Distance from the founder is different, however; it is reflected in how the firm is perceived now compared to the period under the founder.

The longer and more successful the period managed by the founder, the more that distance from the founder is likely to be associated by various stakeholders with a longing for the 'golden years'. In this context (multi-generational, successful family firms), distance from the founder leads to a decrease in commitment and has a negative impact on EO. The success of the first generation is the success of the founder, who addresses and drives at least one of the five dimensions of EO[7] (often more than one, if not all).

As with many other family firms that have enjoyed continued success, the Veronesi Group is at great risk that distance from the founder may have a negative impact on EO for the following reasons.

First, the measure of success (in competitive as well as financial and social terms) achieved by the founder is enormous and resulted in numerous stakeholders at national and international levels (suppliers, consumers, employers and so on). Second, the founder was directly active as the chief of the firm's top management for 50 years. Third, many personal characteristics (especially leadership) were so pervasive as to be contagious and became embedded throughout the organization. Fourth, in the food industry networking with key clients and suppliers, tradition and reputation are central factors of success and are linked to the personality of the founder, his commitment and his beliefs about the social role of entrepreneurship. Finally, the founder not only started and guided the Group to national and international leadership in different market niches, he also presented some of the peculiarities typical of heroes. In fact, several other entrepreneurs in the last 50 years created extremely successful firms in the same region, even in Apollinare's native town, but no one more than he has captured the attention and stimulated the curiosity even of people who never met him.

Apollinare Veronesi has generated myth (in addition to his entrepreneurialism) (Rank, 1909). His parents were champions of honesty, altruism and religious devotion, the three main values of rural society at that time. He shares the name of the patron saint of the city where the Group began and that of a young priest, a family friend, who died the day of his birth. He was estranged from his family and later returned victoriously. Division of the family properties led him to start his entrepreneurial activity in the most undesirable area of the valley.

He is a self-made man of poor origins, who does not compromise to avoid difficulties, who anticipates the future, acts farsightedly and places common welfare above his personal gain. He lives modestly, in an unpretentious house, and does not visibly participate in public social life. He has accepted no important position outside the firm, neither local nor national. Above all, he does not let success change him, his style of living, his ideas, his way of thinking and relating to people, or his values. He inspires admiration and a feeling that 'he is one of us and obtained success!'

Clearly, this case exemplifies the negative impact of distance from the founder on EO. It reflects distance from a history of continuous success, entrepreneurial values, emotions, choices and results. This distance can become fear of losing something considered fundamental when facing new challenges, generate doubts on the right steps to take, create both inside and outside the organization a feeling of insecurity and inertia, and can diminish all five dimensions of EO.

Luckily, and unlike the inevitable succession of generations throughout the years, distance from a successful founder is a perception that can be modified and balanced by intervening both internally (for example, governance) and externally (for example, culture).

Family Governance Mechanisms

Who makes decisions, which decisions are made and how they are made is a critical part of strategy development and execution in the family business context, especially when the number of family members (not only those actively involved in managing the business but also all other shareholders) increases across generations. The first generation founder typically leverages his leadership, guiding resource accumulation, solving conflicts among family members, and providing the firm with a stock of valuable resources (capital, products, commitment, passion, reputation and so on). As more family members are involved in the ownership, governance and management of the business, conflict may result from different family members' various priorities. Resource accumulation, successfully handled in the first generation, can reduce efficiency and efficacy if diverted by continuously changing actors.

If not governed, generational drift may quickly emphasize the distance from a (successful) founder and reduce EO. In particular, the number of family members who are merely shareholders and not involved in management can naturally (and even legitimately) drive attention to their personal needs, far from the financial and strategic necessities of the firm. Conversely, the number of family owners employed at different levels of the organization, especially those in close contact with the founder, can help in sharing his entrepreneurial values and in maintaining homogeneous behaviors that keep EO high at the level of the first generation.

In our case, there are 34 family members: the founder, five members of the second generation, 15 members of the third and 13 of the fourth. Excluding this last generation since they are children, in 2007 13 family owners were involved in the management of the Group and seven were not (see Appendix).

In this situation a number of basic questions concerning relationships among family members may affect the organization's ability to be dynamic in taking risks and be innovative, proactive and aggressive. Who decides? What should the non-active family members know about business decisions before they are taken? How do family members with different roles in the business interact? How does the relationship between active family members and other managers work? The founder made strategic decisions as the Group grew. As the second generation entered the business, the founder created a shared decision-making process to plan for the future in accordance with the core values and competencies of the Group. Four specific balancing mechanisms based on business and family governance structures were implemented.

First, only sons could be owners and managers, not their spouses (no exceptions). This does not mean that spouses are completely out of the business. If they are freelance professionals (banker, lawyer, architect and so on) and the firm needs that kind of service, a fruitful and long-term collaboration can be established.

Second, all sons of the founder are part of the strategic board and participate in defining the strategic goals and discussing the main choices and decisions involving the business. From the 1950s to 1985 only active family members were involved in this process, but things changed to facilitate continuity of 100 percent ownership within the second generation: 'Nobody decides alone: we make a choice all together, and whoever studied and proposed the solution is responsible for all the rest.' The participation of non-active family members in the board allows them to understand the financial needs and long-term expectations that new investment can generate.

Third, although the decision process is conducted by the five members of the second generation, the third generation is also part of the strategic board according to a 'representative mechanism'. One cousin from each of the five families is 'elected' by the other cousins; representation changes each year. In this way, the third generation learns from their antecedents how business strategy is defined and accepted before being implemented. Moreover, brothers and sisters (active and non-active) of the third generation create trust among each other and interact constructively with cousins. Representation on the board is completed by the presence of four non-family members: the CEO, the CFO, the administrative director and the personnel director.

Fourth, in 2002 a family council was created, composed of all members of all generations. The family council manages the estate of the family and not that of the business in order to separate personal needs from business ones, so that all family members may discuss their personal visions of the family/business relationship.

In this way, the firm enlarged the number of persons involved in the strategic decision-making process to leverage the knowledge of all active family members and share strategic goals with non-family members in terms of investment and return on investment over time. Using a representative mechanismin the existing governance structure helped create trust among the increasing number of cousins and prepared them to make decisions for the firm's and the families' future.. The governance mechanisms facilitated listening to each other's suggestions, starting with the founder: 'When I [the director of production] proposed a new method, the founder said: "Let's continue according to the old one." The day after he called me and said: "Mario, I thought last night about what you said and I discussed your solution with the board. Considering the ideas of the other relatives and managers, we decided that is better to do as you proposed."'

Culture

Governance alone is not enough. Governance mechanisms are substantially based on how persons act within the governance structures formalized by the owners. So the effectiveness of these tools in reducing distance from the founder depends on sharing across generations those entrepreneurial values that positively influence EO over time and determine family business culture (Hall et al., 2001; Schein, 1995; Zahra et al., 2008). The implementation of specific family and business governance structures can balance, on one side, the presence of family members actively involved in the business (which reduces distance from the founder since they face similar issues in implementing business strategies year after year and absorb entrepreneurial values from older family members) and, on the other side, the presence of non-active family members (which, in contrast, can reduce sharing entrepreneurial values among shareholders and emphasize distance from the founder).

As the Group grows through internal and external expansion, its activities expand, new companies are started up or acquired, new divisions are created and non-family members are employed as managers at top levels. Sharing those entrepreneurial values that are a core competence of the Group and positively influence EO becomes difficult and the risk of deviation from the successful strategy set up by the founder arises.

In all industries (in particular, the agriculture and food industries in which Veronesi operates) it is important to share entrepreneurial values with a multitude of external stakeholders, such as workers' families, suppliers and clients. Sustaining competitive advantage is related to gaining and maintaining the community's approval.

If family governance is a way to share values within the organization, culture represents an adequate vehicle for conveying the firm's essence to the general public. In successful multigenerational family firms entrepreneurial values are strongly related to the founder. In this case, they also have a relevant and positive impact on the business because they are consistent with the desires of clients in the food industry (both end and chain customers) to maintain health and safety. Some of the founder's and his successor's recurrent slogans are:

'It is not the firm who creates job opportunities, it is the firm's clients who do. Hence, clients are our employers.'
'I would like to hear my employees saying that they are proud to work in our firm since here we work well.'
'You farmers are helping me and I have to respect your ideas.'
'I am proud since I am conscious that we are accomplishing our social duty.'
'Whoever thinks he can be satisfied with the minimum, does not increase his property and wears out the few things he has.'
'You don't have to say you are a gentlemen, you have to act like one.'
'Millers were often accused of cheating: this was simply unacceptable in my family.'

These values directly impact how family members relate to each other, other workers, non-family managers, clients and suppliers, thereby contributing to the culture of the firm. But how are these values shared among all family members, including those not involved in the business? How are they transmitted to other stakeholders inside and outside the firm? How are they transferred from one generation to the next? This case shows that different mechanisms can be used that act in various ways. In particular, a combination of symbols and rituals is useful towards building up a clear view of the firm in the minds of the people in touch with the Group (Table 3.4).

The founder's house is in front of the main factory, so that the address of the firm since 1958 coincides with that of the founder. This signifies a deep-rooted attachment to his native region and devotion to his origins. The address itself works as an effective brand inside the firm's factories; it conveys the proximity between the producer and his products and high standards in the quality of products. One can forget the huge amount of total annual revenues and perceive that the house is the same as the firm and the firm as the house. The founder loves to claim that: 'On Sunday, very early in the morning, when the mills of the factory switch off, I immediately wake up and I can no longer sleep.' The big garden surrounding the factory improves the quality of the workplace and, at the same time, recalls the victorious fight against the scrub and marshland on which the first factory was built.

Several historical objects located near the entrance remind visitors how it all began: the grindstones of the old watermill are followed by the monument to the first hammermill, and the modern firm's production systems,

Table 3.4   *The role of symbols and rituals in sharing entrepreneurial values outside the organization and among family members across generations: selected evidence*

Link to the Past	Rituals and Symbols	Impulse for the Future
'My house represents the heart and the heart can't be sold or left.' The address is the same since foundation in 1958 and coincides with the address of the first factory and of the corporate offices.	The founder's house and address	The old white house, just retouched, and the red field of 'bocce' live together with modern, international, bigger, modernized and technologically advanced plants made of glass and steel.
Represents nature and it is always in order, so as to symbolize victory over the *locus horridus* from where the founder started.	The big garden	According to the modern international concept of the working location, it stands as a *locus amoenus*.
'They are near the entrance in order to recall to everyone how it all began.'	The historical objects	'These objects don't leave space for regrets, since they are visually linked to the modern firm's production system.'
'The first one represents where the Group started and is near the millstones'.	The flags	'the other two tell where the Group operates, that is, Europe, and where it is going, that is, the whole world'.
It has never changed since 1958 and testifies loyalty to the past.	The logo	All other brands created through the narrow diversification are somehow correlated to the original logo of livestock feed, which never changed.
It is not only the same as that of the family (Veronesi) but also of the inhabitants of the founder's native region (Veronesi), who perceive food as personally controlled and at the same time guaranteed by the whole city.	The name of the Group	Has not changed in spite of the recent acquisition of international established brands in pork, beef, and restaurant businesses. The future expansion benefits from being associated with the original brand of the Group, which has a strong reputation in agriculture.

Table 3.4   (continued)

Link to the Past	Rituals and Symbols	Impulse for the Future
Each of the five divisions that form Veronesi Group has its annual meeting. During the meeting all managers and senior employees meet all the top managers and family owners.	The annual meetings	'I do not care so much about the results of the last year and whether we cut a fine figure. You employees are our richness: I care about how you feel and I am touched at seeing your commitment to the Group.'
Every meeting is closed by the leader (for the last two decades by the founder and, since 2004, by his son) who starts speaking always at the same hour. Instead of discussing the results gained during the year, the leader ends every annual meeting by highlighting the core values of the Group and using specific, recurrent expressions and ritual examples related to the origin of the entrepreneurial activities.	The official speeches	'Employees, tell everyone how we work here. Tell everyone that every day we try to work better for the future. Be proud to achieve leadership in a new market.'
'It can appear odd that we do not have intermediate celebrations. But this is why this gold pin is so important: it represents 25 and 30 years of loyalty. Be proud of your past: nowadays it is part of the story of the Group and the base for the future.'	Employee loyalty award	'If we talk about technology or products it is fundamental to drive fast and to be the first to introduce an innovation. If we talk about persons it is fundamental to drive well. This means respect, direct and personal relationships, actions and not celebrations. In building our future we must always remember that this is a Group of persons.'
'The first time, the Group introduces you, a new employee to your business partners'.	The first working day	'but from the second time on it will be you who represents the firm in the world'.

which are 'state-of-the-art'; photos of the track equipped with the wood-wheel from World War I precede those of the three helicopters today utilized to move among the various factories (archetype of the expansion of the Group's activities).

The founder's house, the garden and the historical objects favor the sharing among internal and external stakeholders of some entrepreneurial values which reduce distance from the founder and enhance EO dimensions: daily commitment to work; intellectual and behavioral honesty; the memory and ideal sharing of the efforts and victorious battles of the past; and solidarity with the needs of ordinary people.

The flags in front of the administrative offices are three emblems that have become commonplace, yet still express the original intent. The flag representing the Group and the millstones are on one side (that is, Veronesi in his small native region, in the family), and on the other side are the flag of Italy with a flag representing Europe (indicating the Group in Europe and in the world). Thus is represented both the starting point and at the same time the beginning of the impulse to supersede national boundaries, to discover and create knowledge, to establish companies all over the world.

Even the logo of the first business (livestock feed), although changeable by definition, has not changed since 1958, thanks to a simple and linear image coherent with the more recent trend, but also reflecting loyalty to the past.

The name of the firm (Veronesi Group) is the same as that of the family (Veronesi), the inhabitants of the founder's native area (Veronesi) and the main city of the region where the first farm was settled (Verona). This identification between the family and the territory triggers the perception that products are created and certified not only by one family, but by the whole city, which has a long tradition in agriculture. Over time the Group built additional factories in the same region (Veneto) in order to leverage on this positive connection.

The flags, logo and name of the firm (and a product) favor the sharing among various stakeholders of other entrepreneurial values positively affecting EO. These are the sense of belonging to something important; commitment and devotion to the Group and its activities; decorous behavior in line with the Group's image; a sense of protection implied from working for a successful firm guided by an entrepreneurial family with a blameless past; altruism and identification of personal good with the Group's good, which represents the good of all and not only that of the owners; the stimulus not to rest on (or defend) past laurels, but to meet future challenges by following the guidelines that have inspired, and must continue to inspire, the Group's strategies.

The annual meetings are the official occasion for all managers and senior employees to meet top management and ownership. There are many rituals and symbols, replicated in each of the Group's companies at the end of each year. For instance, the official speeches during every meeting have always, from 1985 to 2005, been concluded by the founder and from 2006 onwards by his son. Each year the speech begins at the same hour, in precise accordance with ritual. Nobody speaks afterwards, in order to let the leader have, literally, the last word. The language is spontaneous and the tone amiable; clearly recognizable behind it all is an established ritual. Although the speech is composed partly of new elements chosen with relation to the public and to some specific situation that occurred during the year, it is composed mostly of ancient, familiar, recurrent, fixed themes and anecdotes recalling the historical key elements and core values of the Group. These speeches never touch on the Group's performance during the past year, but are centered on the deep convictions and behaviors behind all the decisions taken by the ownership and top managers, citing in particular the fundamental role of customers, suppliers and employees in creating new value each year.

During the meeting senior employees with long careers (25 or 30 years) are awarded for their loyalty. The award consists of a gold pin. This pin is a reproduction of the logo of the firm and symbolizes the importance ownership attributes to work in the life of a person, recognizing an employee's loyalty to the history of the Group, which, from that moment on, is now also his history.

Each employee on his first working day in the Group is taken throughout the firm and shown a video describing and reflecting the Group's values. Informal communication represents a ritual within the organization. The office, based on 'open space' typology, becomes a 'community of practices', nourished by the presence of the founder, a constant since the firm's foundation: 'Sunday is the worst day of the week and I am sad, since I can't go to the office and talk to managers and employees.'

The format of the annual meetings and the public speeches, the award created for work loyalty, and the ritual of the first working day are functional to spreading among as many stakeholders as possible the firm's basic ideas and values with a view to sustaining the successful first generation period: the pride in doing good every day through one's work without fear of criticism; attention to people and their individual and personal needs; respect for the ideas of all collaborators; the importance of maintaining a certain standard in relations and of honoring commitments undertaken with clients and suppliers; clarity in expressing and communicating mutual expectations among owners, managers and employees; the importance and centrality of the needs of customers, who represent 'the real employer'. The assimilation of shared values shaping behaviors (of employees, managers and young family members) is given priority as compared to business-related competencies. The transfer of this kind of tacit knowledge into individual competencies that determine relations with colleagues and other stakeholders is acquired by a long-term and valuable network with the firm. This gives internal rather than external managers an advantage: a deep knowledge of firm procedures and culture more important than years spent obtaining strong business-related capabilities working in other firms within the industry. All important positions (including CEO) within the organization are occupied by managers who have spent most of their careers in the Group.

For the founder, this was a factor from the beginning; in fact, he had no choice since the limited financial resources available to him in 1958 meant establishing his factory in an undesirable location. Since then, the founder and the second generation have turned necessity into a virtue, no longer part of an emergency strategy but a deliberate one. This habit of linking the past and the future does not stop with the departure of the founder and continues over time. From the 1960s to the end of the 1990s the founder was the 'face' of the company. During the gradual transition from the first to the second generation only one member of the second generation was appointed to maintain this role. Since all three sons of the founder are close in age and have strong industry-related knowledge and skills, the choice was based on personal characteristics. Giordano (not the oldest or the first to enter the business) was chosen to speak at the annual meeting with managers and employees and, in general, to represent the firm at public events. This aspect is important and impacts performance, since continuity (of the reputation of the firm) is key to success, especially in the food industry. It is essential to indicate and render evident ownership values to external networks, it being better to have only one charismatic member of the family talking with stakeholders for each generation, in order to express firm identity.

This intangible aspect has prevailed also with regard to formal procedures. In fact, the role of president is supposed to pass every five years from one brother to another, but has stayed with Giordano. This helps reduce distance from the founder and creates a 'continuity of founder's values' in the collective imagination, linking tradition across generations.

3.6 CONCLUSIONS AND IMPLICATIONS

Our study provides evidence of how family controlled firms may avoid the trap of the inertial forces deriving from the same resources and capabilities that have determined their success over time. Family firms that have always been successful, mainly thanks to the key roles played by charismatic founders, risk becoming enmeshed in the inertial forces deriving from their own traditions, as both the literature on family business failures and empirical works in the population ecology tradition suggest. Our data reveal that an effective way to escape this pathology is to reduce distance from the founder by replicating its image in the eyes of various internal and external stakeholders (family members, managers, employees, suppliers and customers) through cultural and symbolic actions. Veronesi shows how family controlled firms can enact different balancing acts that prevent inertial forces that may result from performing identical activities and enforcing identical values repeatedly, while at the same time maintaining the value of distinctive resources and competencies stemming from successful tradition. In this regard, distinctive familiness (Habbershon et al., 2003) plays the role of the valuable, inimitable and non-substitutable resources that may allow a family firm to sustain entrepreneurial success over time, as suggested by RBV contributions.

These results have practical implications. Entrepreneurial orientation, and the resulting increased chances of survival and growth, is enhanced by the controlling family's ability to strike a continuous balance between tradition and innovation. This involves acting on three complementary dimensions. First, symbolic action should be performed with the aim of perpetuating the founder's image and creative energy over time, while also balancing the dimensions of the founder's culture that gradually become outdated. Second, family governance mechanisms should be in place with the aim of balancing the increasing number of family members and generations active in the firm, and the tendency toward strategic drift deriving from the presence of multiple, often conflicting, voices. Third, leadership should be exerted with the aim of balancing the need to keep the traditional business activities that have, over time, generated the core resources and competencies driving success, and the addition of new economic activities requiring different resources and competencies.

Our study illustrates several different avenues through which these balancing acts can be performed in a traditional multigeneration family firm active in a single, traditional business. Future research may address the same questions in different industrial and cultural settings. It would be interesting, for instance, to understand the role played by tradition in high-tech family firms, which typically have fewer generations, and which often require quicker adaptation of resources and competencies to their fast-paced environments. In these more dynamic settings tradition may play a different, more problematic role, as preserving old values and ideas may lead to failure more frequently than in traditional settings. Here balancing may result in an exceedingly conservative strategy, while pushing toward continuous innovation. Hence constantly disrupting previous resources and competences may be a more viable approach to preserving the family firm's entrepreneurial potential.

NOTES

1. Ugo Lassini developed the sections on guiding theory, method and empirical testing, analysis and discussion.
2. Carlo Salvato developed the introduction section, conclusions and implications.
3. 'Familiness' is the unique bundle of resources a particular firm has because of the interaction of the family, its individual family members and the business with one another (Habbershon and Pistrui, 2002; Habbershon and Williams, 1999; Habbershon et al., 2003).
4. 'I noticed my father often putting some meal in the bags for poor families. I asked for an explanation, and he told me they were in difficulty. But this happened daily, so I decided that since that moment we would give them everything they needed, but we would also mark down what we were giving to them. In my view it was not right just to consider them as beggars. So I built by myself a table provided with a drawer which could be closed where accounting records could be kept. We did not allow them to make fools of us, we would stop leaving the drawer open, the key was needed, we would be fair.'
5. 'I was conscious that it was not postponed in the interest of progress, but it was going to damage one of my family since it would move the course of farmers. The economic loss we would face oppressed me: so I somehow assumed the role of protector of our small land. The family was big, but I held the reins of it, unfortunately: it was a stressing responsibility, but I had to assume this and so I played the protector rule. I took the country folk on my truck and we came to Verona city in order to plead our case.'
6. 'In 1945 I was confident of my capacity to maintain in the future the whole family sales commercial products. But one Sunday at 10.00 a.m. my brothers called me in order to tell me that they preferred to be independent from me. This traumatic event happened when I had the concrete possibility of starting and expanding lots of activities useful for my nephews, who were more or less my age. One sad and famous Sunday they made my brothers tell me that I had to follow my own way instead of working within the family business. They said that I loved livestock feed but the nephews were not very happy about this. They felt ashamed for me and they did not understand as at that time livestock feed was despised, considered equal to fertilizer! Before getting people used to an innovation, lots of time must pass. With immense sadness I left the family with 10 percent of the value of the family business (I am the ninth of ten sons) and I began the construction of the barn and of my new house.'
7. So defined, and in this context distance from the founder is negatively correlated to EO since we are not considering those situations characterized by a founder who is passing the 'baton of leadership' of a firm not exhibiting good performance.

REFERENCES

Amit, R. and P.H. Schoemaker (1993), 'Strategic assets and organizational rent', *Strategic Management Journal*, **14**, 33–46.

Anderson, R.C. and D.M. Reeb (2003), 'Founding family ownership and firm performance: evidence from the S&P 500', *Journal of Finance*, **58**(3), 1301–28.

Barney, J. (1986), 'Strategic factor markets: expectations, luck, and business strategy', *Management Science*, **32**(10), 1231–41.

Barney, J. (1991), 'Firm resources and sustained competitive advantage', *Journal of Management*, **17**(1), 99–120.

Baum, J. (1997), *Organizational Ecology, Handbook of Organizational Studies*, Chicago, IL: Rand McNally.

Bruderl, J. and R. Schussler (1990), 'Organizational mortality: the liabilities of newness and adolescence', *Administrative Science Quarterly*, **35**, 530–47.

Cabrera-Suàrez, K., P. De Saà-Pérez and D. Garcìa-Almeida (2001), 'The succession process from a resource and knowledge-based view of the family firm', *Family Business Review*, **14**(1), 37–48.

Carney, M. (2005), 'Corporate governance and competitive advantage in family-controlled firms', *Entrepreneurship Theory and Practice*, **29**(3), 249–65.

Carroll, G. (1985), 'Concentration and specialization: dynamics of niche width in populations of organizations', *American Journal of Sociology*, **90**, 1262–83.

Colli, A. (2003), *The History of Family Business, 1850–2000*, Cambridge: Cambridge University Press.

Collins, J.C. and J.I. Porras (1994), *Built to Last*, New York: HarperCollins.

Dierickx, I. and K. Cool (1989), 'Asset stock accumulation and sustainability of competitive advantage', *Management Science*, **35** (12), 1504–11.

Gersick, K.E., J.A. Davis, I. Lansberg and M. McCollom Hampton (1997), *Generation to Generation. Life Cycles of the Family Business*, Cambridge, MA: Harvard University Press.

Grant, R. (1991), 'The resource-based theory of competitive advantage: implications for strategy formulation', *California Management Review*, Special Issue, **33**(3), 114–35.

Habbershon, T.G. and J. Pistrui (2002), 'Enterprising families domain: family-influenced ownership groups in pursuit of transgenerational wealth', *Family Business Review*, **15**(3), 223–37.

Habbershon, T.G. and M.L. Williams (1999), 'A resource-based framework for assessing the strategic advantages of family firms', *Family Business Review*, **12**(1), 1–25.

Habbershon, T.G., M.L. Williams and I.C. MacMillan (2003), 'A unified systems perspective of family firm performance', *Journal of Business Venturing*, **18**(4), 451–65.

Hall, A., L. Melin and M. Nordqvist (2001), 'Entrepreneurship as radical change in family business: exploring the role of cultural patterns', *Family Business Review*, **14**(3), 193–208.

Hannan, M. and J. Freeman (1989), *Organizational Ecology*, Cambridge, MA: Harvard University Press.

Harris, D., J.I. Martinez and J.L. Ward (1994), 'Is strategy different for the family-owned business?', *Family Business Review*, **7**(2), 159–74.

Ibrahim, A.B. (1998), 'Causes of failure in small family firms and strategies to reduce it', *Proceedings of the International Family Enterprise Conference*, Research paper.

Ibrahim, A.B., C. Dumas and J. McGuire (2001), 'Strategic decision making in small family firms: an empirical investigation', *Journal of Small Business Strategy*, **12**(1), 1–11.

Kets de Vries, M.F.R., R.S. Carlock and E. Florent-Treacy (2007), *Family Business on the Couch. A Psychological Perspective*, Chichester: John Wiley and Sons.

Klein, S.B. (2000), 'Family businesses in Germany: significance and structure', *Family Business Review*, **13**, 157–81.

Leonard-Barton, D. (1992), 'Core capabilities and core capabilities: a paradox in managing new product development', *Strategic Management Journal*, **13**, 111–25.

Levinthal, D.A. (1997), 'Adaptation on rugged landscapes', *Management Science*, **43**(7), 934–50.

Ling, Y., Z. Simsek, M.H. Lubatkin and J.F. Veiga (2008), 'Transformational leadership's role in promoting corporate entrepreneurship: examining the CEO-TMT interface', *Academy of Management Journal*, **51**(3), 557–76.

Littunen, H. and K. Hyrsky (2000), 'The early entrepreneurial stage in Finnish family and nonfamily firms', *Family Business Review*, **13**(1), 41–53.

Litz, R.A. (1995), 'The family business: toward definitional clarity', *Family Business Review*, **8**(2), 71–81.

Lumpkin, G.T. and G.G. Dess (1996), 'Clarifying the entrepreneurial orientation construct and linking it to performance', *Academy of Management Review*, **21**(1), 135–72.

Lumpkin, G.T. and G.G. Dess (2001), 'Linking two dimensions of entrepreneurial orientation to firm performance: the moderating role of environment and industry life cycle', *Journal of Business Venturing*, **16**, 429–51.

Lumpkin, G.T., C.C. Cogliser and D.R. Schneider (2009), 'Understanding and measuring autonomy: an entrepreneurial orientation perspective', *Entrepreneurship Theory and Practice*, **33**(1), 47–69.

Miller, D. and I. Le Breton-Miller (2004), *Managing for the Long Run: Lessons in Competitive Advantage from Great Family Businesses*, Boston, MA: Harvard Business School Press.

Naldi, L., M. Nordqvist, K. Sjöberg and J. Wiklund (2007), 'Entrepreneurial orientation, risk taking, and performance in family firms', *Family Business Review*, **20**(1), 33–47.

Nelson, R. and S. Winter (1982), *An Evolution Theory of Economic Change*, Cambridge, MA: Belknap Press of Harvard University Press.

Nicholson, N. (2008), 'Evolutionary psychology and family business: a new synthesis for theory, research, and practice', *Family Business Review*, **21**(1), 103–18.

Poutziouris, P., K. Smyrnios and S. Klein (2008), *Handbook of Research on Family Business*, Cheltenham, UK: Edward Elgar Publishing.

Prahalad, C. and G. Hamel (1990), 'The core competence of the corporation', *Harvard Business Review*, **90**, 79–81.

Rank, O. (1909), *The Myth of the Birth of the Hero*, Germany, Italian edition SugarCo, 1973.

Rauch, A., J. Wiklund, G.T. Lumpkin and M. Frese (2009), 'Entrepreneurial orientation and business performance: an assessment of past research and suggestions for the future', *Entrepreneurship Theory and Practice*, **33**(3), 761–87.

Rumelt, R. (1995), 'Inertia and transformation', in A.C. Montgomery (ed.), *Resource-based and Evolutionary Theories of the Firm*, Norwell, MA: Kluwer Academic Publishers, pp. 101–32.

Schein, E.H. (1995), 'The role of the founder in creating organizational culture', *Family Business Review*, **8**(3), 221–38.

Schein, E.H. (2004), *Organizational Culture and Leadership*, New York: John Wiley & Sons.

Sharma, P. and P.G. Irving (2005), 'Four bases of family business successor commitment: Antecedents and consequences', *Entrepreneurship Theory and Practice*, **29**(1), 13–33.

Singh, J., D. Tucker and R. House (1986), 'Organizational change and organizational mortality', *Administrative Science Quarterly*, **31**, 439–66.

Sirmon, D.G. and M.A. Hitt (2003), 'Managing resources: linking unique resources, management, and wealth creation in family firms', *Entrepreneurship Theory and Practice*, **27**(4), 339–58.

Stein, N. (2001), 'The age of the scion', *Fortune*, **143**(7), 120–8.

Stinchcombe, A. (1965), 'Social structure and organizations' in J. March (ed.), *Handbook of Organizations*, Chicago, IL: Rand McNally, pp. 142–93.

Waldman, D.A., G.G. Ramirez, R.J. House and P. Puranam (2001), 'Does leadership matter? CEO leadership attributes and profitability under conditions of perceived environmental uncertainty', *Academy of Management Journal*, **44**, 134–43.

Wernerfelt, B. (1984), 'A resource-based view of the firm', *Strategic Management Journal*, **5**(2), 171–80.

Zahra, S.A., J.C. Hayton, D.O. Neubaum, C. Dibrell and J. Craig (2008), 'Culture of family commitment and strategic flexibility: the moderating effect of stewardship', *Entrepreneurship Theory and Practice*, **32**(6), 1035–54.

APPENDIX VERONESI FAMILY GENOGRAM

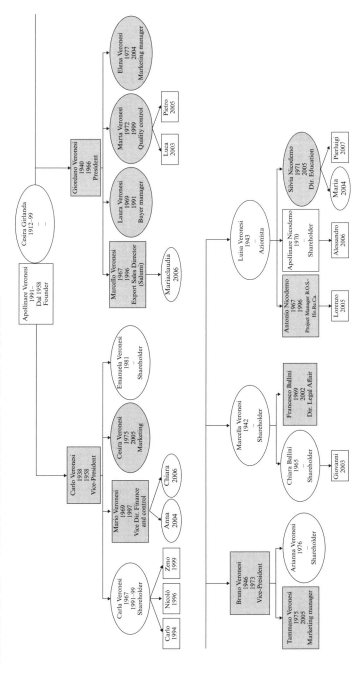

Note: A shaded box (circular for female and rectangular for male) indicates a family member actively involved in the business. Each box contains: name (first line), date of birth and death (second line), date of entry in the company (third line) and current role (fourth line).

4. Portfolio entrepreneurship in the context of family owned businesses

Markus Plate, Christian Schiede and Arist von Schlippe

4.1 INTRODUCTION

In 1986 MacMillan posed the challenge: 'To really learn about entrepreneurship, let's study habitual entrepreneurs.' Habitual entrepreneurs – unlike 'one-shot' or novice entrepreneurs who have entrepreneurial experience in a single business or have just started a business – have multiple entrepreneurial experiences and can be distinguished as either 'serial' or 'portfolio' entrepreneurs. Serial entrepreneurs build and then sell companies, thus usually owning only one company at a time, while portfolio entrepreneurs build or acquire numerous ventures and keep them for a longer period of time.

With this challenge, MacMillan (1986) focused attention on the activities of the entrepreneur, and thus on a new unit of analysis. Scott and Rosa (1996) underlined this new focus by pointing out that firm-level analysis might lead to underestimating the prevalence of portfolio entrepreneurship. More recent studies show that the activities of portfolio entrepreneurs have a significant impact on new venture creation and, thus, on national economics; estimates are that between 12 and 20 percent of newly founded ventures are owned by portfolio entrepreneurs (Carter and Ram, 2003)

Research on portfolio entrepreneurship, which is rooted in the context of small and medium-sized firms, often focuses on the habitual entrepreneur and on differences between habitual and novice entrepreneurs. Although the context of family business is acknowledged, current research does not specifically focus on the influence of a family on its firm. In addition, its focus on a certain size of firm (small or medium), certain industries (for example, farming) or culture (venturing activities of ethnic minorities) limits its scope. In general, process or organizational analyses are scarce.

A second stream of literature is concerned with portfolios of ventures, namely, corporate diversification. Often the medium and large firm or business group (both modern corporate organizations or publicly owned) is the unit of analysis that is examined from the view of strategic management or corporate finance, which deals with the antecedents and consequences of diversification processes.

While MacMillan (1986) focused on the habitual entrepreneur, Gartner (1989) argues that using traits to identify the characteristics of entrepreneurs in contrast to non-entrepreneurs (or habitual versus novice entrepreneurs) is misleading. He defines entrepreneurship as 'the creation of organizations, the process by which new organizations come into existence' (Gartner, 1989, p. 57). Sarasvathy (2004, p. 522) conceptualizes these entrepreneurial activities as firm design. Taking this into account, building up a portfolio of ventures also means building up an organization, or a portfolio of organizations.

To analyse an organization, the resource-based view (RBV) provides a convenient framework, where a firm's resources and capabilities (and the associated strategy and environment) compose and distinguish companies from each other. In portfolio entrepreneurship research this framework is seldomly applied (if at all). Although the RBV of the firm provides acknowledged analytical tools in the field of corporate diversification, it is often applied from a theoretical standpoint to explain the existence and direction of diversification processes. Although empirical studies exist, they do not consider the entrepreneur as a driving force of diversification. The concept of family business is more or less underrepresented in this field of research, as are analyses that deal with process or organizational variables.

In the still young field of research on family firms the notion of portfolio entrepreneurship has not yet been explored. Business portfolios might serve quite different functions for business families, as they arise from certain resources and capabilities provided by (and tied to) entrepreneurs, who might then create special organizations. We thus present a case-based analysis of portfolio entrepreneurship under the frame of organizational design. By applying the RBV, we analyse organizational aspects such as structure or communication of a portfolio entrepreneurship endeavor in the context of family business. Thus we identify the resources and capabilities influenced by the entrepreneurs' family ('familiness'; Habbershon and Williams, 1999) that enable the company's growth and entrepreneurial behavior. Our guiding questions are:

1. Which resources and capabilities tied to the entrepreneur/business family enable the development of successful portfolio entrepreneurship practices?
2. Which resources, capabilities and structure characterize the emerging organization?

We contribute to the literature in three ways. First, our in-depth case analysis focuses on processes and conditions for portfolio entrepreneurship in the context of family business. Second, by applying the RBV, we take a seldom applied theoretical stance in this field of research. Because we focus on special resources and capabilities tied to the business family (familiness), we also contribute to family business research. Third, we highlight aspects of the emerging business and business group, especially of organization and structure.

The chapter is structured as follows. First, we introduce research on the RBV, portfolio entrepreneurship and corporate diversification. Then, we describe the building of a portfolio of ventures of a German family owned business (ALT) and offer a thematic analysis focusing on the unique resources of the entrepreneur and the business group. Finally, we discuss our findings in the light of implications for entrepreneurs from business families.

4.2   THEORETICAL BACKGROUND

In this section we introduce the RBV of the firm and familiness as the specific resource bundle influenced by a business family. Second, we summarize important findings from research on portfolio entrepreneurship and corporate diversification.

The Resource-based View of the Firm

Sources of sustained competitive advantage have long been a major research interest of strategic management (for example, Porter, 1985), which often focuses on the link between a firm's strategy and its competitive environment (industry economics). As a basic assumption, the strategically relevant resources of the firms are assumed to be identical or (if heterogeneous at one time) highly mobile, which eventually leads to the elimination of this heterogeneity.

In contrast, the RBV assumes that firms are, in fact, heterogeneous. This heterogeneity, which could exist over time, is characterized by a different portfolio of firm resources and capabilities and encompasses 'all assets, capabilities, organizational processes, firm attributes, information, knowledge,and so on., controlled by a firm' (Barney, 1991, p.101). Amit and Schoemaker (1993) further distinguish between a company's resources and its capabilities. While resources are regarded as factors (owned or controlled by a firm) that are 'converted into final products and services' (Amit and Schoemaker, 1993, p.35), capabilities 'refer to a firm's capacity to deploy *Resources*' (Amit and Schoemaker, 1993, p. 35, emphasis in original). In this view, capabilities are viewed more as part of the 'organizational structures and managerial processes which support productive activity' (Teece et al., 1997, p. 517).

These resources and capabilities enable the firm to manufacture products or provide services. If the firm acts more efficiently than its competitors as a result, then it gains a competitive advantage. For sustained competitive advantage, these resources and capabilities need to be (1) valuable (that is, exploit opportunities or neutralize threats), (2) rare among current or potential competitors, and (3) imperfectly imitable or substitutable. In this case, heterogeneity and competitive advantage could persist over time.

Unlike resources, capabilities cannot be purchased, as they arise through the dynamic interaction between resources. Hence, if a company declares bankruptcy, the resources of that firm (for example, real estate, machines, patents, employees) could be sold or bought separately, but the capabilities would simply vanish because the interaction that created them would also cease to exist.

Collins (1994) broadly distinguishes three types of capabilities: (1) static, (2) dynamic and (3) creative. Static capabilities refer to the ability to perform basic activities such as producing a product, providing a service or marketing. Dynamic capabilities refer to adapting to changing environments, learning and renewal, while creative capabilities refer to more entrepreneurial or strategic functions. In our analysis we use 'entrepreneurial capabilities' to underline their function.

In particular, factors such as organizational routines, research and development, communication, decision making, culture and strategic management could be regarded as capabilities. Management then faces a special challenge: to choose, build, renew, structure, bundle and leverage crucial resources and capabilities (Makadok, 2001; Sirmon et al., 2007). Hence the management of resources and capabilities could be regarded as an entrepreneurial capability (Mahoney, 1995).

Part of this process is the entrepreneurial activities of innovation. Creating new ventures within or outside the organization leads to an increase of diversification within both the product and the business portfolio. Thus entrepreneurship could be regarded as 'the process by which new organizations are created' (Gartner, 1989, p. 62). In addition to the process, the resulting organization is also of interest. Sarasvathy (2004, p. 523; emphasis in original) underlines 'the notion of entrepreneurship as *firm design*'. From this angle, the resources and capabilities used to build a portfolio of ventures might be different from those of the emerging organization.

According to the RBV, resources and capabilities tied to the family have a good potential to provide sustained competitive advantage due to the uniqueness of each entrepreneur/business family and their socially complex, path-dependent development. These resources and capabilities might be harder to imitate and substitute and, thus, be rare among competitors. Habbershon and Williams (1999) use familiness to describe the specific bundle of resources of a particular firm that is tied to the systemic interaction of individual, family and business.

Portfolio Entrepreneurship

In addition to the vast amount of research on corporate entrepreneurship, a small stream of literature is devoted to portfolio entrepreneurship,which shows a bias toward the small and medium-sized enterprise (SME) sector (Carter and Ram, 2003). It is clear that the classic explanations for company growth (for example, life cycle models) are insufficient to explain the development of small firms, many of which have little chance for modest growth, with only a minority developing into large firms or business groups. Research suggests that small business owners achieve growth in a number of ways (for example, building a portfolio of ventures), but as long as the firm was the unit of analysis this was more or less overlooked. Scott and Rosa (1996) then proposed to focus on the entrepreneur as a unit of analysis.

Regarding portfolio entrepreneurship, results show a great deal of variance. Westhead and Wright (1998) analysed a sample of 621 newly founded British ventures from a broad range of industries and found that 12 percent were owned by portfolio entrepreneurs. Rosa and Scott (1999), analysing three samples of Scottish and English firms, estimated that 20 percent of all business founders and up to 80 percent of the founders of limited companies have ownership and control of at least two firms.

MacMillan's (1986) habitual entrepreneurs own or found multiple ventures. Studies have mostly dealt with the differences between habitual and novice entrepreneurs with regard to sources of finance, personal background, work experiences or personal attitudes toward entrepreneurship (Westhead and Wright, 1998; Westhead et al., 2005).

In general, Carter and Ram (2003, p. 373) conclude that 'Although little is yet understood about the underlying motivations and processes, it is likely that portfolio ownership takes different forms and performs different functions for entrepreneurs in different circumstances and contexts.' A resource-based analysis of a portfolio-building process and the resource base of the emerging organization remains to be undertaken.

Corporate Diversification

The second stream of literature dealing with the establishment of business groups focuses on corporate diversification. For a comprehensive overview of the current literature on diversification, which is outside the scope of this chapter, see Hoskisson and Hitt (1990), Montgomery (1994) or Ramanujam and Varadarajan (1989). We report only main findings here.

Research on diversification has a strong focus on the firm as the unit of analysis and is mostly concerned with large, often publicly held, corporations. Dominant theories that explain diversification are rooted in the market power view, agency view and resource view (Montgomery, 1994). While the market power view relates more to the consequences of diversification (its anti-competitive effects due to conglomerate power; Montgomery, 1994), the agency and resource views relate more to process and conditions of diversification.

In the RBV an 'excess capacity in productive factors' (Montgomery, 1994, p. 167) might be a motive for diversification, provided that they cannot be sold more efficiently in the market. Diversifying into related sectors allows for a transfer of crucial firm-specific resources. Because more widely diversified firms need different resources for these different markets, the possibility of synergistic effects is diminished. In general, this view is seldomly applied in this field of research (Montgomery, 1994). Unrelated diversification often occurs when the company seeks vertical economies or economies in the securing and allocation of financial resources (that is, the exploitation of capital market imperfections).

Ramanujam and Varadarajan (1989) report three main causes of diversification: (1) profit maximization (for example, monopoly power, exploitation of opportunities due to synergies, reduction of risk), (2) managerial growth-maximizing behavior or (3) financial issues, which occur as the result of capital market imperfections. In perfect capital markets investors do not realize benefits from investing in diversified firms, since they could diversify their portfolio themselves more efficiently. As long as transaction costs are higher in the capital market than in the organization, diversification appears to be a viable strategy. High transaction costs might also influence the internal development of competencies usually supplied externally or from buying these competencies (Hoskisson and Hitt, 1990). In addition, new ventures might be established due to declining or maturing markets, which leads to diversification in growth sectors (Montgomery, 1994).

In the context of the modern corporation, agency problems may arise if the diversification process is driven by managerial motives which differ from the owners' motives. Managers' motives are likely influenced by a

Table 4.1   Overview of ALT interviewees

	Kenneth Alt (KA)	Nicholas Alt (NA)	Dr Malcolm Alt (MA)	Dr Hans Smith (HS)	Robert Lorenz (RL)	Mrs Block
Family	X	X	X			
Management	X			X (CEO)	X (CFO)	
Owner	X	X	X			
'Founder'		X				
Supervisory Board		X	X			
CEO	X			X		
Employee						X

reduction of employment risks and an increase of financial compensation, a result of working for a large company (Amihud and Lev, 1981; Hoskisson and Hitt, 1990).

Most (if not all) studies in this field seem to imply that owners are not actively involved in the diversification process. So far, the entrepreneur from a family business has not been considered. Although studies applying a resource-based perspective exist (cf. Mahoney and Pandian, 1992), they lack an explicit in-depth analysis of the portfolio process using the focus of familiness.

4.3   METHODOLOGY

Our primary source of data are semi-structured interviews, while secondary data include web resources and company journals of the ALT group. We conducted seven interviews with six different persons (Table 4.1); two persons were interviewed a second time in a combined interview. Three of the interviewees are family members of the second or third generation; others are long-tenured managers or employees.

Interviews followed the STEP model; that is, semi-structured, with a focus on resources and capabilities (especially familiness) and entrepreneurship practices. New and interesting topics regarding entrepreneurship that arose that were not part of the interview guideline were explored in free interview form. Interviews averaged 114 minutes. Quotes are translated from German into English (we tried to keep as much of the 'tone' as possible). Quoted interviewees are identified by their initials.

All interviews were transcribed and analysed according to the qualitative

Table 4.2   Possible sources of competitive advantage and examples

Resources/Capabilities	Examples
Physical	Plants, raw materials, equipment
Financial	Cash reserves, access to financial markets
Human	Skills and knowledge of individuals
Technological	High quality production, state-of-the-art technological level
Social	Social network, goodwill due to reputation
Organizational/ Process	Organizational competencies, policies, culture, control, decision making, communication, leadership

content analysis approach (Mayring, 2000). In a second step a resource-based framework was applied to identify resources and capabilities tied to the family entrepreneur and the organization. Our primary guiding questions were: (1) 'Which resources and capabilities tied to the entrepreneur/ business family enable the development of successful portfolio entrepreneurship practices?' and (2) 'Which resources, capabilities, and structure characterize the emerging organization?' We focused on physical, financial, human, technological, social and organizational/process resources and capabilities (cf. Grant, 1991; Hunt, 1995), as described in Table 4.2.

To provide further context information, we analysed secondary sources such as websites and company journals of the ALT companies, a documentary describing the development of ALT, miscellaneous Internet articles about the development of environmental laws, politics and so on.

Information regarding entrepreneurial performance and company structure covers the period from 1959 to 2007. (Earlier data were not available; we do, however, briefly summarize ALT's development from 2000 to 2007.) The case analysis covers the period from the 1930s to 1999; in 1999 ALT's three main business fields (waste and secondary resources management, animal waste management and logistics) were established. We do, however, briefly summarize ALT's development from 2000 to 2007.

4.4   CASE ANALYSIS

We analyse the family business, ALT,[1] which is currently owned by two family generations. The father and former lead entrepreneur Nicholas Alt (second generation) owns a minority share, while the four children each own an equal share of roughly 25 percent. In the 1930s Jamie Alt (the first-generation entrepreneur) purchased a small haulage firm in Germany.

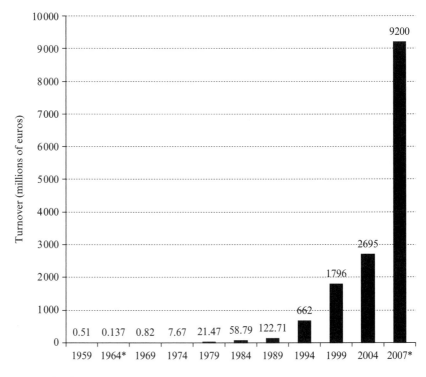

Notes: * Estimated data.

Figure 4.1   *Development of the turnover of the ALT AG from 1959 to 2007*

Nicholas Alt (his son) then initiated exponential growth through foundation and acquisition, whereby the company grew from a turnover of 0.51 million euros in 1959 to 9.2 billion euros in 2007 (Figure 4.1) and grew to more than 32 000 employees.

Presently, ALT is a holding company, with three legally and operationally independent business units (AHLEMANN, BERTRAM and CASSMEIER). All five family members are active in the supervisory board of ALT, while two are active in the executive boards of ALT and the businesses. A third son leads a business unit of AHLEMANN.

AHLEMANN and BERTRAM own several subsidiaries and affiliates, resulting in more than 600 independent worldwide businesses. According to the CFO, 'I think, and I don't exaggerate much, we acquired about 1,000 companies' (HS). AHLEMANN deals with the disposal and recycling of domestic waste, glass, wood, effluents, metal, waste water and so on. Additionally, it specializes in complicated forms of waste recycling (for example, oil residues from gas stations). The company operates subsidiaries in 15 European countries, in addition to China, Japan, Taiwan and Australia. In total, AHLEMANN is active in 24 countries on three continents. BERTRAM, which has 83 subsidiaries in eight countries, specializes in the disposal and reuse of butchery byproducts, fallen stock and food waste. Its production program comprises semi-finished products for animal food and alternative fuels such as biodiesel and biogas. CASSMEIER deals with contract logistics, port logistics, intermodal transport and public transport.

Research on corporate diversification does not take the entrepreneur into account as a driving force. In this field the main units of analysis are medium and large companies. While the entrepreneur is seen as a driving force in portfolio entrepreneurship research, this area mostly deals with minor or small companies. Although ALT is a large corporation, it is driven by entrepreneurs; thus it shares traits recognized or ignored by both streams of research, respectively.

In the next sections we describe the development of ALT from 1930 to 1999, when the actual business structure was finished. We highlight the structural development and the emerging portfolio of ventures, as well as the resources and capabilities tied to the family entrepreneur (familiness) in establishing this portfolio. In addition, we examine the resources and capabilities of the emerging organization.

The Early Years: 1930s to 1976

The business family, Alt, has lived in rural Germany since the early 1930s. Jamie Alt owned a small haulage firm operated with horses and carriages. He transported refuse for the city in which he lived. In the 1950s many cities in rural Germany introduced dust-free refuse collection; thus Jamie Alt bought a special truck to supply this service for his home town. Beginning in the late 1950s, the company began to expand. As most other rural communities faced the same problems and wanted to implement dust-free refuse collection, there were numerous opportunities in the market.

There are two different growth processes which can be described as 'mere growth' (that is, growth within a single organization unit) and 'business propagation' (Sparrer, 2006). Starting with one truck and one city, Jamie and his son, Nicholas, calculated and planned differently from their competitors, allowing them to provide their service more efficiently. This led to unused resources (the capacity of their truck), so they could offer their service to another city. A second truck was then purchased to meet the new demand, yet another city added as a contractor, and so on. The excess in capacity due to a different method of accounting and logistics in a market with high demand led to mere growth. Physical resources (such as trucks and location) were similar to their competitors, but the static capabilities of accounting and planning, tied to and provided by the family entrepreneurs, created a competitive advantage. Access to the necessary financial capital for the growth process was enabled by two resources/static capabilities: (1) the network and reputation of the family entrepreneurs (a social resource) and (2) their accounting methods (a static process capability).

Jamie Alt's good relationship with the director of the local bank was passed on to his son, who negotiated with the director. In those days the financial accounting system was neither very sophisticated (compared to today's standards) nor widespread among small-scale entrepreneurs, but Nicholas learned on his own how to provide a 'state-of-the-art' balance sheet and a sound growth strategy. By offering to report his financial results on a monthly basis rather than quarterly (as usual), he created trust (a social resource), and the bank provided the financial resources needed for expansion.

Nicholas's efforts had a second function. The results of his work enabled him to see on a monthly basis (1) if the organizational routines performed within set parameters on the operational level and (2) if the chosen strategy and its implementation were sound on a strategic level. Thus he could spot deviating parameters (cash flow, costs) quickly. These regular operational and strategic reviews could be regarded as dynamic capabilities that enabled the optimization of operational processes/routines and growth (on a strategic level). The optimization of organizational routines (that is, providing services for the city) led to optimized cash flow, which could be used internally to pay debts and build up equity. Externally, it underlined the trustworthiness of Nicholas Alt (that is, built up social resources) for the bank to consider funding further expansion. These operational and strategic reviews performed during this period of time shaped the ensuing organizational culture.

Nicholas used this contact with the CEO of the local bank to build up his own network (social resource). Due to this contact and reputation (social resource) and the transparency created by regular reviews (dynamic management capability), additional trucks (technological resource) were purchased.

The second growth process, business propagation (Sparrer, 2006), refers to the creation of new organizational units. In our case legally independent units (companies) were either purchased or founded in new areas of Germany.

This regional expansion was also enabled by Nicholas Alt's reputation (social resource). The officials of the cities where he provided his service recommended his work to officials of other cities. To finance expansion, Nicholas's relationship with the manager of the local bank was crucial, since the manager recommended that other banks provide financing to him (financial resource).

A crucial resource (also constraint) for entrepreneurs is their time (Iacobucci and Rosa, 2004): they cannot be everywhere in the organization and cannot deal with everything, although they are 'prone to care'. ALT, consisting of independently operating subsidiaries in different regions of Germany, required local leadership, as Nicholas Alt could not manage everyday operations in different locations. To deal with this problem, he installed certain cultural and decision guidelines for these subsidiaries, according to his motto: 'Assume responsibility, act entrepreneurially.' The local subsidiaries have high levels of entrepreneurial responsibility and freedom. Nicholas Alt emphasized: 'decentralize the company; the ones who are responsible locally make the decision . . . [it's important] that we don't create hierarchies'. To ensure that this entrepreneurial freedom does not lead to unwanted results, a clear framework defines managerial leeway: 'we set the "guardrails". The way they move within these guardrails is in their responsibility' (KA). This decentralization matches an orientation for employees to proactively assume responsibility, as seen by the absence of job descriptions: 'You won't find any job description in the whole company . . .. Manage it, do it, take care of it' (KA). This decentralization of organizational units and a focus on what is necessary for the company led to tremendous entrepreneurial energy in the local subsidiaries and, thus, in the whole company. With this structure, Nicholas Alt built up high levels of dynamic process/organizational capabilities that enabled individuals to adjust to local opportunities and downturns.

In summary, this period is characterized by two growth processes: (1) mere growth within a legally independent organizational unit (that is, a subsidiary providing service to more cities with more trucks) and (2) business propagation, which refers to setting up new, legally independent organizations in other regions of Germany. Within these new units, mere growth could also occur. On the resource level, neither physical capital (for example, real estate) or technological capital (for example, trucks) could be identified as crucial, but as resources and capabilities tied to the entrepreneurs from the business family. The static capabilities of accounting enabled the family to outperform competitors. The second generation (Nicholas) was introduced into the network by the first generation (Jamie). This, in combination with the static capability of accounting, built up trust (social capital) that led to access to financial capital for growth. The network of the city officials and local bankers, then, enabled regional growth. Furthermore, the dynamic capabilities of operational and strategic review (organizational/process capabilities and management abilities) enabled adjustment to changes in business operations and in the environment. The entrepreneurial organization of the separate organizational units also enables dynamic adaptation to local downturns or opportunities.

Diversification: 1976–88

In the 1970s and 1980s environmental issues were increasingly a concern of German society. The German parliament passed several bills regarding waste reduction and to find new ways of utilization. The second oil crisis of 1979 and the report on 'limits to growth' (Meadows et al., 1972) emphasized the limitation of natural resources and the dependence of Western societies upon these resources. To reduce waste and regain resources as an alternative to burning or depositing – that is, recycling – became increasingly attractive.

During this period the pattern of growth became further diversified. First, ALT continued both business propagation and mere growth within Germany by purchasing stakes in established companies, buying companies and founding new subsidiaries. Second, ALT went abroad for the first time; it acquired a local company in another country and provided city waste collection services. Three years later a second subsidiary was opened in another city. The third pattern refers to entry in new business fields that did not result from environmental and political changes, but from an entrepreneurial decision. This development is described below as 'diversification 1'. The fourth pattern refers to a diversification process as a reaction to a dynamically changing environment ('diversification 2'). In addition to these developments on the portfolio level, numerous changes occurred on the organizational and resources and capabilities levels.

Diversification 1 – new business entry

In 1977 ALT entered a completely new market by purchasing a rendering plant. Once again, Nicholas Alt's reputation and network enabled this acquisition. Two different processes are necessary for animal rendering: (1) collection of the fallen stock and (2) disposal (that is, the production of meat and bone meal). Regarding the first, Nicholas Alt could count on his previous knowledge of the logistics of domestic waste collection. The collection of fallen stock was reorganized relatively quickly. The treatment of the carcasses caused a problem as they were not simply a different type of waste, but also raw material for the production of meat and bone meal. For roughly two years, Nicholas oversaw the reorganization of the production process. The collection, disposal and utilization of fallen stock were all conducted by ALT, thereby adding another static capability to the company. The idea of waste as a raw material for production was now incorporated into the company. This sector has been systematically developed ever since.

Diversification 2 – reaction to changing markets
Since the 1960s and 1970s, the amounts and types of waste have grown steadily, causing new business fields to emerge (for example, removal of hazardous waste, pre-processing and disposal of clearing sludge, destruction of data and information media, medical waste and so on). ALT entered this field by opening its first sewage treatment plant at the end of the 1980s.

While this venture focused on waste disposal (although quite different technologies and skills were required), ALT entered the recycling business in 1982. Nicholas Alt followed the idea of recycling broken plastic garbage bins by devoting company (and his own) resources to successfully develop a process of plastic recycling. Next, companies that dealt with the recycling of plastic and, later, of paper or glass were acquired. Moreover, a recycling plant was opened in the early 1980s which sorted paper, glass and plastic parts of industrial, domestic and business waste. The logic of 'production of secondary raw materials' (that is, recycled raw materials) had already been introduced in the animal rendering sector, but was now applied to other types of waste. All these sectors have been systematically developed ever since.

Organizational development
Developments in this period were numerous. ALT entered many unexplored business fields either by foundation or acquisition, adding new physical and technological resources (plants, real estate, machines and so on) and new static capabilities (treatment of hazardous waste and waste water, new products such as meat and bone meal, secondary raw materials such as recycled glass) to the company. Parallel to this development, new dynamic and entrepreneurial capabilities arose (for example, spotting market opportunities and trends, acquisition and integration of companies and so on). Below we analyse the development of the organization under the focus of technological, human and organizational/process resources and capabilities.

Technological resources Innovation is regarded as a major aspect of entrepreneurship. Unique technological resources create competitive advantage and entrepreneurial rents. ALT pursued three strategies to create innovative technological resources: (1) acquisition, (2) collaboration and (3) development.

ALT is not typically an inventor, but enters a market with a new technology, thereby becoming an 'early adopter' (Rogers, 2003): 'We are innovative, without any question. But we don't do research. We use tools that already exist. And then we buy it and realize it' (KA). Technological innovations were often realized in collaboration with the family business DEMPSEY, which was a competitor as well as a strategic partner, a collaboration enabled by the friendly relationship between Nicholas Alt and the elder Dempsey (social resource). Both developed the systems of waste logistics which shaped the whole sector in Germany and built up technological resources and static capabilities that created a huge competitive advantage. Development refers more to organizational capabilities and is described under 'intrapreneurship'.

Human capital   Human capital (people and their knowledge), one of the crucial resources of a company, defines and limits its abilities. In the case of ALT, we observe two important aspects: (1) the development of an entrepreneurial leadership team and (2) highly skilled employees. A third aspect (guidelines for human resource management) is subsumed under 'organizational/process capital'.

Entrepreneurial leadership team: at the end of the 1970s managing the different subsidiaries became very stressful for Nicholas Alt. In addition, he realized that the growth process was limited to his personal resources of time and competence, so he decided to build up an entrepreneurial team. The two new key players were Hans Smith (holder of a doctoral degree), the CEO, who focused on strategy and productivity, and Robert Lorenz, the CFO, who focused on personnel. Nicholas Alt focused solely on distribution and marketing.

Nicholas Alt recruited highly educated, even overqualified (given the size of the company then), persons to enable future growth (human capital). A CEO with a doctorate was a rare occurrence in a sector that was not considered attractive. Nevertheless, Nicholas Alt convinced Hans Smith, whom he knew through his network (social resource), to become ALT's CEO. This 'surplus' in human resources (that is, more than necessary to maintain the status quo) enabled future growth.

Highly skilled employees: in the 1970s and 1980s the business and the logistics of waste management became increasingly important. Nicholas Alt, known as a competent person (social and human resource) in this field, was invited to lecture at universities. There he met knowledgeable students, built up good relationships with them and convinced them to work for ALT: 'I lectured – although I am not an academic! – at several universities. That was fun, I got acquainted with professors. But, what was more important, I got acquainted with good people that were at the university, and we "cherry-picked" them' (NA).

Nicholas Alt and his entrepreneurial team stressed the importance of competent personnel, without which ALT could not grow, as growth required more than normal, everyday capabilities. Most of the time it was not financial but human resources that were the limiting factor for growth: '[New ventures] never were cancelled because of financial reasons, but we asked ourselves very critically: do we have the qualifications that we need for this expansion?' (NA).

In addition, ALT installed an autonomous organization and a special, demanding system of intrapreneurship and communication. Policies regarding human resource management that ensure staff have the necessary competencies are described later.

Organizational and process resources During the early years Nicholas Alt laid the foundation for the later structure of the organization. The entrepreneurial organization of the subsidiaries, the accounting system which provided transparency, the opportunity for operational and strategic review, and the evaluation of these results were crucial factors. This led to a certain type of entrepreneurial team collaboration, intrapreneurship and innovation and the organization of work.

Collaboration of the entrepreneurial team: the entrepreneurial team, consisting of Nicholas Alt, Hans Smith and Robert Lorenz, was crucial for the development of ALT. Their relationship was characterized by respect and cooperation, frank and hard discussions, evaluation of the results of their work on a monthly basis, and testing their ideas in a 'cross-fire' approach. This specific type of dynamic and entrepreneurial process capability enabled ALT's human capital to realize its full potential. The frank discussions allowed an optimal flow of information without personal or organizational defensiveness (Argyris, 1990), and the regular evaluation of results produced a feedback loop which allowed them to monitor organizational processes and react swiftly to deviating results.

Intrapreneurship and innovation: in addition to the strategy of buying inventions or building strategic partnerships, ALT relied on a culture of intrapreneurship to create new technological resources and static capabilities. New products or process innovations were developed by practitioners themselves, not by a specialized R&D department. On an organizational level, this policy was known as 'overqualified people in under-challenging positions' (KA). Competent persons (for example, managers of the subsidiaries) need not use their full capacities to run daily operations, but could devote time to improve products and services or develop new ones. Involvement in daily operations, as well as contact with customers, ensured the economic relevance of these innovations. These new ideas are tested and, if successful, are applied to the whole organization. This special type of dynamic and entrepreneurial organizational resource enables the optimal use of human resources and creates new technological R&D as products to sell on the market.

Work organization: as mentioned previously, an integral part of the communication system of the entrepreneurial leadership team is the regular evaluation of the results of its work (dynamic capability of operational and strategic review). This system is applied throughout the whole organization: 'delegating a lot of responsibilities, giving leeway; but articulating expectancies, measuring the success, and realizing the consequences' (RL).

ALT had built up a sophisticated system to control entrepreneurial dynamics, ensure that the venture was profitable and establish an overview of the organization. This system, which includes a thorough analysis of business processes, is a crucial aspect of their business culture and success pattern: 'That's part of our organizational culture: break down the processes, analyse, formulate tasks and targets, and check the results' (KA). Thus the first goal of this control system is to enable entrepreneurial freedom and regular evaluation of results. The second is to ensure profitability and optimize processes. ALT will not subsidize unprofitable subsidiaries: 'We break down [analytically] the company in small parts until we see the profit even of the smallest part. We want every business unit to earn their money' (KA). This system of entrepreneurial freedom within well-defined guardrails, control and evaluation, and a focus on profitability is a prerequisite for growth: 'This controlling system has been the only possibility for growth. We acquired companies or gained contracts, and when we acquired a small company, we applied the ALT system to it. As we analyse the numbers, we ask: does it work, does it not work, do we have to raise the price, do we have to work on productivity? Then the local manager works within this framework' (KA).

Human resources management   To maintain its special system of intrapreneurship and communication, ALT recruits its top management team from their own staff: 'We try to recruit our managers from our own staff. Normally, this works' (NA). In this way, ALT ensures that the typical organizational knowledge is present when a vacancy has to be filled. In addition, it is important for ALT to ensure that people who are about to be employed are skilled and competent, even if there is no position for them yet: 'If there is somebody who made a good exam or better, we try to employ him "forcefully", even if it's a little bit like "buying ahead", following the motto: "A company is only successful if it has good personnel'" (RL).

The same policy is applied to overseas operations. To ensure that employees in the subsidiaries abroad know the local culture, language and market, ALT prefers domestic managers. To ensure that managers know the company's system of organization and communication, ALT recruits internally. To combine both (seemingly contradictory) demands, managers from abroad are trained in Germany (where they also learn German). Later, these managers run the overseas subsidiaries: 'The persons we employ in Eastern Europe or China all live in our apartments here, this is a multicultural society. They have the chance to go to the university after they learn German, and later they work at ALT. They know exactly how we think, they know our accounting system, our IT systems, and we go abroad with these people' (NA).

The Recent Years: 1989–99

ALT expanded even further in this decade, following its established pattern of growth and propagation. A highlight of this period was the acquisition of CASSMEIER, a logistics company, which is now third among the three big business units of ALT. This entry in the business field of logistics represents a process of unrelated diversification.

One part of CASSMEIER (10 to 15 percent of its revenue) is activities related to collecting glass for recycling. Because CASSMEIER did not want to sell this part separately, the entrepreneurial team decided to buy the whole company, which was a bold move. The recycling activities were integrated into ALT, and CASSMEIER was run solely as a logistics company. This was an unusual move, as ALT usually prefers to stay in related markets where it had built up competencies: 'We attempted to diversify into unrelated markets, but we realized very quickly that that was not the right way; we could earn much more, and faster, from the markets we knew and where we built up competencies' (NA).

Although CASSMEIER's basic physical and technological resources and static capabilities were different, the entrepreneurial team saw the potential of the logistics market, emphasizing that logistics has always been a capability of ALT (that is, the logistics of waste removal). Another major advantage was the experience of organizing an entrepreneurial culture utilizing ALT's system of entrepreneurship, control, evaluation and communication.

The focus on recycling and providing secondary resources (rather than depositing or burning waste) became increasingly important for ALT.

At the beginning of the 1990s a large recycling site was founded, which now includes a 200-hectare area and about 1400 employees; it represents an important part of the circular-flow economy such as the recycling of plastic waste, electronic waste, composting and animal rendering.

In the early 1990s Nicholas Alt left ALT's executive board and became head of the supervisory board, as two of his sons entered the executive board. At that time Hans Smith became CEO. As ALT is a holding company, the leadership of the three main businesses remains in the hands of the family (one son leads AHLEMANN and one leads BERTRAM; Hans Smith leads CASSMEIER).

The Present: 2000–07

The main portfolio, consisting of the three independent business units AHLEMANN, BERTRAM and CASSMEIER was completed in 1998. Nevertheless, as markets changed, ALT continued its growth following the patterns described above. As these last years do not constitute the focus of our analysis and add nothing substantially new, we omit detail here.

Family Involvement

Nicholas Alt has four children. All of them are involved in the company on an operational, governance or ownership level.

Three have held leading positions in AHLEMANN or BERTRAM since the late 1980s and early 1990s. They pursue the same organizational design characterized by small, entrepreneurial, independent units and the same organizational and procedural resources and capabilities. During this period all of the children became owners. Each owns an equal share, while Nicholas Alt retains a minor share. All are active owners, involved in the major strategic decisions and embracing the entrepreneurial design of the organization.

Nicholas led the ALT group until the early 1990s. When two of his children entered the executive board, he withdrew as chairman of the executive board and became chairman of the supervisory board. All four children are actively involved in the supervisory boards of the group or the major companies.

## 4.5	DISCUSSION

We analysed portfolio entrepreneurship in a family owned business. Our two guiding questions were: (1) 'Which resources and capabilities tied to the entrepreneur/business family enable the development of successful portfolio entrepreneurship practices?' and (2) 'Which resources, capabilities and structure characterize the emerging organization?' As these questions are intertwined, we shall answer them jointly.

To understand the growth and diversification process in this case study, we focused on the entrepreneur, which is consistent with research on portfolio entrepreneurship (PE), but not corporate diversification (CD). On the other hand, analysing the resources and capabilities portfolio of the organization provided great insight, a notion common to CD, but not PE. This might underline the importance of family business research as a genuine field, as research on CD and PE has probably led to an artificial disjunction of observed business entities on the basis of size and ownership structure. Family businesses, in which entrepreneurs are prevalent, are not restricted to minor or small businesses. Research on PE, although derived from trait research, emphasizes the importance of reputation and networks as well as a preference for team work approaches. We confirm both in this case study and provide a detailed overview of these approaches from the perspective of communication and resource orientation, thus adding these insights to PE research.

Crucial resources that enabled the growth process were all tied to the family entrepreneur (that is, social resources such as networks, reputation and trust). These provided access to financial capital for growth, human resources (as the precondition for high quality operations) and, under the frame of surplus capacity, technological resources, which provided a crucial competitive advantage.

While the resource-based logic of CD predicts growth and diversification processes in situations of excess (production) capacity, the idea of consciously creating this excess, especially in the field of human resources, offers new insights. Enriching the organization with this surplus of human resources is clearly an entrepreneurial capability that was first provided and later systematically built by the family entrepreneur. An apparent highlight of this process is the creation of the entrepreneurial management team. Here not only the combination of human resources provided by the three leading entrepreneurs (Hans Smith, Robert Lorenz and Nicholas Alt) was important, but also an interaction characterized by regular evaluation of the results of their work, and frank and respectful discussions about these issues. The precondition for these discussions (a dynamic capability of operational review), data provided by the controlling and accounting system (a static management capability), enabled them to react to disturbances in the organizational process relatively quickly. In addition, this culture of communication also enabled discussion about strategic issues (that is, an entrepreneurial capability), such as entering new markets, a pattern also applied in regular meetings with top management. Therefore a culture of evaluation and frank discussion is spread throughout the organization, which enables optimization processes of organizational routines and entrepreneurial processes of new business entry. In our view, these capabilities are clearly shaped by the family entrepreneur; that is, introduced and developed by the second generation and maintained by the third generation.

These patterns are duplicated down to the individual subsidiaries which are run relatively autonomously by entrepreneurial employees. A high degree of responsibility is delegated to local managers, but this leeway is also clearly defined to control the entrepreneurial dynamics. The sophisticated system of controlling and reporting enables optimization of organizational routines and indicates deviations from expectations, which will be discussed accordingly. These dynamic and entrepreneurial capabilities at the subsidiary level also provide a competitive advantage by allowing the best use of crucial resources according to the needs of the local market. In addition, they enable the renewal and innovation of new crucial resources by entrepreneurial managers and employees.

To maintain this organizational pattern, special human resource practices ensure that a qualified person is employed (or even 'bought ahead'), constantly enriching the organization with new human resources. Personnel are systematically introduced into the ALT business system to ensure that this pattern is upheld in newly founded ventures, especially those abroad. In addition, ALT prefers internal recruiting of managers, and delays founding a venture until proper personnel are available. This need for competent personnel creates the necessary static, dynamic and entrepreneurial capabilities.

On the organizational and process levels, dynamic and entrepreneurial management capabilities were crucial for the development and success of ALT. This highlights the importance of 'quality of management' (Prahalad and Bettis, 1986, p. 488) as a factor in the development of the company. Prahalad and Bettis call this the 'dominant logic' of top management, defined as the 'conceptualization of the business and the administrative tools to accomplish goals and make decisions' (Prahalad and Bettis, 1986, p. 491). This dominant logic is shared among the entrepreneurial top management team consisting of the three leading entrepreneurs, subsidiary management and, to a lesser degree, the employees. The dominant logic, its realization in the organizational structure and corresponding practices provide a source of competitive advantage for ALT, which is sustained by careful human resources management (choosing qualified people and providing training) and ongoing renewal of these operations. The family business entrepreneurs all share this 'dominant logic' and uphold it by their strategic decisions as owners/members of the supervisory board, or as top managers on the group level (ALT) and operational level (AHLEMANN, BERTRAM). As this bundle of resources and capabilities is clearly influenced by the business family, it could be regarded as a familiness factor.

In summary, the entrepreneurial processes could be best described by a proactive orientation, based on an organization that is characterized by autonomy. This framework establishes a continuous stream of improvements and innovations, flexible and fast reactions to changing market conditions, and flexible ways to optimize organizational routines. Table 4.3 sums up this argument and gives a short overview.

The growth process per se is described as mere growth and business propagation. While the first refers to growth within an existing organizational unit, the latter refers to establishing new organizational units – first in Germany, then abroad, then in related markets and in unrelated fields such as animal rendering and logistics. The first describes a pattern of 'replication' (new subsidiaries of the same business type in different regions), and the second is a reaction to a differentiating market, which are clearly entrepreneurial moves and entries in new business fields.

Nevertheless, while this added new resources and static capabilities to the company, the ALT system – consisting of the static capability of accounting and dynamic and entrepreneurial capabilities (operational and strategic review, adaptation to local markets, innovation of new products and so on), bundled in independent units and led by entrepreneurial employees – could be applied to all of them.

The propagation of independent subsidiaries or new types of ventures created an organization whose units have quite similar capabilities and organizational structures. The small units are governed by the same logic of entrepreneurship, control and communication that drives the whole organization. This characteristic of 'self-similarity' (that is, the small parts of an object all resemble the whole) results in an organization that resembles a 'fractal' (a concept from the theory of dynamic systems). Fractals are created by iterative processing; that is, basic operations (constructing principles) that are repetitively applied and can be observed in the small parts of the system as well as in the organization as a whole. In this regard, ALT seems to embrace 'fractal entrepreneurship'. This organizational structure, its preconditions and its differences from classic organizational structures might be worth exploring in the future.

For ALT, portfolio entrepreneurship was the crucial growth strategy, which could be due to several reasons. First, its original type of business offers a service that has to be provided locally. The foundation or acquisition of multiple local subsidiaries is a logical consequence of this business model. Establishing them as legally independent entities seems to be more

Table 4.3   *Overview of crucial resources and capabilities in the portfolio*
               entrepreneurship process of ALT

	Resources/capabilities		
	Social	**Human**	**Organizational and Process**
Description	Reputation of Nicholas Alt	Skills of entrepreneurial leadership team (N. Alt, H. Smith, R. Lorenz)	Respectful but frank discussions on a regular basis
	Network and reputation of Nicholas Alt	Skills of employees	Accounting system Thorough process analysis to ensure profitability Operational and strategic review Decentralized autonomy within guardrails
Provides/ Enables	Access to business opportunities (new subsidiaries and business entry)	Competitive advantage through competent entrepreneurial leadership team	Competitive advantage through team work, entrepreneurial organization
	Access to financial capital		Competitive advantage through quick adaptation to changing market
	Access to human resources		Continuous renewal and improvement of resources
	Access to technological resources		
Entrepreneurial performance	Technological leadership Acquisition of up to 1000 companies Turnover growth from 0.51 to 9200 million euros (375 percent per year on average) More than 800 independent subsidiaries on three continents and in approximately 40 countries		

a conscious decision than the result of logical deduction, as the subsidiaries and bigger business units could be organized in a multidivisional form. We only speculate here, but it seems that the autonomous organization of the subsidiaries is fostered by being legally autonomous entities that are also responsible for their own actions and profit. As portfolio ownership 'takes different forms and performs different functions for entrepreneurs in different circumstances and contexts' (Carter and Ram, 2003, p. 373), we conclude that the need to provide services locally, in combination with entrepreneurial freedom and responsibility for results, are major factors in building a portfolio of legally independent companies.

The argument that companies diversify, preferably in related products or markets, was underlined by Nicholas Alt. Knowledge of markets and processes enabled him to earn profits faster than in unrelated markets. The motive of financial risk reduction through unrelated diversification (though a valid one to secure family funds) was also denied by Nicholas Alt. Instead of securing finances, the entrepreneurial notion of generating profit was the driving force, which was much easier to accomplish in known markets.

Arguments in the framework of agency theory and managerial motives seem implausible in a business where the family, as sole owner, provides top-level management and members of the executive and supervisory board. Managers would be unable to decide about mergers and acquisitions without the family; thus managerial motives as the cause for unrelated diversification are very unlikely.

The general argument that excess capacity leads to either related or unrelated diversification (Chatterjee and Wernerfelt, 1988) does not fit this case. It was not excess capacity that led to the initiation of diversification steps, but an entrepreneurial opportunity and the proper personnel to realize it. So in both cases, major diversification steps were entrepreneurial acts rather than the logical consequence of excess capacity and the search for use of this capacity.

4.6 CONCLUSION

Entrepreneurship can be regarded as a source of wealth creation, especially in dynamic environments. In family businesses crucial entrepreneurship practices are often associated with the dominant entrepreneurs from the business family – in our case, Nicholas Alt. An organization that relies solely on the entrepreneurship practices of the single family entrepreneur endangers its existence. First, it limits the growth of the business to the working capacity of the entrepreneur. Second, it limits the resource pool of the firm and, thus, its capability pool. Third, any decline in the performance of the entrepreneur will probably lead to a decline of the performance of the company. Fourth, transgenerational wealth creation (Habbershon and Pistrui, 2002) becomes questionable with each new generation's different entrepreneurship practices.

These arguments point to the importance of organization building. By creating an entrepreneurial organization, entrepreneurial capacities are multiplied and dependency on a single person is reduced. Other family members also have the opportunity to observe an entrepreneurial organization first hand, thus becoming accustomed to this special way of dealing with challenges.

Although the processes of resource picking (by acquisition, cooperation or innovation) and decisions to renew are important for rent creation (for example, a certain patent or technology), capability building is a second, independent, factor (Makadok, 2001, p. 389). While a company can earn rents by superior organizational routines, the dynamic and entrepreneurial capacities of a company enhance the value of resources, either by correction and optimization, adaptation to changing markets, creation of new resources and products or entry in new business fields. For this, qualified personnel are important.

The family plays a crucial role in this firm design by applying and multiplying the appropriate dominant logic on the ownership level. In addition, organizational structure and communication processes should be in alignment with this logic. There seems to be a paradox here. To carry this argument to the extreme, by making the organization entrepreneurial and thus independent from the entrepreneurial capacity of family members, the family entrepreneurs become dispensable. Thus the company needs the family entrepreneur to build up a structure that enables the organization to function without him. By this seemingly paradoxical quality, chances for the continuation of the family business and, thus, continual recreation of the organization by family entrepreneurs are probably enhanced.

As these dynamic and entrepreneurial capabilities seem less content specific (as are resources and some static capabilities), they can also provide a longer lasting effect for transgenerational entrepreneurship. As markets change and competitive advantages due to resources erode, the principles of entrepreneurial organization design might endure and can be applied in other sectors. Building a portfolio in dynamically changing markets can be regarded as the natural result of this strategy. In addition, it might diversify the risk of losses of family wealth.

These considerations underline the importance of family business research as an accepted field. By studying a business family, special bundles of resources and capabilities have to be considered, meaning that new motives, functions and processes of portfolio entrepreneurship might arise. Prevalent literature on small businesses (PE) or large publicly held businesses (CD) covers only certain facets; combining a focus on the person (entrepreneur) and the organization in the context of a family owned business seems to be fruitful. Going back to MacMillan's challenge, we can conclude that building an entrepreneurial organization is a crucial aspect of habitual (portfolio) entrepreneurship. In family owned business the family as keeper of the special dominant logic could provide this source of competitive advantage, which constitutes a familiness factor.

NOTE

1. Names and other characteristics were changed to provide anonymity. Capitalized names refer to companies.

REFERENCES

Amihud, Y. and B. Lev (1981), 'Risk reduction as a managerial motive for conglomerate mergers', *Bell Journal of Economics*, **12**(2), 605–17.

Amit, R. and P. Schoemaker (1993), 'Strategic assets and organizational rents', *Strategic Management Journal*, **14**(1), 33–46.

Argyris, C. (1990), *Overcoming organizational defensiveness*, Englewood Cliffs: Prentice-Hall Inc.

Barney, J. (1991), 'Firm resources and sustained competitive advantage', *Journal of Management*, **17**(1), 99–120.

Carter, S. and M. Ram (2003), 'Reassessing portfolio entrepreneurship', *Small Business Economics*, **21**(4), 371–80.

Chatterjee, S. and B. Wernerfelt (1988), 'Related or unrelated diversification', *Academy of Management Best Paper Proceedings*, 7–11.

Collins, D. (1994), 'Research note: how valuable are organizational capabilities?', *Strategic Management Journal*, **15**, 143–52.

Gartner, W.B. (1989), '"Who is an entrepreneur?" is the wrong question', *Entrepreneurship Theory and Practice*, **13**(4), 47–68.

Grant, R.M. (1991), 'The resource-based theory of competitive advantage: implications for strategy formulation', *California Management Review*, **33**(3), 114–35.

Habbershon, T.G. and J. Pistrui (2002), 'Enterprising families domain: family-influenced ownership groups in pursuit of transgenerational wealth', *Family Business Review*, **15**(3), 223–37.

Habbershon, T.G. and M.L. Williams (1999), 'A resource-based framework for assessing the strategic advantages of family firms', *Family Business Review*, **12**(1), 1–25.

Hoskisson, R.E. and M.A. Hitt (1990), 'Antecedents and performance outcomes of diversification: a review and critique of theoretical perspectives', *Journal of Management*, **16**(2), 461–509.

Hunt, S.B. (1995), 'The resource-advantage theory of competition: toward explaining productivity and economic growth', *Journal of Management Inquiry*, **4**(4), 317–32.

Iacobucci, D. and P. Rosa (2004), 'Habitual entrepreneurs, entrepreneurial team development and business group formation', Paper presented at RENT XVII Managing Complexity and Change in SMEs, 24–26 November, Copenhagen, Denmark.

MacMillan, I.C. (1986), 'Executive forum: to really learn about entrepreneurship, let's study habitual entrepreneurs', *Journal of Business Venturing*, **1**, 241–3.

Mahoney, J.T. (1995), 'The management of resources and the resource of management', *Journal of Business Research*, **33**, 91–101.

Mahoney, J.T. and J.R. Pandian (1992), 'The resource-based view within the conversation of strategic management', *Strategic Management Journal*, **13**(5), 363–80.

Makadok, R. (2001), 'Toward a synthesis of the resource-based and dynamic-capability view of rent creation', *Strategic Management Journal*, **22**(5), 287–401.

Mayring, P. (2000), *Qualitative Inhaltsanalyse. Grundlagen und Techniken.* Weinheim: Deutscher Studien Verlag.

Meadows, D.H., D.L. Meadows, J. Randers and W.W. Behrens III (1972), *Limits to Growth*, Washington, DC: Potomac Associates.

Montgomery, C.A. (1994), 'Corporate diversification', *Journal of Economic Perspectives*, **8**(3), 163–78.

Porter, M.E. (1985), *Competitive Advantage*, New York: Free Press.

Prahalad, C.K. and R.A. Bettis (1986), 'A new linkage between diversity and performance', *Strategic Mangement Journal*, **7**(6), 485–501.

Ramanujam, V. and P. Varadarajan (1989), 'Research on corporate diversification: a synthesis', *Strategic Management Journal*, **10**(6), 523–51.

Rogers, E.M. (2003), *Diffusion of Innovations*, 5th edn, New York: Simon and Schuster.

Rosa, P. and M. Scott (1999), 'The prevalence of multiple owners and directors in the SME-sector: implications for our understanding of start-up and growth', *Entrepreneurship and Regional Development*, **11**, 21–37.

Sarasvathy, S.D. (2004), 'Making it happen: beyond theories of the firm to theories of firm design', *Entrepreneurship Theory and Practice*, **28**(6), 519–31.

Scott, M. and P. Rosa (1996), 'Has firm level analysis reached its limits? Time for a rethink', *International Small Business Journal*, **14**(4), 81–9.

Sirmon, D.G., M.A. Hitt and R.D. Ireland (2007), 'Managing firm resources in dynamic environments to create value: looking inside the black box', *Academy of Mangement Review*, **32**(1), 273–92.

Sparrer, I. (2006), *Systemische Strukturaufstellung*, Heidelberg: Carl-Auer-Systeme.

Teece, D.J., G. Pisaono and A. Shuen (1997), 'Dynamic capabilities and strategic management', *Strategic Management Journal*, **18**(7), 509–33.

Westhead, P. and M. Wright (1998), 'Novice, portfolio and serial founders: are they different?', *Journal of Business Venturing*, **13**, 173–204.

Westhead, P., D. Ucbasaran, M. Wright and M. Binks (2005), 'Novice, serial and portfolio entrepreneur behaviour and contributions', *Small Business Econimics*, **25**, 109–32.

5. Entrepreneurial orientation across generations in family firms: the role of owner-centric culture for proactiveness and autonomy

Ethel Brundin, Mattias Nordqvist and Leif Melin

5.1 INTRODUCTION

The aim of this chapter is to increase the understanding of how entrepreneurial orientation (EO) is transformed by transgenerational processes in family businesses with strong cultures. Based on findings from two in-depth case studies and a theoretical framework that combines insights from the entrepreneurship and culture literatures, we describe and analyse the role of organizational culture in the family business as a key element in how EO travels over generations. More specifically, we show how the EO dimensions of autonomy and proactiveness can both foster and hamper this process and how they interact on different levels. Moving beyond conventional life cycle reasoning, we show that founder-centric cultures can return in later stages of a firm's life cycle. We thus introduce the concept of owner-centric culture as a way of conceptualizing strong family business cultures and their impact on the EO of a business.

We argue that lack of autonomy among family members belonging to the next generation and the firm's top management constrains proactiveness and entrepreneurship in the future. By focusing on the autonomy and proactiveness dimensions in family businesses, we contribute to the EO literature by answering the call for more focused and in-depth studies that address the role of, and relationships between, single dimensions of the EO construct in specific organizational and stakeholder contexts (Lumpkin and Dess, 1996; Lyon et al., 2000). We also contribute to the EO literature by using concepts and insights from the field of organizational culture to examine proactiveness and autonomy.

The remainder of this chapter is organized as follows. We engage in a theoretical discussion about the founder's role in creating the company culture. We also examine the concept of 'familiness' as an advantage or disadvantage for the family business culture. The third section concerns autonomy and proactiveness of EO and relates their importance to the culture perspective. In the fourth section, our case studies illustrate how autonomy and proactiveness work in practice. In the discussion we offer support for our propositions and then conclude by considering implications for theory and practice.

5.2   FOUNDERS, CULTURE AND FAMILINESS

Following Gartner's (1988) view on entrepreneurship as the 'creation of organizations' founders are a key concern in entrepreneurship research. In conventional life cycle models founding is the first phase of a firm that subsequently goes through transitions with age and size that lead to changes in behavior and priorities (Greiner, 1972). Schein (1983) emphasizes the role of the founder in creating organizational culture. For him, culture means underlying assumptions, values and artifacts, such as architecture, office layout and dress codes. It is the founder who introduces the basic assumptions to the organization at its beginning: 'Founders often start with a theory of how to succeed; they have a cultural paradigm in their heads, based on their experience in the culture in which they grew up' (Schein, 1983, p. 14). This perspective means that the founder typically has initial beliefs and convictions about how to organize and compete that stabilize and become part of the organizational culture. As we elaborate below, such founder-driven cultures tend to become strong, sometimes counteracting the adaptive capability to meet challenges that do not fit the culture and leading to inertia when considering necessary changes (Melin and Alvesson, 1989).

   Although some researchers see a risk of oversimplification in focusing solely on the founder, there is consensus that founders are very important to the culture of family businesses (Dyer, 1986; Gersick et al., 1997). According to Kets de Vries (1993), founders share common themes that affect the operation and the culture of their companies. Two such themes are suspicion and the need for control. Because founders are not likely to delegate power, founder-led companies are usually very centralized and dominated by the founder's beliefs and practices. Gomez-Meija et al. (2001) add that long tenures of founders typically mean significant cognitive costs and, therefore, high psychological barriers to turning over daily business operations to others. Even in such situations, founder-centric cultures may foster focused strategic renewal when the succeeding generation interacts with the founding entrepreneur in strategic activities (Hall, 2003).

The family 'is perhaps the most reliable of all social structures for transmitting cultural values and practices across generations' (Gersick et al., 1997, p. 149). According to Garcia-Alvarez et al. (2002), the founder's view of the role of business in the family will influence the process of socialization through which the next generation is embraced into the business. If the founder sees the family business as important for the wealth of the family, the transmission of the values, interests and goals over generations shapes relatively stable cultural patterns in both the family and the business (Garcia-Alvarez et al., 2002). We thus expect that, over time, culture will surpass the founder and express the close connection between the owning family and the business as a result of family values, interests and goals rooted in history and ongoing social relationships. Thus we introduce the concept of owner-centric culture, whereby strong culture often associated with the founder can be a distinct feature in later stages of the family firm's life cycle. Owner-centric culture refers to the organizational and family business cultures being greatly influenced by owners who are also operatively involved as business leaders, even if they are not the founders. Our aim is to broaden the notion of the founder-centric culture that is dominant in the literature.

Although family business cultures are often described as closed and resistant to change (for example, Dyer, 1986; Gersick et al., 1997), flexibility, change orientation and innovation are key cultural characteristics in some family businesses (Hall et al., 2001; Zahra et al., 2004). The core assumption of life cycle models, that firms eventually degrade and die, is directly challenged in corporate entrepreneurship literature, where the possibility of revitalization and rejuvenation instead of predetermined decline is a central thesis (Hoy, 2006). Habbershon and Williams (1999) also have noted, building on the resource-based view, that a family influenced organizational culture may be a source of competitive advantage since it may explain the heterogeneity between firms operating in similar competitive environments. Culture can thus be part of the familiness of a family business, that is, the unique resources that emerge as a result of the interaction between the owning family, individual family members and the business (Habbershon and Williams, 1999).

Culture, however, as other types of familiness and family influenced resources, does not always represent a source of competitive advantage. A specific family influenced resource can either be an 'f+' (facilitating influence), 'f−' (constraining influence) or 'f0' (neutral influence) (Habbershon et al., 2003). The notion of familiness thus aims to capture the source of idiosyncrasies in the resource profile of each family influenced business firm and provides a path for exploring how the family business creates heterogeneous entrepreneurial outcomes (Habbershon and Pistrui, 2002). In this chapter we look at the culture of family business as one such family influenced resource. We examine the impact of culture as either a facilitating or a constraining resource in the transformation of EO by transgenerational processes.

We note that culture is often considered simplistically in the literature. The culture of a business firm is seldom as homogeneous and integrative as the dominant literature suggests. On the contrary, in most organizations culture is a very complex phenomenon, with different meanings and multiple internal competing cultures (Martin, 2002). We adhere to a more multifaceted view on culture through our focus on the relationship between owner-centric culture and the autonomy and proactiveness dimensions of EO.

5.3   ENTREPRENEURIAL ORIENTATION THROUGH AUTONOMY AND PROACTIVENESS

As noted in Chapter 1, we use five dimensions to examine the degree of a firm's EO: proactiveness, risk taking, innovativeness, autonomy and competitive aggressiveness (cf. Lumkpin and Dess, 1996). We focus specifically on the autonomy and proactiveness dimensions of EO, as they show particular relevance to entrepreneurship in family businesses from a culture perspective (Hall et al., 2001; Zahra et al., 2004). In the next section we introduce these dimensions and explain their link to the owner-centric culture perspective.

Autonomy is the freedom of individuals in an organization to be creative, to promote ideas and to change methods. Lumpkin and Dess (1996, p. 140) define autonomy as 'the independent action of an individual or a team in bringing forth an idea or a vision and carrying it through to completion'. Inherent in this definition of autonomy is the role of flexible organizational structures and open communication to support and empower individuals and teams to be creative. On a related theme, Schumpeter (1934) discusses 'mental freedom', where organizations that lack mental freedom become routinized and resistant to change,leading to difficulties in initiating and launching new ventures: 'This is so because all knowledge and habit once acquired becomes as firmly rooted in ourselves as a railway embankment in the earth. It does not require to be continually renewed and consciously reproduced, but sinks into the strata of subconsciousness' (Schumpeter, 1934, p. 85).

Normal activities, then, are taken for granted and transmitted through organizational routines. In this situation stepping outside the boundaries of routine creates difficulties because it challenges the status quo. To escape this situation leadership that questions routines and has 'the capacity of seeing things in a way which afterwards proves to be true, even though it cannot be established at the moment' is needed (Schumpeter, 1934, p.85). In this way, the concept of mental freedom entails that which Martin and Lumpkin (2003) call the ability for organizational members to 'carry ventures through to completion without relying on the support or approval of others'. Here we observe an obvious link to the proactiveness dimension of EO.

Proactiveness essentially implies to what extent an organization and its members act entrepreneurially by anticipating and pursuing new opportunities. This means a forward-looking perspective and search for new opportunities that are accompanied by innovative or new venture activities (Lumpkin and Dess, 1996). An autonomous organization is thus more likely to be proactive, since freedom, mental or otherwise, allows people to pursue more opportunities and anticipate competitors' actions proactively. In other words, if the culture of a family business is characterized by norms, values and attitudes that mean autonomy for people working in the organization, we expect more proactiveness. Proactiveness is fostered not only by cultural values that support the questioning of that which is taken for granted (that is, conventional methods), but also by values that allow foresight, opportunity, creativity and novel strategic actions.

In line with the possible negative influence of the typical family business culture, family business scholars note that family involvement sometimes hampers autonomy, especially mental freedom, particularly if family members' leadership and involvement breed the belief that certain family leaders are irreplaceable, unique resources in their firms (Nordqvist et al., 2008). This situation tends to be most common in founder-centric cultures (Kelly et al., 2000; Schein, 1983).

From our theoretical framework, we propose the following:

1. The concept of a 'founder-centric culture' can be extended to a more generic concept of 'owner-centric culture' in family businesses, which is not restricted to the early generations of family owners.
2. A strong owner-centric culture may hamper as well as foster autonomy and proactiveness in the organization.
3. Owner-centric cultures that foster autonomy and proactiveness are based on a mental freedom that allows individuals to break free of routine patterns and to pursue new opportunities.
4. A low degree of autonomy implies a low degree of proactiveness.

Table 5.1   Interviewees at Novo Footwear and Chem Tech

	Novo Footwear	**Chem Tech**
Owners/family business members active in the firm and interviewed	Father: Greg Arbor Two children: Dennis and Matthew One daughter-in-law: Amy	Father: Paul Wallin Mother: Inga Wallin Three children: Donna, Mark, Mary
Generations	Fifth and sixth	First and second
Non-family members interviewed	Chairman of the board, external member of the board, marketing director	Group CEO, two external members of the board, marketing director

5.4   EMPIRICAL ILLUSTRATIONS

Following the overall research methodology of the STEP Project outlined in Chapter 2, we conducted in-depth case studies in two companies (Chem Tech and Novo Footwear) to address our propositions generated from the literature review. In-depth interviews were conducted with owners, family members active in the business, top executives and members of the board. In addition, half-day sessions were spent with the owners and active family members in order to understand and discuss the business and the business family. Empirical material was collected mainly from 2005 through 2007. In addition, we have been in continuous contact with the business families from 2005 through 2008 to follow new events.

This section presents a short company profile and then describes our findings regarding culture in relation to the autonomy and proactiveness dimensions of EO. Chem Tech illustrates a typical founder-centric culture; Novo Footwear shows that similar cultural patterns may form around a dominant family owner-manager in a much later generational stage of the business, forming our perception of owner-centric culture. Our descriptions illustrate the influence these cultural patterns have on autonomy and proactiveness on the organizational level as well as of individuals working in each firm. Table 5.1 provides a short overview of both companies.

Case: Novo Footwear

Novo Footwear is a medium-size company of 200 employees and a turnover of 25 million euros in 2006 that manufactures and sells safety and occupational footwear for the manufacturing and service industries. The company, which dates back to 1839, is in its fifth and sixth generations. The father, Greg Arbor is CEO, and his sons are Dennis and Matthew). All three hold management positions and have shares in the company; however only Greg is a member of the company board. Greg joined Novo in 1973, which was then owned by his aunt. He became the sole owner in 1995 and, in 2005, Dennis and Matthew were granted shares in Novo Footwear (24 percent each).

Novo Footwear is a highly innovative, dynamic company whose export sales increased considerably at the same time its home market was strengthened. The company's market share has increased steadily over the last few years and currently is 45 percent. It has demonstrated clear entrepreneurial outcomes over the years, including an in-house development department with a special team focusing on innovations. About 3 to 4 percent of turnover is set aside for product development and new markets, and customer groups are approached and expanded continuously. Novo also shows strong financial key ratios.

As owner and CEO, Greg has exerted strong control in the company regarding costs, financial measures, R&D, customer relations and production. In short, he has run the company 'his way'. In recent years Greg's dominance has been questioned by his sons who want to systemize the organizational and decision-making processes. However Greg finds it difficult to grant full responsibility to others. Above all, he does not want to seem to his sons to be less in charge, even though Dennis is Vice-President of Innovation and Design and Matthew is Vice-President of Business Development. Dennis has been with the company for more than ten years and Matthew joined Novo three years ago. Both have academic degrees in business administration. In addition, Dennis has a degree in shoe design and Matthew previously ran his own business.

Autonomy in Novo Footwear

We define autonomy as freedom among organizational members to act independently, present and implement new ideas, and question the status quo. Implicit in this definition are the notions of action and decision making. For autonomy to exist, employees must be allowed to take actions and make decisions. In Novo Footwear the marketing director characterizes decision making as flexible and informal: 'If I want to enter a new market, then the decision can be taken ten minutes later. I just talk to Greg and present my arguments. He knows that I have done my homework.'

Dennis, on the other hand, is troubled that all decisions need his father's approval. Greg is absent a great deal, making it difficult to reach him and obtain approval. Dennis thinks this is quite frustrating: 'I don't like to be dependent on something that I cannot control . . . This is very trying, and takes time.'

Both Dennis and Matthew, however, challenge the status quo. To strengthen their autonomy, Dennis makes some decisions without his father's approval, and Matthew recognizes the boundaries and how to maneuver within them. One of Dennis's decisions is that product development is performed in a department where access is allowed only with an entry code and where development is governed by deadlines. Greg disapproves of this and sees it as a threat to transparency in the organization. According to daughter-in-law Amy, Vice-President of Trading, there is currently much more information shared, referring to Dennis's and Matthew's general briefings about ongoing activities in the organization.

When Dennis is asked whether the organization is entrepreneurial, he says that many people seem to be afraid to challenge existing structures. Because he is reluctant to hurt people, Greg often implements changes slowly. On the other hand, the company is definitely not afraid to introduce and market new products. According to Dennis, people say that there is a lot of 'go' in the company.

Amy's main tasks involve imports and logistics. She claims that it is not difficult to propose changes, since Greg is interested in all ideas, but it often takes a long time for him to approve of and implement changes: 'Because there is one thing that is very typically Greg and that is that time solves all problems.'

On the other hand, according to Amy, some changes are implemented very quickly when Greg has his own ideas. Sometimes things happen so fast that it is hard for her and her group to fully understand the rationale behind the change. To Greg's credit, however, it is acceptable to make mistakes even if the consequences appear too late.

The board of Novo Footwear is small, having two external members, one of whom is the chairman of the board, Greg, and two representatives of the local unions.[1] Dennis and Matthew have been promised seats on the board, but this has not been finalized. The issue of bringing in the sons has been a point of contention among the three owners. Greg admits that it is about power and that his sons need to learn more about the accountability and responsibility that come with ownership. Reliance on informal structures and direct control seem to help Greg to be entrepreneurial, whereas Dennis and Matthew want more structure and formalization. To summarize, autonomy is a strong value that Greg follows in his actions. This, however, limits the ability of others to act in a similar autonomous fashion.

Proactiveness in Novo Footwear
We define proactiveness as the degree to which people and organizations perceive and pursue new opportunities and thereby act entrepreneurially.

Novo Footwear has a clear ambition to grow, and to grow organically. Further, it is as important to be in the forefront of development as it is to be realistic.

According to Matthew Arbor, Novo Footwear occupies a certain segment in a field within normal market conditions. If Novo Footwear moves outside that field, the company and the product will be considered a 'UFO'. If, however, the company develops a product that lies on the border, it will move the whole field in a new direction. Within a certain time frame, if the field has moved, then this product, considered to be on the front edge, becomes desirable and in demand. Unfortunately, Matthew concludes, the company has had unrealistic expectations about being first on the market with new products; they have been outside the field, making expensive mistakes as a result. To Matthew, it is important to systemize development of new ideas and avoid future financial setbacks. Even so, he seems to be satisfied with the bold ventures that he regards as an instinct for survival: 'Our power to be creative is the strongest force we have. It constitutes our ability to survive in the long run.'

Dennis regards Novo Footwear as a proactive company and is convinced that it will always seek to improve present and future products and ideas. Penetrating the vast and novel market of Russia is a sign of proactiveness.

The chairman of the board is very impressed by the courage Greg Arbor shows when it comes to investing in new products and in his ability to grasp new concepts. He mentions novel shoe design, shoe functionalism and branding as examples of Novo Footwear being on the front edge and very competitive in the market. He confirms the urge to be proactive: 'We are among the best safety shoe producers in Europe. And it is a deliberate strategy that we want to lead the development.'

The marketing director also stresses Novo's need to be in the forefront of product development: 'We have to be very competent on innovative product development, focusing on function and ergonomics in the first place but also on design. We must at all times have four or five new products that show the way.'

Novo Footwear's culture reflects its proactiveness as well. There is an urge to continuously improve products in order to add customer value and to attain the highest quality possible. This urge is driven mainly by Greg; his passion creates openness to always seek the 'new'. This is found also in the never-ending activities to combine components in new ways. However new product and business ideas are not limited to the present product portfolio. Greg has a range of ideas that could be put into practice if he could only find the time to devote to their development. Greg wants to prove wrong everyone who does not believe in his ideas. At the same time, he believes in transparency for all employees regarding new product ideas and other important changes.

Case: Chem Tech

Chem Tech is a medium-size firm with 174 employees (as of 2006), developing, producing and selling special chemical products for the pulp and paper industry. Chem Tech is an example of a company that has been very entrepreneurial and growth oriented for several years. Chem Tech was founded in 1973 by Paul Wallin, who has driven the firm's growth strategy with a turnover of 51 million euros in 2006. The founder embodies the typical entrepreneur. He even has the title 'Entrepreneur' on his business card. Being an enthusiastic and energetic sales person, he has managed the positive development of Chem Tech through a niche-oriented competitive strategy and a growth strategy combining acquisitions and organic growth. In the last ten years the Wallin family has worked actively to involve the second generation in the governance and daily operations of Chem Tech. All three children – one son and two daughters – work full- or part-time in the family business. The two eldest also serve on boards within the small group of companies that constitute Chem Tech.

In recent years a new top management team, including a new CEO, has been recruited. The second generation of the family is increasingly involved as well. This means that the family firm is facing a double succession challenge, both within the family and in management. Coinciding with a generally weak industry and falling profitability and growth for the firm, both the family and the firm face important challenges to regain their once outstanding entrepreneurial performance. Being dynamic and ambitious, Chem Tech has grown rapidly due to internationalization, acquisitions and the launch of new products.

Autonomy in Chem Tech

After peak growth in the mid 1990s, Paul Wallin stepped down as CEO, but he and Chem Tech encountered difficulties in replacing him. The first non-family CEO was recruited internally. A very successful marketing director, he was less successful as CEO. Paul was advised by consultants and board members to stay away from the firm and the daily operations as much as possible in order to grant autonomy to the new CEO. However he felt frustrated at not being more involved. Board member: 'The intention was that Paul would distance himself from the daily operations so that the new guy could create an independent platform. But this is one of the fundaments of an entrepreneurial family business, it doesn't work like that. I mean to just exclude the old entrepreneur – the person who has started the business and who has employed all the people. The new CEO tried to close the door on him and Paul felt very bad because of this. For some time we even thought of starting a new company for Paul to take care of.'

The second CEO was recruited externally and accompanied by several other new top managers from a much bigger, competing US firm. The new CEO and top management team pushed for a slightly new strategy, aiming to grow through integrating the company and becoming more unified as a group. Previously, Chem Tech was rather loosely structured as fairly independent companies. The new top management team experienced opposition to slight changes in strategy from the 'old Chem' team, including Paul Wallin. His involvement in daily activities had also been more intensive during the tenure of the second non-family CEO, leading to less autonomy for the new top management team.

Paul's intention, however, is to grant autonomy to both top management and employees. He speaks of 'disciplined creativity'; that is, balancing a 'high degree of discipline oriented culture and a high degree of entrepreneurial spirit'. His son, Mark, explains Paul's current role in the firm: 'He tries to get support for novel thinking in the organization; he tries to get people to be a bit more open. This means giving lectures, participate in discussions, interact with researchers, and take part in sales and market meetings. He tries to make people open their eyes and not think too narrowly. . . I think we are very entrepreneurial when it comes to speed, flexibility and capability to change quickly and adapt to the customer. But then, perhaps, we are not as good when it comes to new ideas for products as we used to be.'

The company's culture is influenced by the relative smallness of the firm, short decision-making processes, and close and informal relationships between people. There are no strict job descriptions or tight chains of command in the organization. Among non-family board members, however, there is fear that the new top management team is not free enough to improve the firm's entrepreneurial performance. There is a similar fear regarding the freedom the next generation of the owner-family will be granted to develop the firm. Members of the second generation, in both the interviews and seminar sessions, claim a lack of freedom to act and develop the firm in the direction of their choice. As they talk about their father having a 'let-go problem', Paul Wallin talks about his children's 'taking-over problem'. He believes that the next generation does not feel ready and hesitates to lead the firm.

Proactiveness in Chem Tech

Mark Wallin says Chem Tech was more project oriented under the previous family top management. This supported proactiveness, since a team was formed very quickly to address customer problems. 'Those that were best suited for the project were quickly involved, regardless of titles.' Today, as a result of the integration of the group, there is more hierarchy, formal structures and processes.

Some respondents argue that the firm could be more proactive by following its chosen niche strategy. Board member: 'We need to have a much better focus on being different. That is entrepreneurship. You identify a problem and then you create a chemical solution to that problem. Then you go out and convince people that what they have taken for granted for many years doesn't have to be like that forever. You have a new and much better idea. This is difficult, but this is really entrepreneurship.'

The same board member claims that the niche strategy means a much clearer focus on some core products: 'We have a good strategy, but still we continue to sell products more widely. We say that we should be a proactive growth firm, become bigger and bigger, but we have not grown the last years. Instead, we have become smaller and smaller. In practice, there has been great pressure here to increase the sales figure without looking so much at the bottom line. We really need to make a radical change in behavior and actually follow the strategy that we have.'

The CEO argues that Chem Tech takes new technical initiatives ahead of competitors: 'That is the creativity, but when it comes to radically make a change from a business standpoint, no, certainly not. This is the next step to work on. Today we manufacture and sell. We could say: why do we need to produce? We could just sell our brain and become consultants. At least we could do this by creating another company next to Chem Tech. But it is difficult to get the support from the owners to do this.'

Mark Wallin adds: 'We are often first, but to be honest there has not been much revolutionary news in our industry lately.'

Paul Wallin says that the firm's relative smallness and flexibility normally make it faster than competitors. Chem Tech has a tradition of introducing new ideas first in the market. To make sure this continues employees are expected to familiarize themselves with the operations of the customers in order to more easily see new business opportunities. In support of this, Chem Tech plans to increase employee/customer interaction to develop a deeper understanding of customer needs.

A top manager describes Chem Tech as a potentially very proactive firm but the potential is not fully realized because of uncertainty regarding taking initiatives. He connects this with the poor self-confidence that he thinks characterizes the organization after several years of low profitability and lack of growth: 'Perhaps one year of good results is enough, and then we'll have many initiatives, because I think that most people working here feel the expectations to actually take initiatives.'

5.5 DISCUSSION

In this chapter we attempt to increase understanding of how EO is transformed by transgenerational processes from a culture perspective. We describe and analyse the role of owner-centric culture as a familiness resource across generations. In particular, we focus on the autonomy and proactiveness dimensions. By introducing the concept of owner-centric culture, we move beyond the conventional life cycle stage model and show how founder-centric cultures can remain or return in later generational stages of family firms. We propose that owner-centric culture is a more appropriate term in family business studies.

The Chem Tech case illustrates a typical founder-centric culture, while the Novo Footwear case shows how similar cultural patterns may form around a dominant family owner-manager in a much later generational stage. Thus our first proposition holds, namely, that the concept of a founder-centric culture can be extended to a more generic concept of owner-centric culture in family businesses. In the remaining discussion we further analyse the dynamics of owner-centric cultures in relation to autonomy and proactiveness.

At Novo Footwear new initiatives are part of the owner-centric culture. Autonomy seems to exist to a high degree, especially when focusing on the activities of the owner-manager, Greg Arbor. He scores very high on autonomy, which implies both that autonomy is a strong dimension of owner-centric culture and that autonomy is limited for other managers. Perceived autonomy, however, seems to be higher for employees compared to family members. The mental freedom (Schumpeter, 1934) to propose ideas and to 'think new' certainly exists. The distinct owner-centric culture, with Greg's need to be in total control, also has, however, a hampering effect, since putting new ideas into practice does not fully exist for other managers, including Greg's sons. Every new initiative must be approved by Greg. When Dennis and Matthew try to exert autonomy such as introducing a new arena for product development, Greg sees it as a breach of the company culture. According to him, the culture advocates openness and transparency and he is afraid of too many formal meeting places from which people may feel excluded. The role of autonomy is full of contradictions in Novo Footwear.

Our interpretation is that the next generation, Matthew and Dennis, has the mental state for proactiveness but not enough opportunity. The freedom to be proactive is clearly expressed and encouraged and, thus, supported by the owner-centric culture. Although Matthew is in charge of business development and Dennis is in charge of innovation and design, Greg still wants to have the last word when deciding which path to pursue, how to do it, and how much time and money is at hand. The owner-centric culture of Novo Footwear has a hampering effect on the systemization of pursuing new opportunities. It is also important to stress that Schumpeter's notion of mental freedom suggests flexible organizational structures in order for entrepreneurship to bloom, which Greg favors. In Novo Footwear the owner-manager has created a strong owner-centric culture that both hampers and supports EO across generations. This supports our second proposition that a strong owner-centric culture may hamper as well as support autonomy and proactiveness in the organization, and our third proposition that mental freedom in owner-centric cultures fosters autonomy and proactiveness.

At Chem Tech autonomy has been nurtured in the culture for many years, but it is unclear to what extent managers and other employees are presently empowered to work autonomously on new projects. Within the owner-family the extent to which the next generation has the freedom to make decisions on long-term issues also is questionable. Chem Tech has an owner-centric culture, where the founder, Paul Wallin, has been the driver of entrepreneurship. But he now seems to both foster and constrain further entrepreneurial development, which is in line with our first proposition. Sustained entrepreneurship in Chem Tech represents becoming less dependent on Paul Wallin, who is still a valuable resource. It seems that the autonomy needed for proactiveness is restricted in this strong owner-centric culture. A cultural change may be needed where top managers, other workers and the next generation of family members are given the freedom to develop the firm proactively. It is interesting to note that the founder still controls a clear majority of ownership voting rights. Our interpretation of the Chem Tech case supports our third proposition, namely, that mental freedom and ability to break free of routine is necessary in owner-centric cultures in order to foster autonomy and proactiveness.

On the basis of both cases, we argue that proactiveness has a relationship to autonomy in so far as that a high degree of autonomy would logically imply a high degree of proactiveness. In Novo Footwear, however, we see that a high degree of proactiveness does not come naturally from a high degree of autonomy. Rather, a high degree of proactiveness does not suffer from a low degree of autonomy, at least not in the short run. But the implications for the transgenerational potential to be entrepreneurial may be more problematic. If the next generation, Matthew and Dennis, are not given enough autonomy (that is, in making their own decisions regarding important investments and bold ventures), it may hamper their future ability to foster EO in the firm. We find a similar dynamic in the Chem Tech case where the children see a 'let-go' problem, as their father

(Paul) does not want to hand over control to them. Simultaneously, however, Paul talks about a 'take-over' problem, as he senses that the next generation does not yet want to assume leadership. In conclusion, our fourth proposition is not given full support, that is, that a low degree of autonomy is followed by a low degree of proactiveness, but a low degree of autonomy seems to hamper EO in the long run.

5.6 IMPLICATIONS

In these firms there are two individuals (Greg and Paul), both with a strong need of control and difficulty handing over responsibility to the next generation of family owners, employees and top managers in the firm. This is in line with previous research on founder-centric cultures (Kelly et al, 2000; Kets de Vries, 1993; Schein, 1983). These owners, however, are very capable of managing flexible structures and have a strong industrial focus that fosters proactiveness in the long run, probably over generations (cf. Brundin et al., 2008). One of these individuals (Greg) needs to prove himself right in pursuing new ideas, which favors mental freedom (cf. Schumpeter, 1934). Viewed this way, an owner-centric culture can be interpreted as hampering, and thus representing an f− on an individual level for members of the future generation, but also supportive, and thus representing an f+ on an organizational level. In both cases the owners are considered inflexible and dominating by their children, resulting in repressed feelings and frustration, leading to a desire, not without fear, to break loose. Their fathers encourage the recognition and pursuit of new opportunities, which benefits the organization. This finding extends the literature on familiness (Habbershon and Williams, 1999; Habbershon et al., 2003) by adding that what is a positive or negative family influence on resources may vary with analysis.

This leads us to the conclusion that proactiveness on the organizational level does not necessarily follow from autonomy on the individual level. For entrepreneurial practices to be successful over generations, though, it seems to be important in owner-centric cultures for people and groups to be able to find a balance between space and place. The transformation of EO by transgenerational processes means finding the equilibrium between letting go and letting in. Such a process is complicated by the complex relationships among family members active in the same business. The retirement and 'edifice complex' (Kets de Vries, 2003), that is, the wish to leave a legacy, may also play a role. In Novo Footwear Dennis and Matthew can be characterized as proactive in their desire for the autonomy not offered by their father. In Chem Tech the father urges his children to exert the autonomy needed to secure a transgenerational entrepreneurial culture, which his children hesitate to do.

Owner-centric cultures seem to create a duality of forces, where culture and future EO are 'opposing forces that must be balanced' (Janssens and Steyaert, 1999, p.122). The challenge is to treat them not as opposing, but as complementary (Achtenhagen and Melin, 2003), including the owner-centric culture that does not directly foster EO but fosters familiness overall. Over time, a strong culture includes defense mechanisms and inertia regarding changing central aspects of the culture. As the owner-centric culture by definition is strongly related to an individual, it is inherently difficult to transfer to the next generation of owners and employees with their own cultural orientations. When the owner-centric culture includes high degrees of autonomy and proactiveness, that is, shows a strong EO, there is momentum for the next generation to be empowered in favor of EO. The 'disciplined creativity' spoken of by Paul Wallin at Chem Tech may adequately describe what should be happening. This, however, is easier said then done, since an owner-centric culture is created by a strong individual and may be traced back to a founder-centric culture where the present owner is a product of company history and its values (cf. Garcia-Alvarez et al., 2002).

A transgenerational entrepreneurial potential does not necessarily imply a need for a next-generation entrepreneur. It might mean that the next generation should be capable of creating a culture that is characterized as entrepreneurial. Further, the dimensions of EO may constitute an f+ and f−, respectively, in different generations and eras. Our findings thus link to the research of Zellweger et al. (2009) on variance of the level of EO across generations. In their view family businesses that are successful across generations know how to manage and adapt, that is, to transform their EO over time. In this chapter we show how the two dimensions of autonomy and proactiveness may work in an owner-centric culture.

Our findings have clear implications for the literature on EO (for example, Lumpkin and Dess, 1996; Lyon et al., 2000) and provide a deeper understanding of proactiveness and autonomy in the context of family businesses. They also reveal how insights from the concept of culture can extend the richness of EO as a theoretical perspective. More specifically, we show that from a cultural perspective there is not a linear transfer of EO, but rather a complex translation and transformation in the transgenerational process of the assumptions, norms and values that provide autonomy and proactiveness. This process also includes a complex interplay among the individual levels of family members, managers, employees and the organizational level of the family business.

Our research provides lessons for practitioners working in family businesses. Owners and managers from different generations who want their family businesses to stay entrepreneurial over time need to pay close attention to culture. Although it is not possible to manage cultures in the traditional sense of control, it is possible to influence them by reflecting on behaviors, norms and incentives. To create an entrepreneurial culture that supports innovation and renewal in established family businesses means to create autonomy for family members and non-family members alike to seize and act upon opportunities. Allowing for autonomy increases the chance for proactiveness that can maintain and sustain competitive advantage. Members of the owning family, especially the senior generation, need to be aware of how important their words and behavior are to the likelihood that others act entrepreneurially and contribute to the growth of the business.

5.7   CONCLUSION

By focusing on autonomy and proactiveness, we attempted to illustrate and discuss the role of owner-centric culture as a key element for EO to travel over generations. As a result, we make the following contributions. We propose a more generic concept for a founder-centric culture by introducing the construct of owner-centric culture that is independent of the business life cycle and the business family generation. Further, taking a cultural perspective, we show how autonomy and proactiveness, as important elements of EO, can both hamper and foster transgenerational entrepreneurship practices, and that there is a need to balance the amount and type of mental freedom. Finally, we show that a low degree of autonomy on the individual level does not necessarily constrain proactiveness on the organizational level.

We raise some new questions for future research. Generally, an owner-centric culture is a very strong force in the organization, as is the will to survive as a prosperous family firm. If a balancing point cannot be found, which force is the stronger – the culture itself or the urge to make EO a bridge to future generations? A more specific question for further exploration is whether a high degree of autonomy on the individual level can be followed by a low degree of proactiveness on the organizational level. We also encourage future researchers to address more explicitly the observation that there is often more than one culture in an organization (Martin, 2002), and often a distinct family culture as well. It would indeed be interesting to further examine the dialectics between family culture and organizational culture and their impacts on transgenerational entrepreneurship in family businesses.

NOTE

1. In Sweden employees are entitled to be represented on the boards of firms with more than 25 employees.

REFERENCES

Achtenhagen, L. and L. Melin (2003), 'Managing the homogeneity-heterogeneity duality', in A.M. Pettigrew, R. Whittington, L. Melin, C. Sánchez-Runde, F.A.J. Van den Bosch, W. Ruigrok and T. Numagami (eds), *Innovative Forms of Organizing: International Perspectives*, London: Sage, pp. 301–27.

Brundin, E., E. Florin-Samuelsson and L. Melin (2008), 'The family ownership logic – core characteristics of family-controlled businesses', Working paper no. 1654-8612, 2008:1, Jönköping International Business School, Jönköping, Sweden.

Dyer, W.G. Jr (1986), *Cultural Change in Family Firms: Understanding and Managing Business and Family Transition*, San Francisco, CA: Jossey-Bass.

Garcia-Alvarez, E., J. Lopez-Sintas and P. Saldana Gonzalvo (2002), 'Socialization patterns of successors in first- to second-generation family businesses', *Family Business Review*, **15**(3), 189–203.

Gartner, W.B. (1988), '"Who is an entrepreneur?" is the wrong question', *American Journal of Small Business*, **12**(4), 11–32.

Gersick, K.E., J.A. Davis, M. McCollom Hampton and I. Lansberg (1997), *Generation to Generation – Life Cycles of the Family Business*, Boston, MA: Harvard Business School Press.

Gómez-Mejía, L.R., M. Nunez-Nickel and I. Gutierrez (2001), 'The role of family ties in agency contracts', *Academy of Management Journal*, **44**, 81–95.

Greiner, L.E. (1972), 'Evolution and revolution as organizations grow', *Harvard Business Review*, **50**, 37–46.

Habbershon, T.G. and J. Pistrui (2002), 'Enterprising families domain: family-influenced ownership groups in pursuit of transgenerational wealth', *Family Business Review*, **15**(3), 223–37.

Habbershon, T.G. and M.L. Williams (1999), 'A resource-based framework for assessing the strategic advantages of family firms', *Family Business Review*, **12**(1), 1–26.

Habbershon, T., M.L. Williams and I.C. MacMillan (2003), 'A unified systems perspective of family firm performance', *Journal of Business Venturing*, **18**, 451–65.

Hall, A. (2003), 'Strategizing in the context of genuine relations', Doctoral dissertation, Jönköping International Business School, Jönköping, Sweden.

Hall, A., L. Melin and M. Nordqvist (2001), 'Entrepreneurship as radical change in family business: exploring the role of cultural patterns', *Family Business Review*, **14**(3), 193–208.

Hoy, F. (2006), 'The complicating factor of life cycles in corporate venturing', *Entrepreneurship Theory and Practice*, **30**(6), 831–6.

Janssens, M. and C. Steyaert (1999), 'The world in two and a third way out? The concept of duality in organization theory and practice', *Scandinavian Journal of Management*, **15**(2), 121–39.

Kelly, L.M., N. Athanassiou and W.F. Crittenden (2000), 'Founder centrality and strategic behavior in the family-owned firm', *Entrepreneurship Theory and Practice*, **25**(2), 27–42.

Kets de Vries, M.F.R. (1993), 'The dynamics of family controlled firms: the good and the bad news', *Organisational Dynamics*, **21**(3), 59–71.

Kets de Vries, M.F.R. (2003), 'The retirement syndrome: the psychology of letting go', *European Management Journal*, **21**(6), 707–16.

Lumpkin, G.T. and G.G. Dess (1996), 'Clarifying the entrepreneurial orientation construction and linking it to performance', *Academy of Management Review*, **21**(1), 135–72.

Lyon, D.W., G.T. Lumpkin and G.G. Dess (2000), 'Enhancing entrepreneurial orientation research: operationalizing and measuring a key strategic decision making process', *Journal of Management*, **26**(5), 1055–85.

Martin, J. (2002), *Organizational Culture: Mapping the Terrain*, Thousand Oaks, CA: Sage.

Martin, W.L. and G.T. Lumpkin (2003), 'From entrepreneurial orientation to "family orientation": generational differences in the management of family businesses', Paper presented at the 22nd Babson College Entrepreneurship Research Conference, Babson College, Wellesley, Massachusetts.

Melin, L. and M. Alvesson (1989), 'Strategic change and entrepreneurship', Working paper, University of Linköping, Sweden.

Nordqvist, M., T.G. Habbershon and L. Melin (2008), 'Transgenerational entrepreneurship: exploring entrepreneurial orientation in family firms', in H. Landström, D. Smallbone, H. Crijns and E. Laveren (eds), *Entrepreneurship, Sustainable Growth and Performance: Frontiers in European Entrepreneurship Research*, Cheltenham, UK and Northampton, MA, USA: Edward Elgar Publishing, pp. 93–116.

Schein, E.H. (1983), 'The role of the founder in creating organizational culture', *Organizational Dynamics*, **5**(1), 13–28.

Schumpeter, J.A. (1934), *The Theory of Economic Development*. Cambridge, MA: Harvard University Press.

Zahra, S.A., J.C. Hayton and C. Salvato (2004), 'Entrepreneurship in family vs. non-family firms: a resource based analysis of the effect of organizational culture', *Entrepreneurship Theory and Practice*, **28**(4), 363–81.

Zellweger, T., C. Mühlebach and P. Sieger (2009), 'How much and what kind of entrepreneurship is needed for family business continuity?' Chapter 8 of this book.

6. Propelled into the future: managing family firm entrepreneurial growth despite generational breakthroughs within family life stage

Alain Bloch, Alexandra Joseph and Michel Santi

6.1 INTRODUCTION

Family businesses have a unique opportunity to mix family expectations and business constraints. Existing literature focuses on cases where succession is (or should be) planned and organized across generations; that is, where family and firm life stages are smoothly linked. In our two case studies the founder (that is, father) dies at a young age, leaving unprepared, and quite young, successors. The two families followed similar stages in perpetuating the father's legacy. Surprisingly, this loss has increased entrepreneurial performance; more surprisingly, both families believe that they are now in a better position than when founders and successors must deal directly with each other. Our goal is to understand the impact of family generational breakthroughs on entrepreneurial growth of the family firm.

If maintaining a transgenerational family firm is not an easy task, it is even more challenging to maintain entrepreneurship across family generations. Habbershon and Pistrui (2002) use 'enterprising families' to describe business families that strive for transgenerational entrepreneurship and long-term wealth creation through new ventures, innovation and strategic renewal. In this context, analysis shifts from the conventional firm-level unit to that of the family. Yet, according to Martin and Lumpkin (2003), as later generations are involved in the management of family businesses, entrepreneurial orientation (EO), representing the materialization and support of this transgenerational entrepreneurship at the firm level, generally decreases, while family orientation, as involvement and inheritance issues become more important, naturally increases.

In this chapter we show that family life stage and entrepreneurial development of family businesses are closely linked through both familiness (Habbershon and Williams, 1999) and EO (Lumpkin and Dess, 1996, p. 135), concepts which will be discussed later.

Our insights are based on two French case studies: the Dick family (owners of the VIRBAC company) and the Leitzgen family (owners of the SALM company). In both families the sudden and early deaths of the father left the children unprepared for leadership. Nevertheless, they strove to keep ownership of the company within the family, regardless of the costs, and tried to develop the business successfully. We note that entrepreneurial development followed a similar path and that the two families passed through an identical succession of steps within their life stage. Of interest is that in both cases firm life stage does not follow family life stage. Although both families faced a breakout in the succession process, both maintained family control of the firm without a family member necessarily occupying a management position and both maintained entrepreneurial growth.

Following a similar pattern, both families and companies experienced the same three phases within their life stage:

1. Initial development. Both companies adopted a founder-centric system, which allowed the spread of a strong entrepreneurial culture. Our analysis shows that EO is a suitable concept to better understand this phase.
2. Professionalization. Both founders/fathers die at an early age, leaving very young and inexperienced successors. For roughly a decade, both companies are run by professional managers who implement the founder's strategic vision. Family influenced resources and capabilities, as part of familiness, are of crucial importance in this phase.
3. Refocusing on entrepreneurship. Successors are now ready to lead the family business. In both cases there is an expressed need to become more entrepreneurial. Again the concept of familiness will play a prominent role.

After a brief presentation of the two families and companies we analyse facts and data in detail. We collected data following STEP methodology: interviews of family members (involved in the firm or not) and non-family managers of board members.

The Dicks and VIRBAC

In 1968 Dr Pierre-Richard Dick founded VIRBAC as a veterinarian office. The company developed rapidly and today is the eighth largest animal health laboratory in the world, and the only independent firm among those eight.

In 1992 Dr Dick dies suddenly. The family decides to keep VIRBAC; however none of the children feel ready to assume their father's position. VIRBAC enters a 12-year phase of professionalization, with external professional management and family control.

Today VIRBAC is a multinational firm with consolidated revenues in 2007 of 438.5 million euros and 2700 employees. VIRBAC has affiliates in more than 100 countries, with 63 percent of its staff posted internationally. Sixty-one percent of turnover is from the market of companion animals and 35.7 percent is from the food-producing animals market. VIRBAC maintains 4000 products and follows a niche strategy. It is a public company, listed on the Euronext Paris stock market since 1985; it is based in Carros, near Nice. (See Appendix 6.1 for a comprehensive description of VIRBAC's main development milestones.)

The Leitzgens and SALM

In 1967 the German business family, Schmidt, opened a French subsidiary: Société ALsacienne de Meubles (SALM). Antonia (the founder's daughter) and her husband, Karl Leitzgen, arrived in Liepvre, France, to operate a factory. Soon the company focused on the production of kitchen furniture and achieved rapid market growth on the French market. SALM followed a dual strategy of both production development (acquisition of the historical German site of Türkismühle and construction of the Selestat site) and branding policy (as of 1985).

The company underwent its first succession in 1995 upon the death of Karl Leitzgen. At that time, his wife, Antonia, decided to become the CEO. From then on she shared management responsibilities with an experienced and talented COO, Jean-Marie Schwab. Antonia actively prepared her daughters, Anne and Caroline, to take over the company. In December 2006 Anne Leitzgen, at the age of 33, was appointed the new CEO.

In 2006 SALM's total sales were 263 million euros, with 1200 employees. Twenty percent of its turnover is outside France, mainly through three foreign affiliates. It operates under two main brand names: Cuisines Schmidt and Cuisinella. Cuisines Schmidt is the French leader in terms of kitchen and bathroom furniture, has more than 450 exclusive distribution centers throughout Europe, and is known for both personalization of its products (in terms of materials, colors, measurement) and quality. Cuisinella is the economy brand of the company.

6.2 INITIAL DEVELOPMENT

Both companies followed a similar entrepreneurial path and experienced the same life stage: rapid growth after foundation and then a difficult second-generation succession due to the unexpected and untimely death of the founding entrepreneur, who had established a strong EO culture within the company.

Lumpkin and Dess (1996) claim that EO reflects 'the organizational processes, methods and styles that firms use to act entrepreneurially'; thus EO defines strategy-making processes and practices of firms that are engaged in entrepreneurial activities (Lumpkin and Dess, 2001). Building on Miller (1983), this established framework has attracted many scholars from the field of corporate entrepreneurship. Nordqvist et al. (2008), however, observe that family firms represent an organizational context that has interesting and specific characteristics that impact EO. Also Hall et al. (2001) and Zahra et al. (2004) specifically demonstrate that culture in family firms potentially promotes and sustains entrepreneurial activities. Our two cases strongly support this point.

We use the five dimensions of the EO construct in our case analyses:

- Proactiveness refers to how a firm takes strategic initiatives by anticipating and pursuing new opportunities. Lumpkin and Dess (1996, p. 136) define proactiveness as 'acting in anticipation of future problems, needs of changes'.
- Stated formally, risk taking refers to 'the degree to which managers are willing to make large and risky resource commitments – i.e., those which have a reasonable chance of costly failures' (Miller and Friesen, 1978, p. 923). Risk-taking firms show a tendency to 'take bold actions such as venturing into unknown new markets' (Lumpkin and Dess, 2001, p. 431).
- Innovativeness refers to 'a firm's tendency to engage in and support new ideas, novelty, experimentation, and creative processes that may result in new products, services, or technological processes' (Lumpkin and Dess, 1996, p. 142).
- Autonomy is the freedom granted to individuals inside an organization to be creative, to innovate and to change current practices.
- Competitive aggressiveness refers to 'a firm's propensity to directly and intensively challenge its competitors to achieve entry or improve

position, that is, to outperform industry rivals in the market place' (Lumpkin and Dess, 1996, p. 148).

Our case analyses give strong support to the EO concept as a dimension that links family and business life stage and development.

Facts and Data from our Two Cases

VIRBAC's early years (1968–92)

Pierre-Richard Dick (1936–92) founded VIRBAC in 1968 together with another veterinarian, Max Rombi. Between the ages of 3 and 17, he was brought up by his mother in Africa. He studied to become a veterinarian and also earned a Master's degree in economics. His initial, innovative idea was to establish a veterinary office within the Cap 3000 mall, near Nice. Malls were new entities at that time, and locating a veterinary office within a mall was not only unusual, but also forbidden by veterinary office business regulations. As a solution, Dr Dick established an entrance from the outside, not through, the mall. After roughly two successful years the office was sold and both entrepreneurs focused on the veterinarian pharmaceutical laboratory business. To Dr Dick the office was merely a job, whereas the laboratory was 'the mission'.

VIRBAC (an acronym of VIRology and BACteriology) was innovative in the marketing of veterinarian pharmaceutical products by specializing in companion animals, thus distinguishing itself from the large veterinarian pharmaceutical companies that targeted food-producing animals. Today VIRBAC focuses on all aspects of companion animals' needs (food, hygiene, vaccines), along with a wide range of products for food-producing animals, some 4000 products in all.

At the end of the 1970s Dr Dick and Max Rombi separated in order to prepare for the succession of their children. Dr Dick kept VIRBAC and Max Rombi created a subsidiary, ARKOVET, where he developed ARKOPHARMA, specializing in phytotherapy and nutrition therapy. Both companies were headquartered in Carros, an industrial area near Nice.

In 1980 Dr Dick diversified his business into a larger, growing market and a more 'noble' activity, the human pharmaceutical industry,with the creation of PANMEDICA. In 1992 this company established PANPHARMA (focusing on the aseptic filling of powders for injection and the manufacturing of parenteral liquid forms), ARDEVAL (specializing in the commercialization of phytotherapeutical products) and a research center.

The international development of VIRBAC began in 1983 with the opening of VIRBAC Egypt and VIRBAC Spain. Within the following decade subsidiaries were opened in the USA (1984), Italy, Brazil, Australia and Germany (1987), Mexico (1988), Poland and Japan (1992), and Belgium (1994). This ever-growing internationalization was supported by internal growth (opening of subsidiaries), acquisitions and a mix of these two modes.

In 1987 VIRBAC acquired ALLERDEN, a US dermatological laboratory. In 1988 IMPERIAL DOG (a German company specializing in the production and commercialization of pet food), UVA (a French company specializing in the production and commercialization of veterinary products) and a Mexican laboratory (later VIRBAC Mexico) were acquired. That same year, VIRBAC Australia bought ARNOLDS, a company specializing in products for horses, and VIRBAC US acquired the assets of Carson Chemicals, an American company. VIRBAC US also created FRANCODEX Inc., to develop pet shops, while VIRBAC Netherlands was created through the acquisition of ANIMED BV.

In 1991 the French companies SOCIETE LABORATOIRES VIGUIE (specializing in companion birds), THALGO SA (specializing in cosmetology) and LABORATOIRES FRERE SA (specializing in beauty care products) were acquired.

In 1992 Dr Dick died in a tragic accident. He leaves behind a solid company as well as an unprepared young family: Marie-Hélène (27 years old), a veterinarian with a HEC MBA, who had worked in PANPHARMA for two years, in charge of marketing; and Jean-Pierre (26 years old), who was working in VIRBAC UK, also a veterinarian with a HEC MBA.

SALM's early years (1967–95)

In 1934 at the age of 27, Hubert Schmidt founded a home-building company in Türkismühle (Saarland, Germany). In 1946, after four years in the German navy and confinement in a British POW camp, he orients production toward furniture, specifically kitchen furniture. At that time (post World War II), the need for equipment is huge. The Schmidt Company prospers in a location under French occupation.

In 1955 the people of Saarland vote in favor of reattachment to Germany. The firm is willing to continue exporting to France; however it faces heavy customs taxes (15 percent). The solution, therefore, is to establish a factory in France.

Hubert Schmidt acquires a factory specializing in material tailing, located in Liepvre, in the eastern part of France (Moselle), close to Türkismühle. In 1967 Antonia, Hubert's daughter, and her husband, Karl, arrive in Liepvre. We consider this year as the establishment of

SALM, as its activity, business model and development were completely different and independent from the Schmidt Company. So different and successful that, some years later, SALM bought back what was supposed to be its German mother company!

Antonia grew up around the family kitchen business. After studying business, she joined the family business and took charge of the sales department. She married Karl Leitzgen, an engineer, who was the son of a furniture businessman from Moselle. Because Hubert Schmidt wanted his three daughters to remain in the family business, he offered his son-in-law the chance to run the Liepvre factory.

In 1967 the couple arrives in Liepvre and Karl takes charge of the development of the company. Antonia assumes public relations responsibilities, which prove to be key to the development of company brands and exclusive distribution centers. Karl and Antonia live in a house just in front of the plant, thus creating a close proximity between the Leitzgens and their employees. Antonia is close to the employees; she is invited to their weddings, baptisms and so on. She is considered both the 'mother' of the Cuisines Schmidt family of employees and the 'boss' of the family business, roles that she takes very seriously.

Cuisines Schmidt is a rapidly expanding company. In 1967 the company had a turnover of 1 million euros and employed 100 people. In 1976 the company experienced its first strategic move: the range of kitchen furniture is completed by the production of kitchen elements. The Liepvre factory grows from 6000 to 32000 m². In 1983 the company becomes SALM (Société Alsacienne de Meubles); turnover reaches 19 million euros, with 270 employees.

In 1985 SALM launches exclusive distributors under the brand names of Promocuisines, Ecocuisines and Gocuisines. As a consequence of this strategic choice, which leads to strong sales, a new plant is opened in 1987 in Selestat, close to Liepvre.

In 1988 the production center of Türkismühle, Germany, is bought. At that time the German plant was run by Antonia's sister. This decision to buy back the German 'nest' generates tensions within the Schmidt family.

In 1989 Cuisines Schmidt becomes 'the' company brand; in a few months 200 exclusive shops are opened. Cuisinella is launched in 1992, positioned as the 'economy' brand for kitchen furniture within SALM'S portfolio. The same year, Cuisines Schmidt began developing bathroom furniture.

In 1995 SALM experiences its first crisis, as Karl Leitzgen dies suddenly. At that time SALM's turnover is 94 million euros, with 732 employees.

Our Analysis

Similarities between our two cases are striking. Each company was founded and developed by a charismatic individual who implemented a very strong EO in the company culture.

VIRBAC has developed as, and is known for having, a 'cowboy' spirit and sees itself as 'the clever warrior or the industry's maverick'.

This competitive and cutting-edge behavior stems from the founding of the first VIRBAC veterinarian office, as well as the market segment (companion animals), which VIRBAC is the only animal health company to target. Taking risks is common in VIRBAC's history: international development and the launch of Leucogen (the first antiretroviral vaccine based on genetic engineering) in 1988 testify to this EO dimension. This requires a high level of autonomy for employees, coupled with and reinforced by a 'right to failure', as illustrated by one of Dr Dick's mottos: 'don't fail twice for the same reasons'. In order to become a leader in the companion animal market, VIRBAC chose to dedicate itself to its customers, namely, veterinarians, and oriented its R&D toward developing 'intelligent products'. Innovation, which was, and still is, based mainly on customers' expectations, is key and has been decentralized to local actors from the beginning. In Japan, for example, the VIRBAC subsidiary manager, who had a background in pet food, proposed creating a new distribution system to deliver products directly to end-customers, thus avoiding the veterinarian as a go-between and opening new opportunities. Even though the proposition was considered highly risky, it was accepted and tested.

SALM developed a branding strategy as early as 1985. 'Karl Leitzgen had this visionary idea: a branding strategy. This was quite a challenge back then but it has proven to be the right choice' (JM Schwab).

This innovative and proactive branding strategy was possible and affordable for SALM only through an exclusive distribution channel. SALM clients are their distributors: the independent franchises of Cuisines Schmidt and Cuisinella. This gives SALM a better balance of power when dealing with its distribution system and allows it to be a cost-effective producer by centralizing production, capitalizing on size and responding quickly to market changes. This branding policy and the development of an exclusive network of branded shops led to the visionary idea of customizing offerings to the personal demands and tastes of clients, thanks to the existence of kitchen showrooms, where customers could personalize their kitchen with the technical help of a sole adviser. 'Karl Leitzgen was a true entrepreneur. In the eighties he launched a kit production; it failed. He, however, kept in his mind this idea which became successful 15 years later. Another example is the branding strategy. In the nineties SALM was in a weak financial situation. He, however, took the risk to launch these brands with heavy investments. He just said "OK let's go"' (JM Schwab).

In order to implement risk-taking behavior, Karl Leitzgen fostered a high degree of autonomy by developing loyalty and trust: 'I will not leave those who trusted us. I trust you and the Executive Board' (Antonia Leitzgen). 'I had a tremendous relationship with Karl Leitzgen. There was a true trusting climate' (JM Schwab).

By choosing customization, SALM relied heavily on innovation in terms of sales and production. Customized sales could be managed only if the production process changed and adapted. SALM has controlled its production process by internally redesigning and developing its production sites (three at present) and implementing an adapted and original management value chain system composed of three phases: conception, production and distribution.

This analysis proves that in the beginning the family and family business life cycles were fully linked thanks to the high level of EO the founder introduced. VIRBAC relies mostly on competitive aggressiveness based on product innovation, and SALM on proactiveness (with the branding strategy). The EO that the founders implemented within their firms is the very basis of their dramatic entrepreneurial development. But will the family business EO survive the end of this family life stage with the death of the founder? During these early years no family succession to the next generation was formally prepared; actions have, however, been taken in terms of succession taxes with the foundation of family holdings. The sudden and unexpected death of the founder caused both families and firms to face an uncertain future and a tremendous challenge. This led both families and family businesses to what we call the professionalization phase.

6.3 PROFESSIONALIZATION

The two families/companies, after the sudden death of the father/founder, faced the challenge of finding a qualified replacement. Both families remained committed to the company and to their father's legacy. Still quite young (in their teens or early twenties), the successors were forced to keep or hire a professional manager to run the company. In both cases this did not represent a dramatic strategic move and is defined as the beginning of the professionalization stage.

During the decade this stage lasts, both families developed and defined strong family values that served as the basis of their firm's strategic vision and context, values which are part of familiness. Drawn from the resource-based view, Habbershon and Williams (1999) define familiness as the unique bundle of resources held by, and particular to, family firms as a result of their unique system of interactions among the family, individual family and non-family (for example, external professionals) members, and the business itself.

The family values we describe refer to these specific and original family influenced resources and capabilities, which impact (positively or negatively) on the firm's entrepreneurial ability, potential and performance.

Facts and Data from our Two Cases

VIRBAC's professionalization phase (1992–2004)

The crucial year for VIRBAC is 1992, with the unexpected death of Dr Dick at the age of 56. At this time Dr Dick's children were in their twenties. To them, this death and its consequences were an earthquake. After a brief and painful mourning period the family unanimously decided to maintain the legacy and the family business. Keeping in mind their father's values of work, independence and consistency, Marie-Hélène Dick became CEO of PANPHARMA. Jean-Pierre, who entered VIRBAC in 1991, remained in the company, though he devoted more and more of his time to becoming a professional wind sailor. Even though the task-related aspect of the succession had been prepared by Dr Dick, an actual managerial succession was not yet in place. The Dick family relied on VIRBAC's team and the most important managers remaining in the company and taking on new responsibilities.

Eventually, the Dick family felt the need to again be actively associated with the managerial and strategic decisions which were mainly the domain of the non-family managers within VIRBAC. The VIRBAC managers, however, considered they had the legitimacy to continue managing and developing VIRBAC according to Dr Dick's will. They had known Dr Dick's children for years and still considered them as 'teenagers' who lacked sufficient management ability. No one within the Dick family appeared to be confident enough in their capacity to serve as general manager at that time, and the Dicks agreed that the best qualified people should manage the company. Therefore, in 1999, after a careful year-long search, the Dick family recruited Mr Eric Maree, an outside and experienced manager, as the new CEO, thus beginning a new era.

VIRBAC continued to follow the strategic path decided upon and implemented under Dr Dick's management.

VIRBAC improved its governance structure in the early 2000s with the reinforcement of its board and the creation of audit and compensation committees consisting of external directors who were non-family and non-VIRBAC members (for example, the CFO of ARCELOR and the former CEO of Bio Merieux).

Eric Maree, who has been and still is the leading actor in this profession-alization move, has a consulting and pharmaceutical professional back-ground. He has dedicated his services tirelessly to VIRBAC and shares strategic development decisions with the Dick family.

This professionalization stage also enabled the family to finally find a new leader. At first, Jean-Pierre Dick (the eldest son) was seen as the natural successor: he had the same veterinarian background as his father and he was already working in the company at a local management level in the UK. After 1992 he actively took part in decisions. However, after a few unsuccessful years, he decided to dedicate most of his time to becoming a world-renowned professional sailor, which he did with the full support of the rest of the family. His position in VIRBAC does not involve executive management; he communicates with clients, the veterinarians who are his peers and for whom his sports image solidifies their relationship.

Only recently did Marie-Hélène (second daughter, elder to Jean-Pierre) accept a leading position within VIRBAC and in the family. Not only did she take charge of PANMEDICA right after her father's death and assumed the presidency of the VIRBAC Board, she also supported and encouraged her siblings in developing their own risky projects. Recently, she replaced her mother as head of the board of Investec and she keeps a very close link with VIRBAC management (she hired Eric Maree).

One decision taken by the family during this professionalization stage was to institutionalize the founder's values. Dr Dick, a true entrepreneur and visionary, embedded profound values within his family, which his family successors did their best to embed as VIRBAC's values and culture. This family culture and these values can be summarized as follows:

- Work. 'Only work pays.' This value could also be seen as consist-ency. Only by working hard on a project, spending time and energy, will you reach your objective. As Jean-Pierre's nephew said, 'I want to be a Dick because a Dick never gives up.'
- Challenge spirit or need of achievement. Always have a difficult to reach goal and do everything possible to attain it. Effort becomes not only necessary, but a true pleasure.
- Excellence. This differs slightly from ambition in that it relies on par-ticipation and the objective to be among the best. The best example of this would be the participation of Jean-Pierre Dick (sponsored by VIRBAC) in the Vendée Globe Race. He demonstrated exceptional individual physical and organizational capabilities, even though he competed with more experienced sailors. In five years he has won

three world sailing races out of the seven in which he competed. Jean-Pierre Dick has also been elected Veterinarian of the Year, a decision that also impacted VIRBAC's image.

- Value of money. The whole family lives frugally, with decent wages, but nothing more. They are not hedonists: 'one penny is one penny'. The pleasure resides in the challenge and the effort required, not on monetary gain.
- Scientific rationality. We saw that the laboratory was seen as a mission. Dr Dick had always given a crucial place to science and discovery, rationalized by the respect and honesty required of a scientific approach.
- Trust and loyalty. 'We learn only by sharing.' Trust is central to VIRBAC and the Dick family and is extended toward those who share the family's and company's values. Trusted individuals are given autonomy and their failures are tolerated. On the same level, loyalty is a valued aspect. Helping employees who are in difficulty is routine, as is training them to strive for promotion. Once recruited and hired, every employee is part of the 'VIRBAC family'.
- Autonomy. One of Dr Dick's sayings is commonly shared and has been repeatedly cited by different respondents: 'do extraordinary things with ordinary people'. It explains why autonomy for employees is so important within VIRBAC.

It took a long time for Dr Dick's successors to find their place in VIRBAC. They had first to accept these values and to embed them in VIRBAC as their father's legacy.

SALM: Antonia's era (1995–2006)
When Karl Leitzgen died suddenly in 1995 (at the age of 56), his daughters, Anne and Caroline, were very young and inexperienced. However Karl wished them to take over the company and assigned the task of preparing them to his trusted general manager, Jean-Marie Schwab. Antonia, Karl's wife and mother of the two girls, did not listen to the banks' advice: she decided to keep the company within the family. 'I was like in a lake: either you swim to the edge or you drown yourself' (Antonia Leitzgen). 'You stay with me or I sell the business' (Antonia Leitzgen to Jean-Marie Schwab).

During the next 11 years SALM followed the successful strategy set by Karl Leitzgen with the support of Antonia, who kept a watchful eye on the development of the firm. Being personally acquainted with almost all employees, she succeeded in keeping a familial atmosphere in the company. Caroline and Anne followed different career paths: Caroline joined the company early as a marketing manager for Germany, while Anne began her career in the advertising industry, first in Paris and then Strasbourg, close to her native region. She later joined SALM, occupying positions in sales, communications and advertising.

It took the Leitzgen family members several years to define their positions in the company. Little by little, Anne and Caroline explored different executive positions. Jean-Marie Schwab fulfilled his promise to prepare Karl's daughters to take over the business. As a result, Anne Leitzgen became SALM's CEO on 1 December 2006.

The family assessed future strategic development of the firm in light of their values, which can be summarized as: 'Head, Heart, Guts'.

- Modesty. This is a key element for the Leitzgen family. 'I don't talk about what I have or what I could have' (Antonia Leitzgen). 'We have educated our daughters in a modest way' (Antonia Leitzgen). While proud of what they have created, the family remains conscious of the hard work, past and present, necessary to continue successfully developing the company.
- Work. Nepotism is no option for the Leitzgen family. 'You will get the position you deserve' (Karl Leitzgen to Caroline). Everyone has to prove their merit to obtain and keep a position within the company. This value especially concerns the family members and is illustrated by the commitment of the two daughters when occupying different positions in the company before succeeding to executive positions.
- Family spirit and priority. Family comes first. The Leitzgen family adopted rules to support and enhance family harmony. Antonia, Anne and Caroline have learned from their experience with the Schmidt family. The Leitzgens strongly value their family spirit and intend to keep it. And SALM is part of the extended family. The position of the family house (in front of the Liepvre site) and the strong link between the Leitzgens and their employees (all personal acquaintances) proves it.

Our Analysis

In both cases we clearly see that the founder still acts as a vivid reference in terms of strategic development. Indeed, for a decade, both companies experienced solid development and growth thanks to professional managers who, on the one hand stayed loyal to the founder's strategic vision and, on the other, implemented a new and modern management system in accordance with the family's desire.

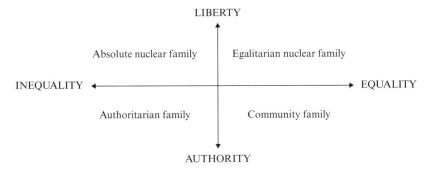

Source: Todd (1985).

Figure 6.1 Typology of family structures

Our two cases show strong similarities, which can be explained by the dramatic structural change they faced after the sudden death of the founder/father. We follow Salvato (2004), who investigated different EOs within different types of family firms. We will prove that what distinguishes our cases is their specific family structure.

The typology of family structures developed by Todd (1985) helps to explain the specificity, and its impact, of our two cases (Figure 6.1).

Todd (1985) has identified four family types.

The 'absolute nuclear family' is liberal and egalitarian. On reaching adulthood, children are expected to establish independent households and means of livelihood. There are no precise conventions of inheritance, since each generation is expected to do as it wishes with its property. In such families children are socialized to be independent and achievement oriented.

The 'egalitarian nuclear family' is characterized by the concepts of liberty and equality. While separation of households is expected, property is divided equally among the children, who are socialized to be somewhat independent and achievement oriented.

The 'authoritarian family' displays the values of inequality and authority. Ultimate authority resides within the senior generation, who anoints one child as heir and treats them different to the others. The association between the senior generation and the chosen heir is close, while other members of the junior generation are expected to establish independent households and means of livelihood.

The 'community family' is characterized by the values of equality and authority. Children live with their parents in extended families, and all next-generation members are treated equally in terms of inheritance. The senior generation leader has the ultimate authority in such families. Our two cases clearly belong to the community family type, especially so after the father's death.

At the same time, this desire to keep the family structure unmodified in spite of a tragic loss has forced both families to reassess their impact on the family business. Both have worked tremendously on their familiness and both have focused on two particular dimensions: culture and relationships.

After the father's death both families kept and reinforced their community family type by thinking of their long-term goals and defining new behavioral rules. They chose to 'organize the family' at a time when they could not 'organize the business', allowing it to be managed by non-family professionals before being returned to the control of the 'prepared' family. It is interesting to note that these two resources also impact the autonomy dimension of EO, a long-term goal.

- Family Culture. The families placed their situation in the firm into question and worked hard to establish their family values, values which are clearly influenced by the father, whose legacy plays a model role. By defining shared family values and institutionalizing them within the firm, the families try to maintain and feed the entrepreneurial development of the business. They are also willing to elaborate the context and, to some extent, the content of the family business strategic future.
- Family relationships and structure. In both cases family harmony, clearly related to community family type, is considered a must. 'I respect my brothers' and sister's expectations and choices; I always keep in mind their personal projects when it comes to take decisions' (Marie-Hélène Dick). Jean-Pierre's sailing prowess is the best proof. Marie-Hélène respected his choice. Nevertheless, she insisted that Jean-Pierre convince VIRBAC to sponsor this endeavor, thereby enhancing the entrepreneurial spirit of the firm and emphasizing links between the employees and the owning family.

Richard, the youngest brother, established his own horse breeding and training business. When each family member may satisfy his own objectives and nurture his own personal interests, familial harmony is assured; the deep-down attachment to the family business acts as an element of internal family fusion. But what will happen to that contextual familial harmony when/if the family firm is not profitable for some years? In that respect, family harmony clearly appears to be dependent on family firm wealth. However this assertion should be nuanced, since during the ten years after Dr Dick's death no dividends have been distributed, demonstrating this generation's high level of sacrifice. But the issue of correlation between family harmony and VIRBAC's wealth is particularly salient for the following generation.

We argue that if, according to Sharma and Manikutty (2005), family culture and structure induce path dependencies that explain strategic decisions (namely, divestment), then in our two cases family structure and familiness changes induce path dependencies that explain strategic decisions.

We might also argue that this stage has been necessary for the families to reach a new life stage and to better understand their business. It would be a mistake to consider this a simple replication of the father's strategic vision. On the contrary, the successors have used their father's legacy to enhance strategic objectives and to generate new entrepreneurial spirit. We argue that professionalization is an example of the link between family life stage and entrepreneurial development. Path dependency (rooted in family structure) negatively impacts this link, but also helps the family overcome their own life stage and gain more experience before forging a new entrepreneurial spirit (that is, to pursue familiness). This supports Aldrich and Kim's (2007) findings: successors take over the family business in their thirties once they have accumulated a capital inherited from their self-employed parents.

6.4   REFOCUSING ON ENTREPRENEURSHIP

As we have seen, both families and companies have taken similar steps: strong entrepreneurial development followed by professionalization, and a founder-centric culture followed by succession preparation. The two families now desire to become more entrepreneurial again. The Dicks are well into this entrepreneurial phase, whereas the Leitzgens are just beginning (Anne Leitzgen became CEO in December 2006). We again use familiness and the mediation of the autonomy dimension of EO to explain this move to a renewed entrepreneurship.

Facts and Data from our Two Cases

'We need to become entrepreneurial again' (Marie-Hélène Dick). 'If we want to remain among the European leaders, we need to be more entrepreneurial' (Anne Leitzgen).

Both families express a strong desire to focus on entrepreneurial development. They are taking similar steps, as we describe below.

VIRBAC and the Dicks

Marie-Hélène Dick is now the acknowledged leader of the Dick family and the protector of its interests within VIRBAC. She officially became chairman in 2006, upon her mother's retirement. Since then, she has developed and opened the company's governance structures to external directors (that is, non-family members and non-VIRBAC members), keeps daily contact with Eric Maree, and closely monitors implementation of plans and actions within VIRBAC. She has not, however, acted alone. Marie-Hélène and her husband, Pierre Madelpuech, are an entrepreneurial team. Pierre and Marie-Hélène met at HEC School of Management, Paris while pursuing their MBA degrees. Pierre has consistently supported Marie-Hélène in her decisions and actions involving VIRBAC and her family. He is an active member of VIRBAC's governance system and is CEO of a French mid-size company. The couple share common views on entrepreneurship, VIRBAC's strategic position and its future.

Both now wish to operate VIRBAC in a more entrepreneurial fashion. They realize that the professionalization stage was a necessary and good thing for the company as well as the family in order to rationalize management and control tools. However Pierre and Marie-Hélène, along with Eric Maree and the Executive Board, feel that it is time to take more risks and to return VIRBAC to its original highly entrepreneurial mindset. Thus, for each of the last three years, three companies have been acquired.

SALM and the Leitzgens

Anne Leitzgen became CEO of SALM in December 2006, replacing her mother, Antonia. The Leitzgens also have recreated an entrepreneurial team. The two sisters, Anne and Caroline (Caroline is in charge of international marketing), are both very active in the company in terms of management as well as strategic vision. They share a common view in that SALM is too focused on the French market. The kitchen industry is now European and is undergoing a concentration phase; therefore SALM now faces increasing competition. Their father's strategic vision has proven to be right so far, but new competition is driving new entrepreneurial developments.

Refocusing on Entrepreneurship: Our Analysis

In order to generate more entrepreneurial growth, both families have modified their familiness and, consequently, impacted their family company development. We focus on the two main dimensions that impact familiness: leadership and decision making.

Leadership issues were resolved over time. Both families understood that a new leader had to emerge from the new generation, without endangering family harmony. Both families underwent a long period of consultation with a coach in order to determine who should assume the leading role, inside and outside the family. But the family business model each chose is quite different: for the Leitzgens the leadership solution is purely familial (Anne is the CEO); for the Dicks a mixed solution has been implemented: a non-family manager (Eric Maree) controls operations and a family member (Marie-Hélène) supervises and controls strategy decisions, together with the Executive Board and the Advisory Board.

As to decision-making processes, the families followed different paths.

On the one hand, there is a centralized decision-making process for the Dicks. Family harmony, which is the principal aim of the whole family, is nevertheless difficult to maintain when decisions regarding the firm have to be made quickly. Therefore the family has built a centralized structure with a strong leadership position. It took several years for Marie-Hélène to accept this role, but it is now clear to all, including her. The trust placed in Marie-Hélène by her family has led to a delegated system concerning the family decision-making process, resulting in constant contact between Marie-Hélène (representing the family ownership) and VIRBAC executives and allowing decisions to be taken very quickly. The family reunion (occurring at least three times a year) enables the whole family to examine the decisions that have been discussed or evaluated with the governance boards and to agree on the decisions that the company and the boards will have to make.

Conversely, the Leitzgens have implemented an open, collective decision-making process. Although a leader is identified, the whole family participates in decision making. So far, there are no familial conflicts, which could be explained by the fact that the three women have all worked as executives within SALM and have a clear understanding of company operations. However, because Anne has been CEO only since December 2006, it might be premature to make conclusions about the family decision-making process, especially since Antonia Leitzgen is known for her strong character and Anne is her 'copycat' daughter.

These familiness resources naturally influence the entrepreneurial development of the family firm through an EO that profoundly impacts the autonomy dimension. As a result, our families express this dimension differently: for the Dicks the priority is trust, which leads to a right to failure; for the Leitzgens the key is respect.

'We can do extraordinary things with ordinary people' (Dr Dick). This motto of VIRBAC's has morphed into the right to failure. Although company troubles should have led to drastic reactions, at VIRBAC failures are understood and forgiven. People are a priority, and if the failure can be rationally explained, there are no negative consequences. This right to failure enhances autonomy, obviously limited by rationality and linked to the relatively loose pressure exerted by shareholders. The following example illustrates this point.

After two products were launched it was discovered that they were ineffective on dogs and cats and the products had to be recalled. Although 6 million euros were lost, there was no direct impact on the organization or on the responsible executives.

If failure is admitted, repetition of the same or a series of different failures by the same manager is not acceptable. But the reason for this acceptance of failure is the desire for managers to become innovative and autonomous, and the belief that behaving as entrepreneurs means not only risking failures, but also accepting these failures to avoid 'freezing' entrepreneurship.

Respect is a key word for the Leitzgens. Karl Leitzgen used to tell his daughters: 'Respect the coworkers that make you live'. During our interviews we were struck by the strong level of respect between members of the family. While being loyal to Karl's legacy, they have managed to build their own lives inside SALM in their own way. Antonia has attained a sense of equilibrium between developing SALM and maintaining her character. The tremendous commitment of the whole family to the company has not hindered the development of personal skills or characteristics.

SALM is also like an extended family where Antonia is the mother (many employees refer to her as such during the SALM convention) and loyalty is paramount. During our interviews we had lunch with the three family members and Jean-Marie Schwab in the company's restaurant. Each of them knew all the employees we met, whatever their position. When visiting the production site at Liepvre, we also met cheerful and respectful workers. Although this may be only anecdotal, we believe it strengthens our thesis of the importance of respect within the Leitzgen family and the family firm. Family and employees are very close, as symbolized by the family house located nearby. This symbolism is so strong that during the SALM convention, great concern was expressed about Antonia moving away from this house.

These two elements show that a change has occurred in terms of autonomy in both family firms. Following a new life stage the next generations in both cases have undergone a painstaking transgenerational entrepreneurship process. Even though we might not consider the right to failure and respect dimensions as strictly resources, they considerably enrich our understanding of the family business entrepreneurship field. Indeed, we see that EO remains a vivid, dynamic model for later generations,

whereby changes are implemented without endangering the first generation's inheritance.

6.5 CONCLUSION

Both our stories begin in 1967–68 with an extraordinary entrepreneur
who, via a very centric management system, builds and develops a strong
company. Both founding 'fathers' die abruptly within a few years of each
other (1992–95) and at the same age (56). The companies and families
are unprepared for succession; in both cases neither wife nor children feel
experienced enough to manage the family business.

The families decide that, for roughly a decade, the company will be run
by professional managers who stay loyal to the founder's strategic vision.
These managers put a new management system in place, yet maintain a
strong link with the family in order to ensure that family succession will
take place successfully.

Both families define strong family values on which their firm's strategic
vision and context are set. During this ten-year period a family leader
emerges who takes new responsibilities within the firm and expresses a
strong desire for the company to become more entrepreneurial again, following the father's model.

These two cases clearly demonstrate a strong link between family life
stage and family firm life stage in terms of entrepreneurial development,
a link that is impacted by different factors. Entrepreneurial orientation
analysis shows us how the founder develops the family business and at
the same time impacts and shapes its future. Path dependency, surprisingly, explains the professionalization stage when the family business is
run by professional managers who follow the founder's strategic vision.
Familiness explains the desire of family successors to refocus on entrepreneurial development.

Our analysis contradicts Martin and Lumpkin (2003). Here family orientation does not overwhelm EO with the arrival of the next generation. Our
explanation is rooted in family structure, following Todd's (1985) typology
and giving some support to Salvato (2004) when it comes to distinguishing
family firm types and EO. We demonstrate that community families (characterized by the values of equality and authority) suppress family orientation (where issues of involvement and inheritance arise) when considering
the future. Because the main goal for both families is to develop transgenerational potential, EO is a crucial step in that process. Our findings
also support Hall et al. (2001) and Zahra et al. (2004), for whom culture
promotes and sustains family firm entrepreneurial activities.

Table 6.1   Findings: a 3-stage process

	Phase 1: Early Days	Phase 2: Professionalization stage	Phase 3: Refocusing on Entrepreneurship
Timing	1960s to mid 1990s	Mid 1990s to mid 2000s	Today
Business challenge	Foundation and strong development within a founder-centric system	Organizational rationalization with professional, non-family leadership	Balance between family entrepreneurship and professional management
Family challenge	Creating and developing a family firm	Sustaining family harmony and building the new family culture	Choosing a family leader and maintaining family harmony
Analysis of company development	High levels of entrepreneurial orientation enable organizational growth	Familiness resources to ensure continuity and family control: ● family culture ● family relationships	Familiness resources to refocus on entrepreneurship: ● leadership ● decision-making process

Following Habbershon and Pistrui (2002) we use the family level of analysis to better understand the complex family firm context and better apprehend the evolution of EO, since family life stages directly influence business life stages.

Other important research considerations are the relationships between EO dimensions and family resources. In our two examples the autonomy dimension is more important when considering family firms. Following previous research (Hall et al., 2001; Zahra et al., 2004), we root our explanation in the culture of the family firm as a specific resource. This influence is mixed, since it stems from the complex interrelation of two systems, family and business.

Moreover, in exploring family life stage and entrepreneurial growth, we discovered a specific family development phase, that of professionalization. As family businesses frequently face the issue of external management, we recommend that future research focus on the strategic impact of professional managers (that is, non-family members) on business family development. In our two cases these professional managers strictly continued the founder's strategic vision. Nevertheless, it appears that entrepreneurial development cannot occur without the existence of a strong entrepreneurial mindset specific to the families (at least in our cases). It would be interesting to know if these professional managers were recruited based solely on their management skills to help prepare a family successor to take over the company, as in SALM. If so, then managers may not be chosen for their entrepreneurial ability or for the sake of firm growth. Entrepreneurial development, therefore, should be the sole focus of the families whose specific capabilities (for example, familiness) are relevant.

Finally, our two examples help us to understand how 'enterprising families', as defined by Habbershon and Pistrui (2002), are in a much better situation than normal families to overcome the hurdles related to the succession process. Table 6.1 summarizes our findings.

REFERENCES

Aldrich, H. and P. Kim (2007), 'A life course perspective on occupational inheritance: self-employed parents and their children', in M. Reef and M. Bloomsbury (eds), *The Sociology of Entrepreneurship*, Oxford: Elsevier JAI, pp. 33–82.

Habbershon, T.G. and J. Pistrui (2002), 'Enterprising families domain: family-influenced ownership groups in pursuit of transgenerational wealth'. *Family Business Review*, **15**(3), 223–37.

Habbershon, T.G. and M.L. Williams (1999), 'A resource-based framework for assessing the strategic advantages of family firms', *Family Business Review*, **12**(1), 1–25.

Hall, A., L. Melin and M. Nordqvist (2001), 'Entrepreneurship as radical change in family business: exploring the role of cultural patterns', *Family Business Review*, **14**(3), 193–208.

Lumpkin, G.T. and G.G. Dess (1996), 'Clarifying the entrepreneurial orientation construct and linking it to performance', *Academy of Management Review*, **21**(1), 135–72.

Lumpkin, G.T. and G.G. Dess (2001), 'Linking two dimensions of entrepreneurial orientation to firm performance: the moderating role of environment and industry life cycle', *Journal of Business Venturing*, **16**(5), 429–51.

Martin, W.L. and G.T. Lumpkin (2003), 'From entrepreneurial orientation to "family orientation": generational differences in the management of family businesses', in *Frontiers of Entrepreneurship Research, 2003*. Babson Park, MA: Babson College, pp. 309–21, available online at http://www.babson.edu/entrep/fer/BABSON2003/XII/XIIP2/XII-P2.html

Miller, D. (1983), 'The correlates of entrepreneurship in three types of firms', *Management Science*, **29**, 770–91.

Miller, D. and P. Friesen (1978), 'Archetypes of strategy formulation', *Management Science*, **24**, 921–33.

Nordqvist, M., T.G. Habbershon and L. Melin (2008), 'Transgenerational entrepreneurship: exploring entrepreneurial orientation in family firms', in H. Landström, D. Smallbone, H. Crijns and E. Laveren (eds), *Entrepreneurship, Sustainable Growth and Performance: Frontiers in European Entrepreneurship Research,* Cheltenham, UK and Northampton, MA, USA: Edward Elgar Publishing, pp. 93–116.

Salvato, C. (2004), 'Predictors of entrepreneurship in family firms', *Journal of Private Equity*, **7**(3), 68–76.

Sharma, P. and S. Manikutty (2005), 'Strategic divestments in family firms: role of family structure and community culture', *Entrepreneurship Theory and Practice*, **29**(3), 293–311.

Todd, E. (1985), *The Explanation of Ideology, Family Structures, and Social Systems*, Oxford: Basil Blackwell.

Zahra, S.A., J.C. Hayton and C. Salvato (2004), 'Entrepreneurship in family vs. non-family firms: a resource-based analysis of the effect of organizational culture', *Entrepreneurship Theory and Practice*, **28**(4), 363–81.

APPENDIX 6.1 VIRBAC MAIN DEVELOPMENT MILESTONES

Year	Event
1968	Foundation of VIRBAC
	Two associates: Dr Dick and Max Rombi
1975	New French regulation concerning access to markets
End 1970s	Separation of Dick and Rombi: Dr Dick keeps VIRBAC
1980	Creation of PANMEDICA: Panpharma and Ardeval and a research center
1983	Creation of VIRBAC Egypt and Spain
1984	Creation of VIRBAC US
1985	VIRBAC is listed on the French Stock Exchange
1987	Creation of VIRBAC in Italy, Brazil, Australia, Germany
	Acquisition of ALLERDEN in the USA
1988	Launching of Leucogen vaccine (first antiretroviral vaccine worldwide)
	Creation of VIRBAC Mexico
	Acquisition of Imperial Dog (Germany), UVA (France), Arnolds (Australia), Carson Chemicals (USA)
1991	Acquisition of French companies: Laboratoires VIGUIE, THALGO SA, Laboratoires FRERE SA
1992	Creation of VIRBAC in Poland and Japan
	Dr Dick's death, Mr Boissy (former CFO) becomes the new CEO
1994	Creation of VIRBAC in Belgium
	In France VIRBAC reunites all the different brands on the market
1999	Merger of VIRBAC US with AGRINUTRITION
	VIRBAC Corp is listed on NASDAQ
	Creation of VIRBAC South Africa through the acquisition of Logos Agvet
	Mr Maree becomes the new CEO of VIRBAC
2004	Acquisition of VIRBAC Corp.
2006	Acquisition of the first veterinarian laboratory in India (GlaxoIndia)
	VIRBAC Corp. exits NASDAQ: acquisition of the 46 percent minority shares
2007	Acquisition of Bio Solution International in Thailand

APPENDIX 6.2   SALM MAIN DEVELOPMENT MILESTONES

Year	Event
1934	Hubert Schmidt creates a company specializing in home building in Türkismühle, Germany
1946	The company starts to produce furniture
1959	First kitchen cabinets are produced
1967	Acquisition of the Liepvre factory
	Antonia and Karl Leitzgen arrive in Liepvre
1976	Kitchen elements are produced
	Liepvre factory is developed
1983	Creation of SALM (Société Alsacienne de Meubles)
1985	New distribution policy: exclusive centers (Promocuisines, Gocuisines, Ecocuisines)
1987	Construction of the Selestat plant
1988	Acquisition of the Türkismühle plant
1989	Cuisines Schmidt becomes a brand
1992	Cuisinella is launched
	Bathroom furniture for Cuisines Schmidt
1995	Karl Leitzgen dies, Antonia Leitzgen becomes CEO
1998	Creation of EMK, kit furniture
2006	Anne Leitzgen becomes CEO

7. Dealing with increasing family complexity to achieve transgenerational potential in family firms

Eugenia Bieto, Alberto Gimeno and María José Parada[1]

7.1 INTRODUCTION

Empirical research on family business performance suggests several paradoxical results worthy of discussion. Among the extensive work on the superior performance of family firms versus non-family firms (Anderson and Reeb, 2003) superior performance varies according to the generation and the family's degree of involvement in the family business (Pérez-González, 2006; Villalonga and Amit, 2006). In that sense, the family has an influence on family business performance, which seems to be positive in general terms, but can also be negative. This family influence has been termed familiness by Habbershon and Williams (1999), who define it as 'the unique bundle of resources a particular firm has because of the systems interaction between the family, its individual members, and the business' (p. 11).

Superior performance due to the familiness advantage has been partially challenged by some authors (for example, Chrisman et al., 2003), who point out the weaknesses of family businesses. Limited understanding of the different components of the familiness concept and how it affects the firm's behavior has been highlighted as a clear gap in the family business literature. Chrisman et al. (2005, p. 238) state: '[T]he organizational consequences of familiness in terms of the way decisions are made, functions are performed, and strategies and structures are set, are not known. In other words, we do not know much about what family firms look like, why they are often so successful, or why its success is often limited in terms of size and scope.'

Knowledge of how familiness evolves over time is also lacking. There is some evidence that family businesses tend to underperform over time (Gimeno et al., 2006; Villalonga and Amit, 2006), which dilutes the familiness advantage. Results of our study suggest that over time, as complexity increases, family businesses may sustain their familiness advantage by changing their family business model (Gimeno et al., 2009). To do so, they would be required to evolve from a sole owner model or a top management team (TMT) model into an entrepreneurial family team (EFT).

TMTs are composed of a limited number of managers who run the company together. In the family business TMTs are generally composed of siblings or cousins who do not choose each other, do not necessarily share the same vision, nor agree on each others' roles or equally support entrepreneurial behavior. When family members aim to manage the company as equals using a TMT model, the result may be disagreements and underperformance (Gimeno et al., 2006). The EFT is defined by a specific structuring of participation of all family members that form the owning family coalition in the business. All of them feel they belong to the family business, stress value creation over value preservation and participate in the entrepreneurial endeavor in a structured way.

The family understands that value is added not only by the family members who act entrepreneurially in the management sphere, but also by other family members who voice opinions and support the entrepreneurial activities of the company in the ownership sphere. In this model ownership roles are respected and valued as part of the familiness advantage, while owners assume the responsibility of empowering management to act entrepreneurially. Entrepreneurial behaviors are positively valued by the owners, though not all owners act as entrepreneurs. Although an EFT has no role in the beginning when the entrepreneur unifies management and ownership roles, it is needed in later stages when family complexity increases.

This chapter seeks to contribute to the family business and familiness/ RBV literature by approaching the familiness advantage dynamically, proposing an explanation of how some resources that create a familiness advantage are sustained or diluted over time. The introduction of EFTs as a way of sustaining familiness may also contribute to the growing literature on entrepreneurship in family firms (for example Dyer and Handler, 1994; Habbershon et al., 2003; Kellermanns et al., 2008). This chapter identifies some of the problems that sole owners and TMTs face when complexity increases over time. We suggest that the EFT is key to transgenerational entrepreneurship that sustains the familiness advantage over time.

First, we provide a literature review that leads to four propositions, subsequently supported with the findings of case studies and further developed in the conclusions. Next, we explain the methodology, followed by findings and discussion. We conclude with a discussion that leads to further research opportunities.

7.2 THEORETICAL FRAMEWORK

Family Complexity and Succession

Although there is growing interest in the transmission of entrepreneurial behavior in the family business, little research exists in the family business and entrepreneurship domains. Different conceptual frameworks in the management literature make possible the understanding of these complex processes.

Succession in family business traditionally has been approached as a passing of the baton from an entrepreneur (often a retiring CEO) to a successor to continue the entrepreneurial endeavor (Handler, 1990). Moreover, succession has been approached in terms of change in the top leadership of the organization (Alcorn, 1982). Attention is devoted to the successors by identifying their most important attributes (Chrisman et al., 1998), comparing their aspects in different countries (Sharma and Rao, 2000), and examining how the desires and attitudes of both the retiring CEO and the successor affect the succession process (Sharma et al., 2003).

Succession problems have been described as a main factor that weakens family companies (Bird et al., 2002) due to the psychological profile of a powerful entrepreneur (Kets de Vries, 1993), the dynamic relationships between parents and children (Mathews et al., 1999), the loss of leadership (Lansberg, 1999) and the lack of planning (Carlock and Ward, 2001; Lansberg, 1988; Ward, 1988b). Successful succession planning has been associated with a quantitative performance dimension (company results, post-succession) and a qualitative and personal dimension (family satisfaction with the succession process as a whole) (Morris et al., 1997; Sharma et al., 2001).

The ownership dimension of succession has been insufficiently addressed (Ayres, 1990). The link between management and ownership succession has been approached only indirectly with the three-dimension model (Gersick et al., 1997), which defines an ownership dimension and a family dimension that are more properly a management succession dimension. Succession is a consequence of time. Management succession is common to all organizations (Christensen, 1953), but in family businesses ownership succession is also associated with individual life cycles. Succession impacts different aspects of family companies and has been approached from a variety of perspectives, including the transition to a non-family CEO (Bennedsen et al., 2007; Wasserman, 2003), the departure of founding entrepreneurs due to the imbalance of founders' competencies with company needs (Boecker and Karichalil, 2002) and gender differences (Bennedsen et al., 2007; Davis and Tagury, 1989).

With the succession process, there is often an increase in members of the dominant coalition (Chua et al., 1999), which also has a qualitative impact due to their differences. Thus there is increased diversity in the roles played by the various individuals (Tagiuri and Davis, 1996), along with an increase in the differences in their competency profiles (McClelland and Boyatzis, 1982), objectives and values (Ward, 1997), trust between the various players (McCollom, 1992), which may diminish shareholder commitment to the company (Thomas, 2002), and eventual loss of entrepreneurial capacity (Payne, 1984). The increase in family complexity caused by generational transition changes the family business dynamics and, therefore, may affect familiness and may diminish family business performance (Gimeno et al., 2006).

Increasing family complexity also means the involvement of more family members who are from different branches, with different levels of closeness and different competency profiles and interests. This high family complexity may reduce the familiness advantage, given the effort needed to solve increasing conflicts of interests among individuals and family groups, the slower decision-making process and conflicts in the mission of the company. Block holders in the family shareholder group (for instance a family branch) may emerge to defend particular interests, or showing willingness to leave the business, given the tight and closed ownership control.

This leads to our first proposition:

Proposition 1   Increase in family complexity due to generational transition tends to reduce the familiness advantage.

Founders and Top Management Teams

Family firms in their early stages are run by their founders, who by definition are entrepreneurs who create new products, processes, markets and so on (Schumpeter, 1934). A founder is the soul and engine of the business, and, with their experience and networks, develops the company and gives the business a unique resource that leads to competitive advantage. A founder, over time, tends to become more conservative and unwilling to take risks (Morris, 1998), for fear of jeopardizing the family wealth (Sharma et al., 1997). Moreover, a founder realizes that they will have to pass the baton and will not run the business forever. Thus the founder's competitive advantage disappears over time.

Even though sole founders may be key company resources, over time they may be negative resources, limiting the familiness advantage. Organizations depend heavily on founders' experience, knowledge, decision making, values and practices, and are created around them and their unique style. The distinctive marks of founders on companies may be weaknesses.

In later stages family firms tend to be managed by TMTs, as siblings are incorporated into the business. The literature suggests that teams have potential positive effects on new ventures (Colombo and Grilli, 2005; Timmons, 1999), given their knowledge diversity (Clarysse and Moray, 2004) and their superior capacity for acquiring resources (Brush et al., 2001). One of the difficulties that teams experience, however, is combining the positive differences among team members with the necessary cohesion that action-driven teams should have. Departures of team members may be a way of adapting to this contradiction (Ruef et al., 2003). In that sense, teams may incorporate new members to add new, valuable resources (Kamm and Nurick, 1993; Sandberg, 1992; Ucbasaran et al., 2003) or to create a highly cohesive kin-related group (Bird, 1989; Ruef et al., 2003).

The criterion of equality between generations that families tend to apply (Lansberg, 1988; Linares, 1996) is likely to affect team performance in family businesses. This means that the owning family members feel that they have the same rights as other family members of their generation. The family condition as a criterion for entering top management does not mean that new members will add valuable competencies to the team, neither will they add greater cohesion. This incorporation does not necessarily mean a negative team dynamic in the short term, due to the hierarchical (parental) relations among family members. Although the presence of parents, as hierarchy, maintains order and unity of action, in the case of a relationship between equals (siblings or cousins), the hierarchy disappears, which tends to make teams less effective (Ensley and Pearson, 2005).

Lechler (2001) describes six characteristics of successful teams (communication, cohesion, work norms, mutual support, coordination and the balance of member contributions). These characteristics seem to be more difficult to develop in teams composed of siblings and cousins if they have been appointed because of their family condition and not for their contribution to the management team. This may lead to weaker cohesion, as family cohesion does not necessarily mean management team cohesion. These relational conflicts limit the performance of management teams, which seem to be related to the founder's life cycle and can be understood as a capability life cycle (Helfat and Peteraf, 2003). As explained by Helfat and Peteraf (2003), '[A] capability involves coordinated effort by individuals-teams' (p.999). Thus, '[T]he capability lifecycle depicts the evolution of a capability that resides within a team' (p.999). Consequently, the advancing age or death of the founder leads to the disappearance of both the founder's capabilities and the hierarchies inside the team, resulting in a misuse of team resources. Thus TMTs may hamper the familiness advantage, given the high probability of disagreements in vision, interests and profiles, and rivalry in assigning different management positions. Equality, as a guiding principle, prevents the TMT from taking advantage of the different profiles, competencies and interests of its members, which hampers the capacity to accept differing roles and positions and precludes the possibility of changing roles.

Few efforts have been made to link entrepreneurship and TMT literature with the mainstream approach in the family business literature. Time affects family complexity (Gimeno et al., 2006), resulting in multiple role dynamics (Tagiuri and Davis, 1996); separation of ownership and management (Fama and Jensen, 1983); loss of cohesion (Beckhard and Dyer, 1983; Davis and Harveston, 2000); differences in values (Ward, 1988a), entrepreneurial attitude (Gimeno et al., 2006), competency profiles (Boyatzis, 1984) and interests (Schultze et al., 2001); and the reduction of familiness (Ensley and Pearson, 2005). This increase in family complexity tends to reduce alignment between the management team and the whole owning family, which supports the idea that the transition from founding to following generations tends to weaken familiness as a pool of family resources. Eventually, it transforms a positive resource in the first generation into a negative one in the following, thus reducing family business performance (Minichilli and Corbetta, 2007).

This leads to our second proposition:

Proposition 2   Founders and TMTs cannot sustain the familiness advantage over time.

Development of Governance Structures as a Source of Sustainability Over Time

The main principle of the agency theory-based approach (Daily and Dollinger, 1993; Kang, 2000) is that the identification between ownership and management in family businesses avoids agency problems in family businesses. More recent approaches, however, admit the existence of agency problems (Chrisman et al., 2005; Gómez-Mejía et al., 2001; Lubatkin et al., 2007; Schulze et al., 2001). Differences in interests, information and power emerge inside the family group, which makes governance a relevant issue.

The evidence of the superior performance of family firms as opposed to other types of companies (for example, Anderson and Reeb, 2003) has been refined by different authors, who claim that superior performance occurs only in the founding generation, due to the passing of the CEO position to family members (Miller and Le-Breton-Miller, 2007; Pérez-González, 2006; Villalonga and Amit, 2006). Superior performance is maintained, however, if there is a differentiation between the CEO and the chairman position, and the former is occupied by a non-family professional.

As mentioned earlier, the sole owner tends to be the cornerstone of the organization, providing leadership, risk taking, decision making and control, and developing their skills, knowledge and networks. In that situation it makes sense to have a very simple governance structure, as management and ownership is the same, and the strength of the business depends on the capacity of its leader. Over time, as both family and business complexity increase, more developed governance structures are needed. No single person represents both ownership and management who has the legitimacy to lead both the family and the business.

Differences in interests, decision-making power and information appear, not as typical agency problems (Jensen and Meckling, 1976), but as more complex ones. The problem is not between two homogeneous groups (agents and principals), but among the many different groups of interest identified by Tagiuri and Davis (1996). The problem of how to align interests, deal with different levels of decisions and information asymmetries, and develop accountability is raised (Gimeno et al., 2009). Governance arises as a key element for generating order and efficiently managing the family and business spheres (Neubauer and Lank, 1999). In fact, a governance structure composed of three tiers – owning family (family council), business governance (board of directors) and management (executive committee) – has been suggested by the family business literature (Lansberg, 1999; Neubauer and Lank, 1999; Schwartz and Barnes, 1991; Ward, 1991; Ward and Handy, 1988). Thus governance structures should be adapted to family business characteristics (Corbetta and Salvato, 2004), which represent a factor of family business performance (Miller and Le Breton-Miller, 2006).

In the three-tiered family governance structure the family council aligns ownership, the board of directors assesses and controls management, and the executive committee manages the company. Gimeno (2006) supports the positive impact of both family and business governance structures in family business performance, measured by profit growth of the business and by family satisfaction. This means that governance structures maintain the superior performance of family businesses over time, consequently sustaining the familiness advantage.

This leads to the third proposition:

Proposition 3   Over time the development of governance structures tends to strengthen the familiness advantage.

Relations Among Family Members

One of the issues frequently addressed in the family business literature deals with relationships among family members (Dyer and Sánchez, 1998). Family businesses have frequently been associated with poor communication that leads to conflict (Kaye, 1999; Kets de Vries, 1993). Nevertheless, the family business literature has devoted little attention to the basics of communication theory, created under a 'transmission paradigm' (Shannon and Weaver, 1949), which subsequently incorporates a relational aspect (Bateson, 1958; Birdwhistell, 1952; Jackson, 1968; Ruesch, 1987; Watzlawick, 1986; Watzlawick et al., 1981). These authors define human communication on two different levels: content (information that is exchanged) and relational (relations that are established) (Watzlawick et al., 1981).

This approach has been used extensively in the literature on negotiation and conflict resolution (Fisher and Ury, 2002). In a negotiation both levels become mixed and distorted, so that maintenance of the relationship may affect the agreement on content or, on the contrary, negotiating content may affect the relationship. Good communication skills require the capacity to differentiate both levels of communication.

It is especially important to differentiate between the two levels in family businesses, due to the strong links between content and relationships. Logically, relations are of great importance, as they constitute the basis of the family system. Content is also important, since a family must be able to discuss business matters effectively. Bateson (1958) and Watzlawick et al. (1981) suggest two types of relational patterns: symmetry and complementarities. In the first case two people consider themselves to be equal, while in the second case one person places themself in a superior position in respect to the other. Alternation is the capacity to change the relational pattern according to the situation.

A complex business family needs to practice alternation in order to develop functional governance structures and to maintain entrepreneurial leadership. The governance bodies (family council and board of directors) require a symmetric relationship (members relate to each other as equals), but with complementary relations between them (the family council is 'superior' to the board of directors and the latter is 'superior' to the CEO) (Gimeno et al., 2006). Therefore, in many cases, rivalry is the result of disagreement between two individuals regarding the kind of relationship they have. For instance, one may propose a symmetrical relationship (equal to equal), while the other may put themself in an upper-hand position in a complementary relationship. Hence many communication problems are grounded not on differences in content, but in relationships. Due to the multiple roles they play in the family business, individuals need to develop a capacity for alternation, so that they can relate to others from different positions. The expansion of the business family over time requires the family also to develop this capacity, so that it can change its relational pattern according to the context (Gimeno et al., 2006).

Sustaining entrepreneurial leadership in a family business requires family members to relate to each other symmetrically (all shareholders are equal), but also complementarily (inferior members follow superior members in the entrepreneurial hierarchy). If the family is unable to break a rigid pattern, the family business is dominated by a symmetrical pattern that is natural between siblings and cousins (Lansberg, 1988). If all family members are equal in all contexts, no one will follow others (putting one's self in an inferior position), and no one will lead others (putting one's self in a superior position). This means that most of the entrepreneurial family members will transform their entrepreneurial leadership not into entrepreneurial performance, but into rivalry,[2] which may explain the loss of the familiness advantage.

This leads us to the fourth proposition:

Proposition 4   Maintenance of the familiness advantage in complex family businesses requires family members to develop the ability to switch positions and roles in family relational patterns.

7.3   RESEARCH METHODOLOGY

This study forms part of the STEP Project, which focuses on the transgenerational potential in family businesses. One of the main issues highlighted is the importance of the pool of resources that are idiosyncratic and unique to the family business, defined as familiness (Habbershon and Williams, 1999), the focus of this chapter. Given the nature of the research and the early stage of topic development, the research strategy is based on an exploratory qualitative study. To better understand the phenomena we use a case-based study to explore in depth the history, development and relationships among members (Stake, 1994). A qualitative approach

Table 7.1 Interviewee profile

	Case 1	Case 2	Case 3
Company	Pharma Co.	Construc Co.	Tourism and Leisure Co.
Number of interviews	8	9	5
Owning family interviewed	1 of the fourth generation 5 of the fifth generation	2 of the first generation 5 of the second generation	1 of the second generation 2 of the third generation 1 of the fourth generation
Other family members interviewed	1 top executive 1 member of the board	2 top executives	1 former advisor
Generations	Fourth and fifth	First and second	Second, third and fourth

allows us to study the topic in its natural setting (Rossman and Rallis, 1998), understand the main actors and obtain more details about individuals for further study (Yin, 1994).

More than 60 hours of open-ended and flexible interviews were conducted with a total of 22 people. Profound conversations were generated, revealing feelings and stories embedded in the family and the business, and allowing in-depth exploration of the topic. Key, strategically relevant actors in the family business were interviewed, taking in perspectives of both family and non-family members. Family members from different generations were interviewed, given the importance of transgenerational potential and the maintenance of unique resources through generations to sustain the business over time. See Table 7.1 for details.

All interviews were tape recorded and transcribed. From the interviews and secondary sources case studies were written that allowed further comparison. In addition, a wide range of archival data are used to support the investigation, along with a ten-year longitudinal analysis of all three companies. Archival data was collected from the Internet, newspapers, public databases and other sources. This multiple data collection strategy allows for triangulation, which is important for further analysis, as it provides stronger substantiation of the topic being studied (Eisenhardt, 1989).

Purposeful sampling allowed a selection of three family owned Spanish firms that complied with STEP criteria: a pharmaceutical group in the fifth generation, a tourism and leisure company in the third generation, and a

Table 7.2　Company profile

	Case 1	Case 2	Case 3
Company	Pharma Co	Construc Co.	Tourism and Leisure Co.
Industry	Pharma	Construction and energy	Services (tourism and leisure)
Age of company	> 100 years	> 40 years	> 50 years
Generation in control	Fifth	First	Third
CEO age	48	70	46

construction and energy group in transition from the first to the second generation (Table 7.2).

7.4　FINDINGS

The three cases differ in their level of family complexity as well as in the structures they have created to cope with this complexity. All three have sustained and developed their familiness advantage through a combination of business leadership teams, governance structures and relational patterns. The oldest of these has developed a stable model by evolving into an EFT, meaning that the family is involved in the business from different positions, not necessarily that of management or governance. Although they also have different interests and profiles, all support and foster the entrepreneurial behavior of those in charge.

'Even though I'm not working in the company, I am involved in it as I take part at the family council. I support my brothers in the decisions they make. I know they are doing their best effort in managing the company for all of us. On the other hand I know I don't have the same experience and background as they have, and I know they have the profile to run the business' (M.U.).

'My father has been very generous and he has given space to my brothers to manage the company. He has always supported them, even if he might not have agreed always 100 percent' (M.U.).

'We moved up to the Board of Directors and left space to my brother so he could form his own team and run the business according to his experience' (Q.U.).

The companies in the other two cases are in the process of searching for a stable combination. We identify clear common patterns that are key for sustaining the familiness advantage.

Evolution of the Familiness Advantage

A broad time span is shown in Case 1, with a company history of 170 years. From the first generation the family developed a policy for reducing family complexity by giving ownership of the company only to male offspring. At the same time, they maintained control of the company by giving the majority of shares (51 per cent) to the firstborn. The family genogram permitted this during the first four generations in which the firstborn had only one son, with a varying number of daughters. By the fourth generation the family owner controlled 51 percent of the stock; we will call him Dr Jum.

These policies were based on the belief that family complexity could weaken the company (reducing familiness advantage, according to our present conceptual framework). In the fourth generation the controlling family members held 51 percent of ownership, and the remaining 49 percent was split between eight second cousins.

At the same time, the eight owners made up the top management of the company; thus there was no differentiation between ownership and management. Because top management positions were reserved for owning family members, it was increasingly difficult to deal with day-to-day operations, not to mention the impossibility of developing entrepreneurial decisions that went beyond replicating existing strategies, policies and business practices.

Dr Jum explains: 'I haven't explained this, but I have had up to eight family members working with no defined functions. This situation sometimes generated confrontation among family members and confusion among the lower levels within the organization'.

Realizing the risk that family complexity was causing the company, Dr Jum decided to buy out all of his cousins, which automatically excluded them from management positions. By returning to the sole-founder position and becoming the company's key source of competitive advantage, Dr Jum believes it unlikely that the company would have survived without this ownership concentration. 'My father realized that the family was not rowing in the same direction. If his cousins might have been more entrepreneurial, possibly he would not have bought out. Even though all the family was very respected by the employees, they also noticed that there was not a consensus or support from the other family members towards the entrepreneurial vision my father had' (JUT).

Case 1 shows a family company with a long history and a very solid position that was losing its familiness advantage due to increasing family complexity. The family business rebuilt its family resource pool by pruning the ownership tree.

Case 2 shows a family run company that has been exploiting the resource of the sole founder as a clear familiness advantage, and which created an entrepreneurial company. Now the family is in transition, with the founder losing vigor but not his entrepreneurial attitude, and the children having to 'take up the reins'. Three of the five children are interested in occupying top management positions in the company, while the other two want professional careers, not only outside the family business, but in quite different fields.

The family is aware that increasing family complexity may jeopardize the future of the company, as a result of the separation of ownership and management through the equal split of shares and the differences in interests, competencies, needs and personal circumstances of all five siblings. They are aware of the potential loss of the familiness advantage that may be produced in the short term and are actively working toward creating the conditions to avoid this, as we will explain later. 'We are five siblings. We have different interests and backgrounds. Given some anecdotes we had, you realize that my parents generate harmony within the family. Thus, whenever they will not be around we might have some big disagreements. In other words, chaos would emerge at some point if we do not start working it out soon' (R.C.).

Case 3 shows a different pattern. It is a third-generation family business that has not weakened its familiness advantage over the years, but, on the contrary, has strengthened it. This case does not reject the first proposition, given that the increase in complexity has been quite small. The founder had only one child; that child, in turn, had only two children, who act as a unit. 'My brother and I discuss important decisions, but we also know that each one has his own expertise and that we are good at what we do, so we trust completely in each other' (C.R.).

Founders and TMTs

In Case 1 the company was founded by a single owner; in later generations it evolved into a TMT, where all owners occupied top management positions. These positions were directly related to the fact of being an owner, given that there was no differentiation between management and ownership.

Family members were either part of the family business (owners and managers) or not (neither managers nor owners), as was the case of female family members. Thus the company was managed by a TMT composed of members who were not chosen according to their competencies, interests or personal fit, but by their family relation, which tends to diminish entrepreneurial capacity.

Differences among family members hindered the creation of new entrepreneurial projects appropriate to new markets and competitor situations. The cousins, organized as a team, had difficulty developing strategies that were not a continuation of previous generations. It was not the leadership capacities of Dr Jum, but the 'followship' capacities of the family members that paralyzed company development.

After the buyout and the return to the sole-entrepreneur model, Dr Jum proposed a TMT model, based on equality, to his sons (excluding his two daughters), thus maintaining the family tradition. After five years as a TMT the four brothers decided that they were hindered entrepreneurially under the current regime, and that it would be more effective to select one of them to become CEO.

In Case 2 the sole founder proposed that the next generation form a TMT composed of the three sons interested in managing the company, with ownership split equally among all five children. Currently, the family is aware that this TMT model raises two issues that should be addressed in order to maintain entrepreneurial behavior. The first is how to organize owner-manager relationships and the second is how to avoid the disadvantages that might arise from a TMT composed of the three brothers.

The main questions are how to coordinate decision making among them, how to disagree and how to make decisions. The different backgrounds and responsibilities in the family group gave them their own perspectives on identifying opportunities and risks. In the following sections we concentrate on the actions the family is taking to address these issues.

The third case successfully replicates the sole-entrepreneur model from the founder to his only child. The transition from the second to the third generation evolved into a TMT model, in which the two siblings shared ownership and the CEO position. The company has continued to grow, adding an important international dimension to the two CEOs. In this case the two siblings working as a TMT performed quite well. Compared to the other two cases, we infer that their success is based on three elements: their competency profiles, shared values and collaborative relationship.

Their competency profiles are complementary. While one sibling constantly challenges the organization to move forward, the other structures and consolidates the developments made by the other CEO. The researchers observed that both siblings share the same values related to growth, austerity, hard work, quality of service, development of individuals inside the company and value creation for the community. The relationship between the two siblings is described in the section on relations below.

Governance Structure

In Case 1 the governance structure was very simple during the first 120 years. The identification between management and ownership and the TMT as a management model made it unnecessary to develop a governance system that went beyond the management sphere. As previously explained, this resulted in a major loss of familiness advantage. When Dr Jum bought out his cousins' shares, he started a process of conceptually differentiating ownership from management. His creation of an advisory board to advise him as CEO started the succession process, which suggested to him that it was time to hand over the reins to his children.

When his children took charge of management and Dr Jum moved up to the position of chairman, the advisory board suggested that it be replaced with an executive board of directors that would monitor the TMT formed by the siblings. A board of directors was created, composed of Dr Jum, the four brothers, and three highly competent and demanding outsiders. Afterwards a family council was set up to represent ownership.

The governance structure the four brothers created has allowed the siblings to break the TMT that was established in the company. The siblings appointed a very entrepreneurial and demanding board, which recommended that the family break the TMT model and select one of the siblings as CEO. In parallel, the board, as a governance body, offered the other three brothers privileged positions to participate in, empower and monitor the development of the company.

The high functioning board of directors allowed the siblings to relate with the company not only as managers but also as 'governors'. This permitted three of them to abandon top management positions and concentrate on their duties as directors, while one simultaneously holds CEO and board positions. He is well supported by the board, but also receives pressure from board members to act entrepreneurially.

Without a high functioning board of directors, the siblings would have had enormous difficulty in leaving their top management positions. The board offered the siblings another way to participate more effectively in the family business. As a result, the board has been a strong factor that has allowed the company to increase the familiness advantage and avoid the negative impact that sustaining the TMT would have had on the familiness advantage.

Case 2 has some similarities with Case 1 in the early stages of the fourth generation, after the buyout. As the founder is aware, he cannot replicate the sole-entrepreneur model and has started a process of separating management from governance by creating an effective board of directors that includes himself, his three executive sons, and two independent and highly respected external board members. According to the founder, the board should be an instrument to cope with the possible challenges of five siblings owning the company and three of them acting as a TMT. The board is functioning quite effectively, with more emphasis placed on its advisory rather than its monitoring duties.

We believe this case will follow the pattern seen in Case 1, where the board invites the family to break the TMT model during the second generation. The family is interested in establishing a family council to orient and monitor the board's development and maintain the entrepreneurial development of the company, which should sustain the familiness advantage.

Case 3 is quite simple from the governance point of view because, as mentioned previously, the two family shareholders are a very effective TMT. The two siblings also are conscious that the success of the TMT is limited to their generation and are considering ways to maintain the familiness advantage.

Relations

Case 1 shows two clearly differentiated stages, the first from 1868 to 1984, and the second from 1984 to the present. In the first stage relationships were based on the pre-eminence of the firstborn principle and equality among the remaining brothers, as well as the exclusion of women.

This system worked for three reasons. First, it clearly defined who had utmost authority and guaranteed the ability to make decisions. Second, the exclusion of women reduced complexity. Had this not been the case, it would have been difficult to maintain order by the third generation. Third, it was accepted by all family members. Women accepted their exclusion, the younger sons accepted the firstborn's privileges and the firstborn sons also accepted their roles.

The relational pattern was complementary, in the sense that the firstborn occupied a higher position, while the rest of the TMT occupied lower positions. Acceptance was due largely to the model being coherent with the social values of the time and avoided the competition that usually appears when the TMT model is applied in complex business families.

When Dr Jum began to make way for the fifth generation, he changed some of the traditions that were key to maintaining low complexity, such as including women, changing the firstborn principle and establishing equality among siblings. Four sons implied four managing directors, which represented a new way of maintaining relations. With respect to ownership, the criterion to transfer ownership was based on equality.

Dr Jum proposed an egalitarian relationship model to his children as members of the TMT by following modern-day egalitarian culture. The alternative would have been to choose one child over the others, a difficult decision for a father and one that would have been difficult to accept by those not chosen. This problem had been avoided in the previous model with the firstborn principle.

The siblings, helped by the board, transformed the relational pattern. They realized that one of their most interesting characteristics was their differences – in competency profiles, interests and personal situations – and not what made them equal; they were equal as siblings and as owners. Instead of letting themselves be distracted by rivalry, they decided to take advantage of these differences by appointing one as CEO, establishing relations as equals among themselves both on the board of directors and on the family council. They also established actual hierarchical relations between the board and the CEO. A clear indicator that the board was in an upper position in relation to the CEO was that the board could be demanding and, as the interviewees pointed out, in the event of underperformance, it could replace the family CEO.

In Case 2 the family followed a different pattern. The founder was in an upper position in relation to his children, but in recent years the three children occupying CEO positions have established an equal relationship with the founder. The relational pattern between the CEO siblings and the other two non-active siblings is unclear, but it is evolving into a complementary (hierarchical) pattern, given that the CEO siblings have information, decision powers and management education that gives them superiority over the two non-managing siblings.

Despite having a board of directors, it remains unclear whether the board is capable of gaining a superior position. The pattern of equality that dominates the CEO-sibling relationship, among themselves and with the founder, does not allow the CEO siblings to put themselves in inferior positions in relation to the board. This relational pattern allows the board to take on an advisory function, but not a monitoring function. Therefore the familiness advantage in this case is still sustained by the founder. If the family is unable to evolve in its relational pattern, it is likely that sibling rivalry will arise in the internal dynamics of the TMT and in the relations between managing and non-managing owners.

In Case 3 relationships are very clear. The two siblings have a symmetrical relationship, in that each considers the other as an equal. They have established a collaborative relationship that has been key to the success of the TMT. As mentioned previously, the success of the co-management arrangement is based on the division of responsibilities and, generally speaking, equality between siblings. In matters related to operations and expansion, the sister takes a subordinate role to her brother. In matters of finance, law and information systems, however, she takes the dominant role. 'My brother and I work together well. We make decisions together and we support each other as we trust in the other's capacity to do the things each one is good at' (C.R.).

This system of collaboration has allowed both siblings to build up and complement their skills. In this case, very clearly, the familiness advantage has been reinforced in the third generation. Nonetheless, the siblings are aware that the complexity of the fourth generation (six children) could jeopardize the current familiness advantage. The separation of ownership and management, and the differences between the children (ages, competencies, interests and so on), will make it impossible to replicate the TMT model. 'My brother and I have a relationship that may be difficult to imitate in the next generation, not only because they are more, but also because of their interests and profiles' (C.R.).

7.5 DISCUSSION

The four propositions (Table 7.3) have been basically supported by the observations obtained in all three cases.

The natural evolution of a family business is to pass from a sole owner to a TMT in the next generations, which means that different family members join the management of the company with the desire of being in a TMT. This natural evolution to management teams, due to the tendency to apply the criteria of equality between generations (Lansberg, 1988; Linares, 1996), tends to increase family complexity, thus weakening the familiness advantage. The TMTs are formed mainly by the successive incorporation of next-generation family members according to their life cycles.

The entrance of the next generation into the management of the family business makes it difficult to sustain the familiness advantage and leads to diminishing shareholder commitment to the company (Thomas, 2002) and eventual loss of entrepreneurial capacity (Payne, 1984). This is caused by increased diversity of roles (Tagiuri and Davis, 1996), and increased differences in competency profiles (McClelland and Boyatzis, 1982), objectives and values (Ward, 1997) and trust (McCollom, 1992).

On the contrary, limiting access of all owning family members to management of the company breaks the identification between management and ownership, which also challenges the familiness advantage. Our research shows that companies can avoid the negative effect of family complexity on the familiness advantage by evolving into our model, EFT. There are different models to which a family business can conform, as suggested by Gimeno et al. (2009), and the EFT can be a way for a

Table 7.3   Propositions

	Proposition	Support
P1	Increase in family complexity due to generational transition tends to reduce the familiness advantage.	• Case 1: Family history shows that family complexity was weakening the familiness advantage. This led to the buyout by Dr Jum, which reduced family complexity. • Case 2: The family expects a loss in the familiness advantage due to family complexity, if the model does not change. • Case 3: The familiness advantage did not weaken with time, but grew stronger, mainly due to low family complexity.
P2	Founders and TMTs cannot sustain the familiness advantage over time.	• The three cases started with a sole founder. • Case 1: It evolved into a TMT until the model collapsed. • Case 2: It is evolving from a sole founder into a TMT and is about to collapse. The family is trying to adapt the TMT in order to make it work in the second generation. • Case 3: The TMT has been highly successful until now, but the family recognizes that the model cannot be replicated into the next generation.
P3	Over time the development of governance structures tends to strengthen the familiness advantage.	• Case 1: The governance structure has been a determinant factor in strengthening the familiness advantage. • Case 2: The family has created a board of directors to play a role in the evolution it is trying to create. • Case 3: The family does not have a board of directors nor needs one so far, due to the lack of family complexity and the circumstances that are making the TMT model work very efficiently. Nevertheless, the family is thinking of establishing a board to help the next generation maintain its entrepreneurial performance.
P4	Maintenance of the familiness advantage in complex family businesses requires the ability to switch positions and roles in family relational patterns.	• Case 1: The governance system cannot be explained without the relational capacity that the family developed. • Case 2: This is one of the main obstacles the family faces to avoid creating a TMT. • Case 3: Relations between the siblings explain to a great extent, the success of the TMT model.

complex family business to maintain that familiness advantage as a team, as Nordqvist (2005) claims.

Case 3 may disclaim this conclusion, because it has successfully evolved from the sole-founder model to a TMT. The characteristics that, in this case, made the model so successful are that family complexity is relatively low, being a third-generation family business with two siblings who share values, interests, and competency profiles. Because the siblings agree on relational patterns, they collaborate to develop the familiness advantage.

We suggest that these characteristics are not idiosyncratic in this case, and that they can be proposed as common to successful EFTs in family businesses, which can be synthesized in:

- limited family complexity
- shared values and interests
- matching of competency profiles
- agreement on relational patterns that leads to collaboration.

Despite not having these characteristics, both Cases 1 and 2 have maintained their familiness advantage successfully by moving in the same direction.

Case 1 implemented the TMT model over four generations, until it failed due to the loss of the four characteristics previously cited. Family complexity increased, the competency profiles no longer matched, the values and interests differed fundamentally and the relational pattern no longer led to collaboration. By analysing how Case 1 overcomes the dysfunction of the TMT in complex families, we identify the EFT. We observe that Case 2 is also in the process of abandoning the TMT model and evolving into an EFT.

The different ways of reinforcing the familiness advantage, thus improving performance, are canalized through a developed ownership structure, defining ownership, governance and management spheres (Gimeno, 2004; Lansberg, 1999; Neubauer and Lank, 1999; Schwartz and Barnes, 1991; Ward, 1991; Ward and Handy, 1988), creating different ways to participate. The family members relate mainly through the ownership sphere, thus maintaining equal relationships (Bateson, 1958; Watzlawick et al., 1981). They also interact at other levels (Bateson, 1958; Watzlawick et al., 1981; Gimeno et al., 2006) if this supports the entrepreneurial development of the business. This means that management positions are not reserved for family members because they are family, but are reserved for highly entrepreneurial managers, under the control and advice of the board. These managers may or may not be family members; they are selected by the board, following family desires.

We suggest that the EFT model clearly differentiates roles that allow a CEO to be seen as a professional manager without the overlapping of their role as owning family member. This means that management positions are not held indefinitely, only temporarily, according to the competency profile of the CEO.

EFTs are also characterized by the alternating relations among its members. Family members do not see themselves as 'being' a position (CEO, chairman and so on); they 'hold' a position, so they can hold different positions simultaneously. This allows them to avoid rigid relationship patterns, always 'up' or 'down' or equal, varying instead according to the roles they play each moment and their context.

A person can hold different positions (owner, board member, management team member) and change their relation with others according to the position that the context proposes. This allows members to have equal relationships with other owners who have professional careers outside the family business and who feel they are members of the EFT, despite not working in the company.

7.6 CONCLUSIONS

We propose that the EFT is a good way to leverage the familiness advantage in some specific circumstances, as Case 3 shows. Trying to maintain this model when circumstances do not allow it to develop can weaken the familiness advantage and, consequently, business performance. Case 1 shows how a family business experiencing increasing family complexity can maintain the familiness advantage over time by evolving into an EFT. In Case 2 a family business realizes that the TMT will eliminate the familiness advantage and is attempting to develop an EFT model.

From a prescriptive point of view, this research suggests that entrepreneurs follow a sole-owner model, which is then replicated into the next generation by substituting a TMT for the sole owner. Our research shows that this model is not functional when family complexity increases because it weakens the familiness advantage. Results suggest that, over time, successful family businesses may evolve into an EFT model, an evolution that may allow the family business to sustain the familiness advantage over time (Table 7.4).

7.7 LIMITATIONS AND FUTURE RESEARCH

This study's qualitative methodology is a sound method to examine previously unexplored concepts and ideas in depth. It is also a good tool to

Table 7.4   Main conclusions about the models

	Solo Owner	**Top Management Team (TMT)**	**Entrepreneurial Family Team (EFT)**
Family complexity	Low	Low	Medium and high
Composition	Founder	Siblings or cousins (usually 2–5 family members)	All family members involved in the family business (in management, ownership or future ownership)
Main values	Individual project	Team project	Family project
Role of the family	Follow the entrepreneur	Follow the TMT	Family fosters and supports the entrepreneurial endeavor
Relational pattern	Complementary (sole owner has a dominant position)	Symmetry among team members	Symmetry inside the governance bodies and complementary between the bodies
Governance	No governance structure: the entrepreneur is everything	Weak governance structure: the executive committee coordinates the team	Structured governance: differentiation between ownership sphere, governance sphere and management sphere
Management and ownership	Identification	Confusion (no clear identification)	Clear differentiation
Management positions	Permanent	Permanent	Non-permanent
Main threat to familiness advantage	Entrepreneur life cycle and rivalry among heirs	Rivalry in the management team and with non-manager owners	Maintenance of family cohesion around the entrepreneurial project

develop theory, which is the focus of this chapter. The drawback is that the findings are not generalizable, as the cases are studied in a specific context. Moreover, purposeful sampling can result in narrow theory (Eisenhardt, 1989). Another limitation is subjectivity in the interpretation of the interviews, mainly influenced by the culture and background of the researchers.

The EFT model opens a new framework that needs further conceptual study and more in-depth analysis. For that reason, qualitative and quantitative methodologies can be used to determine the validity of this framework. It may represent a new dimension of familiness affecting firm behavior, which remains unexplored (Chrisman et al., 2005); this fresh component may be one of the key elements that support family firm performance over time.

The evolution from sole founder to TMT and, finally, to EFT opens up new avenues for research as well, pointing out the need to better understand which elements foster or hinder this evolution. This may be linked to succession issues, as the increase in members belonging to the dominant coalition (Chua et al., 1999) has a qualitative impact due to increased diversity in the roles of various family members (Tagiuri and Davis, 1996), combined with differences in competency profiles (McClelland and Boyatzis, 1982) and objectives and values (Ward, 1997), among other issues.

Furthermore, new questions arise as to what extent the dimensions identified in this research reflect the key elements of an EFT, if an EFT performs better than a TMT and under what circumstances. Another interesting issue to be analysed is the extent to which complex family businesses evolve into EFTs and the life expectancy of EFTs compared to TMTs.

NOTES

1. Authors have equally contributed to the elaboration of the chapter, therefore they are ordered alphabetically. We are very thankful to Thomas Zellweger and Mattias Nordqvist and to an anonymous reviewer for their very valuable comments and suggestions on this chapter.
2. We call this phenomena 'entrepreneurial rivalry'.

REFERENCES

Alcorn, P. (1982), *Success and Survival in the Family Owned Business*, New York: McGraw-Hill.
Anderson, R.C. and D.M. Reeb (2003), 'Founding-family ownership and firm performance: evidence from the S&P 500', *Journal of Finance*, **58**(3), 28–38.
Ayres, G. (1990), 'Rough family justice: equity in family business succession planning', *Family Business Review*, **3**(1), 3–22.
Bateson, G. (1958), *Naven: The Culture of the Lamut People of New Guinea as*

Revealed Through a Study of the 'Naven' Ceremonial, Stanford, CA: Stanford University Press.

Beckhard, R. and W.D. Dyer (1983), 'Managing continuity in the family-owned business', *Organizational Dynamics*, **12**(1), 5–12.

Bennedsen, M., K. Meisner, F. Pérez-González and D. Wolfenzon (2007), 'Inside the family firm: the role of families in succession decisions and performance', *Quarterly Journal of Economics*, **122**(2), 647–91.

Bird, B. (1989), *Entrepreneurial Behavior*, Glenview, IL: Scott Foresman and Co.

Bird, B., H. Welsch, J.H. Astrachan and D. Pistrui (2002), 'Family business research: the evolution of an academic field', *Family Business Review*, **15**(4), 337–50.

Birdwhistell, R.L. (1952), *Introduction to Kinesics (An Annotation System of Body Motion and Gesture)*, Louisville, KY: University of Louisville Press.

Boecker, W. and R. Karichalil (2002), 'Entrepreneurial transitions: factors influencing founder departure', *Academy of Management Journal*, **45**(14), 818–26.

Boyatzis, R.E. (1982), *The Competent Manager: A Model for Effective Performance*, New York: John Wiley & Sons.

Brush, C., P. Greene, M. Hart and H. Haller (2001), 'From initial idea to unique advantage: The entrepreneurial challenge of constructing a resource base', *Academy of Management Executive*, **15**(1), 64–78.

Carlock, R., and J. Ward (2001), *Strategic Planning for the Family Business*, New York: Palgrave.

Chrisman, J.J., A. Bauerschmidt and C.W. Hofer (1998), 'The determinants of new venture performance: an extended model', *Entrepreneurship Theory and Practice*, **23**(1), 5–29.

Chrisman, J.J., J.H. Chua and S.A. Zahra (2003), 'Creating wealth in family firms through managing resources: comments and extensions', *Entrepreneurship Theory and Practice*, **27**(4), 359–65.

Chrisman, J., J. Chua and L. Steier (2005), 'Sources and consequences of distinctive familiness: an introduction', *Entrepreneurship Theory and Practice*, **29**(3), 237–47.

Christensen, C.R. (1953), 'Management succession in small and growing enterprises', PhD dissertation, Harvard University, Cambridge, Massachusetts.

Chua, J., J. Chrisman and P. Sharma (1999), 'Defining the family business by behavior', *Entrepreneurship Theory and Practice*, **23**(4), 19–39.

Clarysse, B. and N. Moray (2004), 'A process study of entrepreneurial team formation: the case of a research-based spin-off', *Journal of Business Venturing*, **19**(1), 55–79.

Colombo, M. and L. Grilli (2005), 'Founders' human capital and the growth of new technology-based firms: a competence-based view', *Research Policy*, **34**(6), 795–816.

Corbetta, G. and C. Salvato (2004), 'The board of directors in family firms: one size fits all?' *Family Business Review*, **17**(2), 119–34.

Daily, C.M. and M.J. Dollinger (1993), 'Alternative methodologies for identifying family- versus nonfamily-managed businesses', *Journal of Small Business Management*, **31**(2), 79–81.

Davis, J. and R. Tagiuri (1989), 'The influence of life stage on father-son work relationships in family companies', *Family Business Review*, **11**(1), 47–74.

Davis, P. and P. Harveston (2000), 'Internationalization and organizational growth: the impact of internet usage and technology involvement among entrepreneur-led family business', *Family Business Review*, **13**(2), 107–20.

Dyer, G.W. and M. Sánchez (1998), 'Current state of family business theory and practice as reflected in *Family Business Review* 1988–1997', *Family Business Review*, **11**(4), 287–97.

Dyer, W.G. and W. Handler (1994), 'Entrepreneurship and family business: exploring the connection', *Entrepreneurship Theory and Practice*, **19**(1), 71–83.

Eisenhardt, K. (1989), 'Building theories from case study research', *Academy of Management Review*, **14**(4), 532–50.

Ensley, M. and A. Pearson (2005), 'An exploratory comparison of the behavioral dynamics of top management teams in family and nonfamily new ventures: cohesion, conflict, potency, and consensus', *Entrepreneurship Theory and Practice*, **29**(3), 267–84.

Fama, E.F. and M.C. Jensen (1983), 'Separation of ownership and control', *Journal of Law and Economics*, **26**, 301–25.

Fisher, R. and W. Ury (2002), *Obtenga el Si: el Arte de Negociar sin Ceder*, Barcelona: Gestión 2000.

Gersick, K.E., J.A. Davis, M.M. Hampton and I. Lansberg (1997), *Empresas Familiares: Generación a Generación*, Mexico: McGraw-Hill.

Gimeno, A., G. Labadie, W. Saris and X. Mendoza (2006), 'Internal factors of family business performance: an integrated theoretical model', in P. Poutziouris, K. Smyrnios and S. Klein (eds), *Handbook of Research on Family Businesses*, Cheltenham, UK and Northampton, MA, USA: Edward Elgar Publishing, pp. 145–64.

Gimeno, A., G. Baulenas and J. Coma-Cros (2009), *Modelos de Empresa Familiar: soluciones prácticas para la familia empresaria*, Bilbao: Editorial Deusto.

Gómez-Mejía, L.R., M. Nunez-Nickel and I. Gutiérrez (2001), 'The role of family ties in agency contracts', *Academy of Management Journal*, **44**(1), 81–96.

Habbershon, T. and M.L. Williams (1999), 'A resource-based framework for assessing the strategic advantages of family firms', *Family Business Review*, **12**(1), 1–25.

Habbershon, T., M. Williams and I. MacMillan (2003), 'A unified systems perspective of family firm performance', *Journal of Business Venturing*, **18**(4), 451–65.

Handler, W.C. (1990), *Managing the Family Firm Succession Process: The Next Generation Family Member's Experience*, Boston, MA: Boston University School of Management.

Helfat, C. and M. Peteraf (2003), 'The dynamic resource-based view: capability lifecycles', *Strategic Management Journal*, **24**(10), 997–1010.

Jackson, D.D. (ed.) (1968), *Therapy, Communication, and Change*, Palo Alto, CA: Science and Behavior Books.

Jensen, M.C. and W.H. Meckling (1976), 'Theory of the firm: managerial behaviour, agency costs and ownership structure', *Journal of Financial Economics*, **3**, 305–60.

Kamm, J. and A. Nurick (1993), 'The stages of team venture formation: a decision making model', *Entrepreneurship Theory and Practice*, **17**(2), 17–27.

Kang, D.L. (2000), 'Family ownership and performance in public corporations: a study of the U.S. fortune 500, 1982–1994', Working Paper No. 00-0051, Boston: Harvard Business School.

Kaye, K. (1999), 'Mate selection and family business success', *Family Business Review*, **11**(2), 107–15.

Kellermanns, F., K. Eddleston, T. Barnett and P. Pearson (2008), 'An exploratory study of family member characteristics and involvement: effects on entrepreneurial behavior in the family firm', *Family Business Review*, **21**(1), 1–14.

Kets de Vries, M. (1993), 'The dynamics of family controlled firms: the good and the bad news', *Organizational Dynamics*, **21**(3), 59–62.

Lansberg, I. (1988), 'The succession conspiracy', *Family Business Review*, **1**(2), 11–19.

Lansberg, I. (1999), *Succeeding Generations*, Boston, MA: Harvard Business School Press.

Lechler T. (2001), 'Social interaction: a determinant of entrepreneurial team venture success', *Small Business Economics*, **16**(4), 263–78.

Linares, J.L. (1996), *Identidad y Narrativa*, Barcelona: Paidós Terapia Familiar.

Lubatkin, M., Y. Ling and W. Schulze (2007), 'An organizational justice-based view of self-control and agency costs in family firms', *Journal of Management Studies*, **44**(6), 955–71.

Matthews, C., T. Moore and A. Fialko (1999), 'Succession in the family firm: a cognitive categorization perspective', *Family Business Review*, **12**(2), 159–70.

McClelland, D. and R. Boyatzis (1982), 'Leadership motive pattern and long-term success in management', *Journal of Applied Psychology*, **67**(6), 737–43.

McCollom, M. (1992), 'The ownership trust and succession paralysis in the family business', *Family Business Review*, **5**(2), 145–60.

Miller, D. and I. Le Breton-Miller (2006), 'Family governance and firm performance: agency, stewardship, and capabilities', *Family Business Review*, **19**(1), 73–87.

Miller, D. and I. Le Breton-Miller (2007), 'Kicking the habit: broadening our horizons by studying family businesses', *Journal of Management Inquiry*, **16**(1), 27–30.

Minichilli, A. and G. Corbetta (2007), 'Top management teams in family controlled companies: the impact of familiness', Paper presented at FERC Conference, Monterrey, Mexico.

Morris, M.H. (1998), *Entrepreneurial Intensity*, Westport, CT: Quorum Books.

Morris, M.H., R.O. Williams, J.A. Allen and R.A. Ávila (1997), 'Correlates of success in family business transitions', *Journal of Business Venturing*, **12**, 358–401.

Neubauer, F. and A.G. Lank (1999), *La Empresa Familiar*, Barcelona: Ediciones Deusto.

Nordqvist, M. (2005), 'Familiness in top management teams: commentary on Ensley and Pearson's "An exploratory comparison of the behavioral dynamics of top management teams in family and nonfamily new ventures: cohesion, conflict, potency, and consensus"', *Entrepreneurship Theory and Practice*, **29**(3), 285–91.

Payne, P.L. (1984), 'Family business in Britain: an historical and analytical survey', in A. Akio Okochi, Y. Shigeaki (eds), *Family Business in the Era of Industrial Growth; Its Ownership and Management*, Tokyo: University of Tokyo Press, pp. 171–206.

Pérez-González, F. (2006), 'Inherited control and firm performance', *American Economic Review*, **96**(5), 1559–88.

Rossman, G. and S. Rallis (1998), *Learning in the Field: An Introduction to Qualitative Research*, Thousand Oaks, CA: Sage Publications.

Ruef, M., H. Aldrich and N. Carter (2003), 'The structure of founding teams: homophily, strong ties, and isolation among U.S. entrepreneurs', *American Sociological Review*, **68**(2), 195–222.

Ruesch, J. (1987), 'Values, communications and culture', in J. Ruesch and G. Bateson, *Communication. The Social Matrix of Psychiatry*, New York: W.W. Norton & Company, pp. 3–200.

Sandberg, W.R. (1992), 'Strategic management's potential contributions to a theory of entrepreneurship', *Entrepreneurship Theory and Practice*, **16**(3), 73–91.

Schultze, W.S., M.H. Lubatkin, R.N. Dino and A.K. Buchholtz (2001), 'Agency relationships in family firms: theory and evidence', *Organization Science*, **12**(4), 473–91.

Schumpeter, J. (1934), *The Theory of Economic Development*, Boston, MA: Harvard University Press.

Schwartz, M.A. and L.B. Barnes (1991), 'Outside boards and family businesses: another look', *Family Business Review*, **4**(3), 269–85.

Shannon, C. and W. Weaver (1949), *The Mathematical Theory of Communication*, Urbana-Champaign: University of Illinois Press.

Sharma, P. and A.S. Rao (2000), 'Successor attributes in Indian and Canadian family firms: a comparative study', *Family Business Review*, **13**(4), 313–30.

Sharma, P., J.J. Chrisman and J.H. Chua (1997), 'Strategic management of family business: past research and future challenges', *Family Business Review*, **10**(1), 1–35.

Sharma, P., J.J. Chrisman, A. Pablo and J.H. Chua (2001), 'Determinants of initial satisfaction with the succession process in family firms: a conceptual model', *Entrepreneurship Theory and Practice*, **25**(3), 17–36.

Sharma, P., J.J. Chrisman and J.H. Chua (2003), 'Succession planning as planned behavior: some empirical results', *Family Business Review*, **16**(1), 1–16.

Stake, R. (1994), 'Case studies', in N.K. Denzin and Y.S. Lincoln (eds), *Handbook of Qualitative Research*, Thousand Oaks, CA: Sage, pp. 236–47.

Tagiuri, R. and J.A. Davis (1996), 'Bivalent attributes of the family firm', *Family Business Review*, **9**(2), 199–208.

Thomas, J. (2002), 'Freeing the shackles of family business ownership', *Family Business Review*, **15**(4), 321–31.

Timmons, J.A. (1999), *New Venture Creation. Entrepreneurship for the 21st Century*. Boston, MA: McGraw-Hill.

Ucbasaran, D.A., M.W. Lockett and P. Westhead (2003), 'Entrepreneurship founder teams: factors associated with team member entry and exit', *Entrepreneurship Theory and Practice*, **28**(2), 107–28.

Villalonga, B. and R. Amit (2006), 'How do family ownership, control and management affect firm value?' *Journal of Financial Economics*, **80**(2), 385–419.

Ward, J. (1988a), *Keeping the Family Business Healthy*, San Francisco, CA: Jossey-Bass.

Ward, J. (1988b), 'The special role of strategic planning for family businesses', *Family Business Review*, **1**(2), 105–17.

Ward, J. (1991), *Creating Effective Boards for Private Enterprises: Meeting the Challenges of Continuity and Competition*, San Francisco, CA: Jossey-Bass.

Ward. J. (1997), 'Growing the family business: special challenges and best practices', *Family Business Review*, **10**(4), 323–38.

Ward, J. and J.L. Handy (1988), 'A survey of board practices', *Family Business Review*, **1**(3), 289–308.

Wasserman, N. (2003), 'Founder-CEO succession and the paradox of entrepreneurial success', *Organization Science*, **14**(2), 149–72.

Watzlawick, P. (1986), *El Lenguaje del Cambio: Nueva Técnica de la Comunicación Terapéutica*, Barcelona: Herder.

Watzlawick, P., J. Beavin and D. Jackson (1981), *Teoría de la Comunicación Humana: Interacciones, Patologías y Paradoja*s, Barcelona: Herder.

Yin, R. (1994), *Case Study Research: Design and Methods*. Second edition, Thousand Oaks, CA: Sage.

8. How much and what kind of entrepreneurial orientation is needed for family business continuity?

Thomas M. Zellweger[1], Philipp Sieger and Corinne Muehlebach

8.1 INTRODUCTION

One of the key concepts in entrepreneurship research is entrepreneurial orientation (EO), which describes the attitudes, values and beliefs of entrepreneurial organizations that tend to engage in strategy making characterized by actively pursuing opportunities, taking risks and innovation (Dess et al., 1997; Lumpkin and Dess, 1996; Miller, 1983). EO comprises five salient dimensions (innovativeness, risk taking, autonomy, competitive aggressiveness and proactiveness; Lumpkin and Dess, 1996). These dimensions are separate but related constructs; that is, the degree of each dimension may vary, even though the constructs are positively correlated (Nordqvist, 2008). They have received wide support in entrepreneurship research and have proven to be very prolific as antecedents to the success of small and medium-sized businesses, often recently founded and fast-growing (Wiklund and Shepherd, 2003). EO, which is one of the main building blocks of the transgenerational entrepreneurship research model underlying this chapter, is also viewed as an important factor that contributes to organizational success in more general terms (Kellermanns and Eddleston, 2006).

Based on recent calls by researchers to apply concepts established in entrepreneurship theory in the family business context in order to advance both fields of research, this chapter examines to what degree the EO construct explains business activity of transgenerational firms. In particular, we challenge the fundamental claim by entrepreneurship scholars that the more entrepreneurial the firm, the higher it scores in the five EO dimensions and the more successful it should be over time. Indeed, a wide stream of literature proposes that entrepreneurial attitudes and behavior are crucial antecedents for a company's short- and long-term success (Dess et al., 2003; Zahra and Covin, 1995).

A closer look at the development of entrepreneurial firms in practice, however, reveals that often the opposite is true. During the economic era lasting from the 1990s to roughly 2002 many new firms appeared in the marketplace. Through the theoretical lens of corporate entrepreneurship and, in particular, EO, these companies were considered highly entrepreneurial: they were very innovative, for example, in terms of applying new Internet technology. Even the design of the organizational structures was often intended to be original, as reflected by a stimulating living room-like workspace design. Furthermore, their owners and employees strove for high levels of autonomy (for example, stock ownership plans that included lower echelon employees). Because they challenged large and established industry giants, they were considered as aggressive by their competitors and proactive in occupying new markets and introducing new products. Last, but not least, these organizations displayed a high risk propensity in terms of personal financial and non-financial resource commitment by owners and managers. In summary, these firms ranked high on all EO dimensions. However, even though a few became established, large firms (for example, Google), many were unable to survive over time, declaring bankruptcy or losing independence in the ensuing economic downturn.

We label this type of EO pattern as 'score high and die'. Examples of firms that were truly entrepreneurial at the beginning of their organizational lives but were unable to survive more than a few years abound. In light of these firms'entrepreneurial behavior, we suggest EO as a satisfactory concept to describe their short-term organizational rise. However the explicative power of EO seems to suffer when predicting long-term firm survival. In the context of long-term, multigenerational, firms, therefore, the question arises whether EO is a suitable concept to determine performance and transgenerational potential.

In the context of these considerations this chapter will explore the extent to which EO is *sine qua non* for long-term organizational success, as implicitly suggested by many corporate entrepreneurship studies (for example, Dess et al., 2003). Using the STEP case study methodology we will explore whether EO can be excessive and, accordingly, whether organizational performance and transgenerational potential are feasible with moderate or even low levels of EO. Challenging accepted wisdom that EO is key for a family firm's long-term success, we propose two predominant and, in certain aspects, conflicting theoretical perspectives, with the first rooted in entrepreneurship theory and the second ingrained in family business literature. Whereas entrepreneurship theory, by definition, stresses that behavior (as captured within the EO construct) and growth are key for long-term success, family business literature

Table 8.1   The different views of traditional entrepreneurship and family business literature

Traditional Entrepreneurship Literature	**Family Business Literature**
Type of firm	*Type of firm*
Young, newly created, often fast-growing small and medium-sized firms	Established, traditional, often multigenerational and larger firms
Type of industry	*Type of industry*
Growing and dynamic industries and markets	Mature industries and saturated markets
Type of ownership	*Type of ownership*
Owner-managed / first generation partnerships	(Multigenerational) family ownership
Main focus of research	*Main focus of research*
Entrepreneurial behavior (family relationships are widely neglected)	Family relationships in a business context (entrepreneurial behavior is widely neglected)
Resource challenge	*Resource challenge*
Adding resources to establish an organization in the competitive environment	Reconfiguring and shedding resources to continue and readjust an organization in the competitive environment
Planning horizon	*Planning horizon*
Short	Long
Measures of success and performance	*Measures of success and performance*
Growth and financial performance; taking advantage of opportunities in the market	Survival and family succession; meeting a mixed goal set of financial and non-financial performance dimensions

has traditionally emphasized succession and continuity as antecedents. Table 8.1 provides a prototypical overview of these respective theoretical perspectives.

Both perspectives are considered typical for their respective fields, and both represent a specific perspective on entrepreneurship in the context of family firms. Just as much as each one of these perspectives brings light to a specific side of the object of investigation, both viewpoints seem to be blind on certain aspects, probably most on those aspects where the other viewpoint is able to see something. To examine entrepreneurship in the context of multigeneration family firms, we will perform our analysis using the theoretical lens of entrepreneurship and, more specifically, the EO construct. To this end, we refer to three qualitative Swiss case studies from 2006 and 2007 consisting of family firms between 75 and nearly 180

Table 8.2 Overview of selected cases

Company Name	Health Pharma AG	Taste SA	Technics AG
Industry	Pharmaceuticals	Consumer goods	Printing and filtration technology
Employees in 2007 (*c.*)	340	175	2000
Company age (*c.*)	140 years	80 years	175 years
Annual Sales 2007 (*c.*)	60 million euros	30 million euros	200 million euros
Export orientation	5% of sales	30% of sales	Subsidiaries in 21 countries, representations in 75 countries
Ownership	Completely family owned (two branches, 51%:49%)	Owned by the Taste brothers (51%:49%)	Owned by 150 descendants of the nine founding families and some employees
Family involvement	CEO and CFO, members of the supervisory board	Only the Taste brothers (CEO, Director of Marketing)	CEO and members of the supervisory board
No. of interviews	5	4	4
Family generation	Fifth	Third	Seventh

Note: Names changed for anonymity purposes.

years old that are still controlled by the founding families (for interview details, see Appendix).

Using STEP case study methodology we selected cases according to the following criteria: at least second generation family ownership, ownership group of at least two family members and one family member in management, majority family ownership control in at least one company, at least one business controlled by the family of medium to large size (that is, 50 or more employees) and, finally, firms that see themselves as family firms. According to STEP interview guidelines, we conducted interviews with between four and five representatives in each company. The interviewees were both family members and non-family members in top management team positions (CEO, CFO, president of the supervisory board, head of marketing, head of production and so on; see Appendix). We transcribed the interviews and wrote the actual case study using the STEP guidelines, thereby addressing family influence on different resource pools, EO, entrepreneurial performance and transgenerational potential. The resulting case studies form the basis of the following considerations.

8.2   ENTREPRENEURIAL ORIENTATION REVISITED

Scholars have raised concerns that entrepreneurship, in general, has been under-researched in the family business context (for example, Eddleston et al., 2008). However, as the EO construct gains increasing acceptance in the entrepreneurship literature (and beyond), there is an inherent risk that this key construct is increasingly applied or misunderstood as a normative concept that is equally relevant in any corporate context, in small, newly created firms as well as in older, established firms. While the relationship between EO and general firm performance is positive (Rauch et al., 2004), the inherent danger of applying EO research to the family firm context is that the five dimensions of the EO construct are seen as the 'right' entrepreneurial behavior, regardless of competition, life stage, industry, size and, in particular, family related characteristics.

Recent studies provide controversial findings as to whether family firms constitute a context supporting or constraining EO (Naldi et al., 2007; Zahra, 2005). While some authors claim that family businesses are a hospitable environment for entrepreneurial activities (Aldrich and Cliff, 2003), others claim that certain firms are introverted, becoming resistant to change and conservative over time (Shepherd and Zahra, 2004). Nordqvist et al. (2008) identify three 'dualities' that are related to EO dimensions in family firms: historical/new path, independence/dependence and formality/informality. As a result, the authors conclude that family firms do not have to be entrepreneurial across all five dimensions of EO to reach the desired entrepreneurial outcome. Regarding context, business culture plays an especially important role. For instance, a strong, family related business culture may impact the ability to create and maintain EO (Nordqvist, 2008). Explicit and open business cultures are assumed to facilitate entrepreneurial change (Hall et al., 2001). Zahra et al. (2004) claim that business culture can promote and sustain entrepreneurial activities, a view that is supported by Habbershon and Pistrui (2002).

Another important contextual factor is the type of family firm. Individual CEO characteristics, governance and organization-related factors as well as ownership structure have an impact on EO (Salvato,

2004). Martin and Lumpkin (2003) stress generational involvement, as family orientation can overtake EO when successive generations assume control. These considerations on contextual factors refer back to Lumpkin and Dess (1996), who first noted that environmental factors (for example, industry, dynamism, munificence) or organizational factors (for example, top management team characteristics, strategy-making process) might impact EO. However, beyond this assertion, it is unclear how the context of multigeneration family firms influences EO.

To this end, we will analyse all five underlying dimensions of EO in detail. For each dimension we start with a definition and a brief literature review, then discuss the related findings from our cases. Thus we will critically assess the five dimensions and ask whether they capture the full range of entrepreneurial patterns we detected in the firms under investigation.

Innovativeness

Innovativeness refers to 'a firm's tendency to engage in and support new ideas, novelty, experimentation, and creative processes that may result in new products, services, or technological processes' (Lumpkin and Dess, 1996, p. 142). There is typically a continuum of innovativeness, regarding both the scope and pace of innovation in products, markets and technologies. Schumpeter (1934, 1942) emphasized the central role of innovation in the entrepreneurial process in terms of 'creative destruction', by which wealth was created when existing market structures were disrupted by the introduction of new goods or services that shifted resources away from existing firms and caused new firms to grow. The key to this cycle of activity was entrepreneurship: the competitive entry of innovative 'new combinations' that propelled the dynamic evolution of the economy (Schumpeter, 1934). In the context of family firms, innovativeness is regarded as a highly important dimension of EO for long-term performance, together with autonomy and proactiveness (Nordqvist et al., 2008). In addition, family firms that invest in innovation have greater potential for high performance (Eddleston et al., 2008; McCann et al., 2001).

In the context of the family firms we examined, these organizations did not score high on the innovativeness sub-scale throughout their history, despite the presumably pivotal role of innovativeness to long-term success (Lumpkin and Dess, 1996; Schumpeter, 1934, 1942). For example, when questioned about the relevance of innovativeness, Frank Taste, the CEO of Taste SA, pointed out that innovativeness was 'truly important since the introduction of their top-selling product in the 1940s was a true innovation at the time. At the same time customers are slow in accepting new products and often show a high preference for a product they had known for years. Consequently, the introduction of new products and the entrance to new markets has been rather slow. Still, the company earns the largest part of its sales volume with the chocolate bar.'

Hence the slow acceptance of new products by customers, the high marketing costs and risks associated with introducing new products, and the long-term success of existing products did not create much short-term pressure for product innovation.

Similarly, Technics AG did not constantly score high on the new products and new market-oriented innovativeness scale over their nearly 180 years of existence. Rather, revolutionary phases are interspersed with evolutionary and incremental phases. Big innovations seem to come in waves, and they 'always have to be digested', as the CEO, Mr Keller states.

Health Pharma AG managed to grow to roughly 60 million euros in sales by entering a highly regulated niche market with little innovation in new products or development of new markets. According to the CEO, Mrs Julia Klemer, the firm is 'not very innovation-driven' regarding products, production processes or technology. Innovativeness is restricted by family heritage to a certain extent, with change occurring slowly (for example, changing product names that carry the name of the former CEO). When Regula Blinzli, Head of Marketing, asks 'why is that so?' the answer is often: 'that has always been like that, it comes from the old CEO'.

Whereas most firms did not score high on the traditional innovativeness measures (for example, in terms of new products, new markets, new technological processes), we find higher levels of innovation within these firms in forms that are less visible from the outside and not captured by traditional measures of entrepreneurship. Thus innovativeness is represented by developing improvements that generate value through renewal from within. According to Julia Klemer, innovation comes 'rather from the introduction of new management systems and structures than from the product or production side'. Specifically, firms have concentrated on implementing new management techniques such as fostering internal improvement processes or financial management systems (Health Pharma AG), introducing a balanced governance structure that represents the owning families with a committed management board, which is difficult for competitors to imitate (Technics AG), or implementing an umbrella brand strategy (Taste SA).

Beyond the risks and costs associated with innovation, the slow acceptance of new products by customers, the use of proven technologies in a stable environment and protection from a regulated market niche, we consider that low innovativeness levels are also related to the discretionary scope of action for the owner-managers of these firms. Due to higher degrees of freedom internally and lower degrees of freedom in the industrial context dominated by large multinationals, internal changes were more easily conceivable than changes that immediately affected the marketplace.

Finally, we find that the family dominated life cycle of management and ownership structure can also impact innovativeness. Within Health Pharma AG and Taste SA we find high degrees of internal innovation during the first years after the transfer of control from one family generation to the next. Often the preceding generation's management style was highly personalized. Therefore later generations assuming control first had to resolve issues surrounding the reorganization of the leadership team and style. Only after these challenges had been met could external product and market innovations be tackled.

In summary, we find that the family firms under investigation scored modestly on the innovativeness scale when measured in terms of new products, markets or technological processes as defined by traditional EO literature. However, in contrast to these traditional measures, we found that firms displayed higher innovativeness levels from within the organization, not necessarily represented by technological processes, but through value-generating renewal (for example, management and governance structures, exploitation, increasing the efficiency of existing solutions). In addition, we also discovered that innovativeness was not always low, but varied over time, often in line with the transition of organizational control and, therefore, with the life cycle of the family.

Competitive Aggressiveness

Competitive aggressiveness refers to a firm's propensity to directly and intensively challenge its competitors to achieve entry or improve position; that is, to outperform industry rivals in the marketplace (Lumpkin and Dess, 1996, p. 148). Competitive aggressiveness can be reactive as well. For instance, a new entry that is an imitation of an existing product or service would be considered entrepreneurial if the move implies an aggressive, 'head-to-head' confrontation in the market. According to Lumpkin and Dess (1996) competitive aggressiveness also embraces non-traditional methods of competition, such as new ways of distributing or marketing products.

In this context, the works of Martin and Lumpkin (2003) are of crucial relevance. They found that as later generations are involved in a family business, competitive aggressiveness decreases because family orientation (FO) overtakes EO as successive generations assume control. Accordingly, founding generations are characterized more by entrepreneurial concerns, while later generations are increasingly characterized by family concerns, which decreases EO in terms of competitive aggressiveness, risk taking and autonomy (Martin and Lumpkin, 2003). Similarly, Nordqvist et al. (2008) propose that competitive aggressiveness is less important in family firms when the three dualities are in place.

Indeed, in our Swiss cases we found that family firms did not exhibit a high level of competitive aggressiveness according to our definition; they try to avoid direct competition and prefer striving for a unique position within, and dominance of, a market niche. Simon (1996) calls this being a 'hidden champion', with hidden understood not in terms of invisibility due to smaller size but rather as a competitive posture that avoids direct confrontation. In this regard, Werner Mueller, the family CFO of Health Pharma AG points out: 'Being aggressive would not fit our company at all. I prefer a differentiation of our company that is based on our basic values and on our tradition as a Swiss family business. We have to be cautious with our outside appearance; we have to avoid aggressiveness and pomposity. We prefer being small but nice – a pearl in the market. The aim is sustainable success and not short-term profit maximization.'

Furthermore, it is important to note that Taste SA and Health Pharma AG are competing against industry giants. Thus pursuing an aggressive marketing strategy would probably not be the wisest course of action given differences in resource availability (for example, financial capital).

In addition, whereas aggressive firms direct their organizational energy toward challenging competitors (that is, externally), we find that firms directed a large part of their energy internally. This 'live and let live' and 'to each his own' posture allowed them to focus on their own issues and on improvements to internal efficiency. For example, Markus Taste, marketing director of Taste SA, mentions that one of their big competitors, whose nationwide marketing campaign that implied repackaging of existing chocolate products in a new and presumably fashionable manner, failed to gain support from customers.

Furthermore, whereas young firms may act aggressively toward competitors in general ('liability of newness'), more established organizations might challenge their competitors purely to assure their own survival ('liability of oldness'). In this context, aggressiveness might not be seen as an active posture, but rather as a reactive move to avoid the decline of the product portfolio or the company.

Finally, we found that family managers often displayed a negative attitude toward any aggressive behavior. Due to the negative connotation of the word aggressiveness, most entrepreneurs were hesitant to identify themselves with it. This concern could be related to the research design; that is, questioning entrepreneurs on aggressiveness during personal interviews, which might induce a negative social desirability bias. Beyond this effect, family managers might be particularly hesitant to be seen as aggressive, since a negative corporate reputation for aggressive firm behavior might negatively affect the reputation of the family and the manager, due to identity overlaps between firm, family and individual, reinforced by an inability to leave the family or easily switch the organization (Dyer and Whetten, 2006).

Thus our case-based findings partly support Martin and Lumpkin (2003), who argue that, as later generations are involved in a family business, competitive aggressiveness decreases. However, unlike them, we do not find increasing FO as the main reason for the observed low levels of competitive aggressiveness.

Risk Taking

Entrepreneurial firms are often said to take risks. Heavy debt and large resource commitments in relation to a new entry are examples of risky behavior. Stated formally, risk taking refers to 'the degree to which managers are willing to make large and risky resource commitments – i.e., those which have a reasonable chance of costly failures' (Miller and Friesen, 1978, p. 932). Risk-taking firms show a tendency to 'take bold actions such as venturing into unknown new markets' (Lumpkin and Dess, 2001, p. 431).

Recent research in the family business arena draws a more nuanced picture of risk taking in family firms (Gómez-Mejía et al., 2007; Zellweger, 2006). These authors find that family firms take decisions based on reference points. Specifically, Gómez-Mejía et al. (2007) state that for family firms the primary reference point was the loss of socio-emotional wealth; that is, non-financial aspects that meet the family's affective needs such as identity, exercising family influence and perpetuating the family dynasty. To protect this wealth, family firms accept a significant risk to their performance while avoiding risky decisions that aggravate that risk. In addition, Martin and Lumpkin (2003) found a decreasing level of risk taking as later generations assume control. Similarly, Nordqvist et al. (2008) view risk taking as a less important dimension in family firms and that less risk taking does not necessarily imply less innovativeness and proactiveness.

Naldi et al. (2007) prove statistically that risk taking in family firms, defined as within the EO construct, is smaller than in non-family firms; it is positively associated with proactiveness and innovation and, surprisingly, negatively related to financial performance. One reason may be that less formal control systems and pressure from external parties lead to less analysed and calculated entrepreneurial decisions. They emphasize that the existing literature has not sufficiently addressed the role of the organizational context in which risk taking takes place. Rauch et al. (2004) state that risk taking has a positive but significantly smaller correlation with performance than with other EO dimensions. Furthermore, Zahra (2005) suggests that family ownership and involvement promote entrepreneurship, while long tenures of CEO founders discourage it.

Considering these diverse findings on risk taking in family firms, it might be useful to step back and reconsider what is actually being measured. In line with the finding that family firms are not uniformly risk averse (Gómez-Mejía et al., 2007; Zellweger, 2006), we find differing types of risk orientation along three different dimensions. Investigating these different facets might produce a more nuanced understanding of risk taking in family firms.

First, we found that firms took what Frank Taste, CEO of Taste SA, labeled 'calculated business risks', often due to family influence. Business risks are associated with decisions relating to the ongoing management of the firm, as captured in the EO understanding of risk taking. By calculated business risks, we mean balancing the risks associated with management decisions against existing solutions so that a project's failure does not threaten the firm's survival. This rather thoughtful approach can be found elsewhere. As the president of the supervisory board of Technics AG states, 'We will only engage in projects that do not endanger the company as a whole. The shareholders prefer a stable dividend with stable risk.' This clearly illustrates the family's influence on the company's attitude toward risk. The CFO of Health Pharma AG claims that making a major step forward in a family business is difficult, 'as only little risk with debt capital is taken'. A member of the supervisory board claims that it is better 'to muddle through with an existing concept without making large resource commitments. Being active in niches with amortized machines is a typical profile of small and medium-sized companies.'

Second, we found that most family members assumed a high ownership stake in the firm. Accordingly, ownership risk (holding only one or a few assets with no or limited diversification) was high among all owners in our case studies.

Third, we found that most of our firms displayed very high levels of equity from total assets. These low leverage levels could be interpreted in light of a low control risk, hence a low risk to owners of losing control over the company.

Accordingly, instead of generally speaking about low or high levels of risk aversion in family firms we need to differentiate between types of risk, keeping in mind that socio-emotional aspects of ownership and family control are valued by family owners. More specifically, in the family business context any assessment of a firm's business risks (as captured by the EO construct) will yield only a fragmentary picture. Family firm owners were willing to make risky resource commitments in terms of undiversified allocation of their wealth tied to their shareholdings. However the risk of failure of this investment was intended to be mitigated by taking management decisions that did not endanger the firm's survival or the family's control over the firm.

Proactiveness

Proactiveness refers to a firm's efforts to seize new opportunities. Proactive organizations monitor trends, identify the future needs of existing customers, and anticipate changes in demand or emerging problems that can lead to new venture opportunities. Proactiveness involves not only recognizing changes but also being willing to act on those insights ahead of the competition (Dess and Lumpkin, 2005, p. 150). Together with autonomy and innovativeness, proactiveness is regarded as an important dimension in family firms (Nordqvist et al., 2008).

More recent developments within the companies we studied must be characterized as evolutionary rather than radically proactive. Frank Taste, CEO of Taste SA, admits that his company has lived off its two top-selling products 'for a bit too long'. Exhibiting a similar non-proactive approach, a member of the supervisory board of Health Pharma AG claims that 'you should rather postpone construction and work with fewer people if the outlooks are rather uncertain'.

However, at Taste SA, along with the transition from the second to the third generation, there is a new entrepreneurial spirit. The two Taste brothers and their team have successfully introduced new product lines, increased exports and reorganized the firm's product portfolio under a new umbrella brand strategy.

All firms under investigation have been willing to invest proactively, that is, moving from trading activities to building up their own production facilities and repeatedly increasing their capacities (Taste SA and Health Pharma AG) at certain points in time. Within the management teams of Taste SA, Health Pharma AG and Technics AG we find an entrepreneurial and proactive mindset. However, to date, it remains unclear to what extent family shareholders would be willing to support proactive investments associated with large and even risky resource commitments. Family shareholders struggling with inner conflicts (Health Pharma AG) or a conservative family shareholder group with a safety oriented mentality similar to a family internal pension fund (Technics AG) are likely to hinder bold proactive moves. This underlines the importance of including family and ownership considerations in assessing proactiveness in the family business context.

This being said, it should be noted that even though a high degree of proactiveness is desirable according to the EO construct, under certain circumstances (that is, high insecurity), firms might have good reasons for adopting 'a wait and see' posture. For example, being a first mover is not necessarily the best strategy in rapidly changing technical environments in which the dominant design for production is unclear. Similarly, in certain contexts (for example, cyclical industries) waiting for the right moment to acquire, develop or shed critical resources (for example, real estate) can be a source of competitive advantage in contrast to more short-term oriented investors. Hence persisting on a course of action with uncertain short-term gain can be an important antecedent to long-term success.

In summary, recognizing changes and acting rapidly on those insights ahead of the competition can be a source of competitive advantage. However forgoing short-term activity while closely monitoring movements in the industrial context and persistently pursuing a defined strategy can be sources of advantage over competitors in the long run.

Autonomy

Autonomy as captured in the EO construct refers to the independent action of an individual or a team in bringing forth an idea or a vision and carrying it through to completion. In general, it means the ability and will to be self-directed in the pursuit of opportunities. In an organizational context it refers to actions taken free of stifling organizational constraints. Thus, even though factors such as resource availability, actions by competitive rivals or internal organizational considerations may change the course of new venture initiatives, these are not sufficient to extinguish the autonomous entrepreneurial processes that lead to new entry: throughout the organizational player remains free to act independently, to make key decisions and to implement policy (Lumpkin and Dess, 1996).

Martin and Lumpkin's (2003) considerations are also relevant, as they found that the level of autonomy decreases as later generations assume control. Regarding long-term entrepreneurial performance, autonomy is regarded as an important dimension, as outlined by Nordqvist et al. (2008), who suggest considering autonomy as having both an internal and an external dimension. Internal autonomy is related to empowering individuals and teams within an organization and external autonomy is related to stakeholders such as banks, suppliers, customers and financial markets. Family firms are less likely to use formal monitoring and other control mechanisms than non-family firms, which are good preconditions for individual autonomy (Eddleston et al., 2008).

Our family and non-family interviewees agreed on the importance of internal autonomy as a driver of entrepreneurial activity. Our in-depth interviews reveal that the younger generations of the Taste SA and Health Pharma AG families successfully managed to overcome the more patriarchal and authoritarian leadership style of their parents (that is, fathers). The non-family managers of Taste SA feel that open communication in the management team and the new style of management and leadership are positive developments.

Our interviewees assigned great importance to external autonomy as a necessary precondition for internal autonomy. Their first and foremost goal is to secure the independence and autonomy of the organization. According to Markus Taste, shareholder and marketing director of Taste SA, the company will only take decisions that will not endanger its independence and family control. External autonomy, in turn, provides owners and managers with the freedom to implement a unique strategy that does not have to satisfy short-term oriented shareholder demands. Indeed, Regula Blinkli, non-family marketing director of Health Pharma AG, points out that 'the wish for autonomy on the company level has always been a major driving force in the development of the company'.

Internal autonomy is a more recent management practice that has arisen as the third and fifth generations have taken control (Taste SA and Health Pharma AG). It does not, therefore (at least retrospectively), explain performance or transgenerational potential. In contrast, the wish and need for external autonomy and independence have been present in all three organizations throughout generations. For example, Werner Merz, CFO of Technics AG, points out that 'independence of the organization from external parties has always been very important'. Indeed, a few years ago the 150 family shareholders chose not to open up shareholder structure to the public for autonomy reasons and because there was no need for external funds. At the same time, Technics AG managers are aware of the danger related to considering external autonomy as the ultimate goal of a firm. Rather, they consider it as a means to create the internal autonomy of managers, which is ultimately aimed at generating further entrepreneurial development.

In summary, individual autonomy is a more recent management practice introduced by younger family generations. However external autonomy is a predominant theme within these firms across generations and has more explicative power with regard to transgenerational potential than internal autonomy.

8.3 CONCLUSION

Reaching beyond Lumpkin and Dess's (1996) argument that EO depends on environmental and organizational factors, we find distinct patterns of entrepreneurial behavior in the context of multigeneration family firms.

First, we find that the family firms under investigation did not score high on the five salient dimensions of the EO construct. Our theoretical considerations and the results of our case studies reveal that for this type of firm it might not always be the most promising strategy to strive for a maximum score on each of the five EO dimensions. 'The more the better' is not necessarily true. For example, while many new economic firms should have scored high on all EO dimensions (that is, they were autonomous, aggressive, innovative, risk taking and proactive), they did not survive more than a few years. Instead, the right level of EO at the right time seems to indicate long-term success, which is clearly present in the firms we investigated. Beyond Lumpkin and Dess's (1996) assertion that EO depends on external (that is, market) conditions, our case studies show that the level and the composition of EO is clearly dependent on family background. Second, we find that certain scales are inappropriate in the family firm context since they are not sufficiently defined and applicable. For example, our considerations on differing aspects of risk (business, financial, control) call for a more fine-grained understanding of risk aversion. Similarly, firms show a distinct pattern of autonomy that calls for a differentiation between internal and external autonomy. Whereas we do not find a common pattern with regard to internal autonomy, the majority of the firms we studied strove for high levels of external autonomy. In addition, the applied innovativeness scale is not perfectly suitable in the family firm context. Although our firms scored low on a scale measuring new products, markets and technologies, they scored high when measuring internal and 'invisible' innovations such as exploiting existing solutions, management systems, internal processes and procedures.

Third, we find that key aspects (for example, the persistence or perseverance in implementing and pursuing a defined strategy) are missing on the EO scales (opposing an aggressive approach). Many 'hidden champions' (Simon, 1996) have grown in the shadow of large, established companies by focusing on niches not specifically targeted by these competitors. The reason why the notion of persistence is not captured within the EO construct could be that EO is an inherently static construct, developed and used to measure entrepreneurial behavior at a certain point in time. Studying entrepreneurship in a multigenerational family business context (as opposed to that of young firms) is a unique opportunity to track entrepreneurial behavior and its success across time, hence, in a longitudinal manner, as suggested by Dess et al. (2003). Studying EO in family businesses might assist us in developing measurement tools that capture the dynamic dimension of entrepreneurial behavior, which better explains transgenerational potential.

To conclude, we must note an important limitation. In our attempt to investigate entrepreneurship in the context of family firms and business families we follow a 'common denominator' approach, which is limited in terms of its explicative power. If the goal is to study family businesses through the lens of entrepreneurship, then that common denominator, entrepreneurship, will define what actually can and will be studied in the family firm context. However specific family related aspects, which are not covered by the individual and organizational aspects represented within entrepreneurship and EO, cannot be studied with this approach. One way of overcoming this difficulty is by describing EO as a set of options. A company, in response to its capacity and external challenges, has to find the optimal position on a set of continua. As we followed the evolution of our firms through time, we noticed that they continuously adapted their entrepreneurial posture. For example, periods of high risk taking were followed by periods of consolidation. Periods of low levels of innovation in terms of new products were followed by periods of renewal, radical changes and product innovations. In this context, entrepreneurship could be seen as two extremes that need to be balanced: autonomy and swimming with the stream, aggressiveness and patience/persistence, innovativeness and tradition, risk taking and risk aversion, proactiveness and 'wait and see'.

This approach opens up a way for future research to examine how EO in family firms is transformed over time. Thus we would like to return to the case of the new firms mentioned at the beginning. Referring to the EO construct and its sub-dimensions, we find that Technics AG, Taste SA and Health Pharma AG did not 'score high and die'. Rather, it seems that each forged its own path to entrepreneurial success. Based on our theoretical

Autonomy	*Swim with stream*
Aggressiveness	*Patience/persistence*
Innovativeness	*Tradition*
Risk taking	*Risk aversion*
Proactiveness	*Wait and see*

Figure 8.1   Entrepreneurial orientation continua

considerations and findings we might label this achievement 'score clever and stay forever'.

NOTE

1. Corresponding author.

REFERENCES

Aldrich, H.E. and J.E. Cliff (2003), 'The pervasive effects of family on entrepreneurship: toward a family embeddedness perspective', *Journal of Business Venturing*, **18**(5), 507–25.

Dess, G.G. and G.T. Lumpkin (2005), 'The role of entrepreneurial orientation in stimulating effective corporate entrepreneurship', *Academy of Management Executive*, **19**(1), 147–56.

Dess, G.G., G.T. Lumpkin and J.G. Covin (1997), 'Entrepreneurial strategy making and firm performance: tests of contingency and configurational models', *Strategic Management Journal*, **18**(9), 677–95.

Dess, G., R. Ireland, S. Zahra, S. Janney and P. Lane (2003), 'Emerging issues in corporate entrepreneurship', *Journal of Management*, **29**(3), 351–78.

Dyer, G., and D.A. Whetten (2006), 'Family firms and social responsibility: preliminary evidence from the SP 500', *Entrepreneurship Theory and Practice*, **30**(6), 785–802.

Eddleston, K., F. Kellermanns and T. Zellweger (2008), *Corporate Entrepreneurship in Family Firms: A Stewardship Perspective*, Paper presented at the 2008 USASBE Conference, San Antonio, CA, USA.

Gómez-Mejía, L.R., K. Takacs Haynes, M. Nunez-Nickel, K.J.L. Jacobson and J. Moyano-Fuentes (2007), 'Socioemotional wealth and business risks in family-controlled firms: evidence from Spanish olive oil mills', *Administrative Science Quarterly*, **52**, 106–37.

Habbershon, T.G. and J. Pistrui (2002), 'Enterprising families domain: family-influenced ownership groups in pursuit of transgenerational wealth', *Family Business Review*, **15**(3), 223–37.

Hall, A., L. Melin and M. Nordqvist (2001), 'Entrepreneurship as radical change in family business: exploring the role of cultural patterns', *Family Business Review*, **14**(3), 193–208.

Kellermanns, F.W. and K.A. Eddleston (2006), 'Corporate entrepreneurship in family firms: a family perspective', *Entrepreneurship Theory and Practice*, **30**(6), 809–30.

Lumpkin, G.T. and G.G. Dess (1996), 'Clarifying the entrepreneurial orientation construct and linking it to performance', *Academy of Management Review*, **21**(1), 135–72.

Lumpkin, G.T. and G.G. Dess (2001), 'Linking two dimensions of entrepreneurial orientation to firm performance: the moderating role of environment and industry life cycle', *Journal of Business Venturing*, **16**(5), 429–51.

Martin, L. and T. Lumpkin (2003), 'From entrepreneurial orientation to "family

orientation": generational differences in the management of family businesses',
Paper presented at the 22nd Babson College Entrepreneurship Research
Conference, Babson College, Wellesley, Massachusetts.

McCann, J.E., A.Y. Leon-Guerrero and J.D. Haley (2001), 'Strategic goals
and practices of innovative family businesses', *Journal of Small Business
Management*, **39**(1), 50–9.

Miller, D. (1983), 'The correlates of entrepreneurship in three types of firms',
Management Science, **29**(7), 770–91.

Miller, D. and P.H. Friesen (1978), 'Archetypes of strategy formulation',
Management Science, **24**(9), 921–33.

Naldi, L., M. Nordqvist, K. Sjöberg and J. Wiklund (2007), 'Entrepreneurial orientation, risk taking and performance in family firms'. *Family Business Review*,
10(1), 33–47.

Nordqvist, M. (2008), 'Entrepreneurial orientation in family firms', *Zeitschrift für
KMU und Entrepreneurship*, **55**(1), 62–78.

Nordqvist, M., T.G. Habbershon and L. Melin (2008), 'Transgenerational entre-
preneurship: exploring entrepreneurial orientation in family firms', in H.
Landström, D. Smallbone, H. Crijns and E. Laveren (eds), *Entrepreneurship,
Stable Growth and Performance: Frontiers in European Entrepreneurial Research*.
Cheltenham, UK and Northampton, MA, USA.

Rauch, A., J. Wiklund, M. Freese and G.T. Lumpkin (2004), 'Entrepreneurial
orientation and business performance: cumulative empirical evidence', Paper
presented at the 23rd Babson College Entrepreneurship Research Conference,
Glasgow, UK, 4–6 June 2004.

Salvato, C. (2004), 'Predictors of entrepreneurship in family firms', *Journal of
Private Equity*, **7**(3), 68–76.

Schumpeter, J.A. (1934), *The Theory of Economic Development*, Cambridge, MA:
Harvard University Press.

Schumpeter, J.A. (1942), *Capitalism, Socialism, and Democracy*, New York:
Harper & Brothers.

Shepherd, D. and S. Zahra (2004), 'From conservatism to entrepreneurialism:
the case of Swedish family firms'. Unpublished paper, University of Colorado:
Boulder.

Simon, H. (1996), *Die heimlichen Gewinner (Hidden Champions): Die
Erfolgsstrategien unbekannter Weltmarktführer*, Frankfurt: Campus.

Wiklund, J. and D. Shepherd (2003), 'Knowledge-based resources, entrepreneurial orientation, and the performance of small and medium-sized businesses',
Strategic Management Journal, **24**(13), 1307–14.

Zahra, S.A. (2005), 'Entrepreneurial risk taking in family firms', *Family Business
Review*, **18**(1), 23–40.

Zahra, S.A. and J.G. Covin (1995), 'Contextual influences on the corporate
entrepreneurship–performance relationship: a longitudinal analysis', *Journal of
Business Venturing*, **10**, 43–58.

Zahra, S.A., J.C. Hayton and C. Salvato (2004), 'Entrepreneurship in family
vs. non-family firms: a resource based analysis of the effect of organizational
culture', *Entrepreneurship Theory and Practice*, **28**(4), 363–81.

Zellweger, T. (2006), 'Investitionsentscheidungen von Familien- und
Nichtfamilienunternehmern', *Zeitschrift für KMU und Entrepreneurship*, **54**(2),
93–115.

APPENDIX   INTERVIEW DETAILS ABOUT THE THREE SWISS CASES

Case 1: Health AG

No. of interview	1	2	3	4	5
Job description	CEO	Marketing director	CFO	Member of supervisory board	Head of quality assurance
Management	X		X		
Family	X		X (in-law)		
Generation	Fifth		Fifth		
Supervisory Board	X		X	X	
Owner	X				
Date of interview	12.03.2007	12.03.2007	12.03.2007	12.03.2007	12.03.2007
Duration	93 min	70 min	91 min	74 min	47 min

Case 2: Taste SA

No. of interview	1	2	3	4
Job description	CEO	Export director	Production director	Marketing director
Management	X	X	X	X
Family	X			X
Generation	Third			Third
Founder				
Supervisory Board	X			X
Owner	X			X
Date of interview	27.02.2006	27.02.2006	27.02.2006	27.02.2006
Duration of interview	100 min	85 min	88 min	97 min

Case 3: Technics AG

No. of interview	1	2	3	4
Job description	CEO	CFO	President of supervisory board	Member of supervisory board
Management	X	X		
Family	X			X
Generation	Fourth			Fourth
Founder				
Supervisory Board	X		X	X
Owner	X	X		X
Date of interview	06.03.2006	06.03.2006	06.03.2006	06.03.2006
Duration of interview	71 min	80 min	77 min	75 min

Index